The Charles Eliot Norton Lectures, 1973

THE UNANSWERED QUESTION

Six Talks at Harvard

Leonard Bernstein

Harvard University Press   Cambridge, Massachusetts and London, England   1976

The pages that follow were written not to be read, but listened to; and the fact that they do now exist in book form seems to me a moving testimony to the fidelity and creative involvement of numerous colleagues.

It has been a long four years from the day I made my first notation in the flyleaf of Chomsky's *Language and Mind* to this moment of publication. From the beginning, these six Norton lectures were intended to be experienced aurally, accompanied by visual aids and extended orchestral performances on a film screen, plus a near-continuous stream of musical illustration at the piano—with never a care for how it might all look some day on the printed page. And with never a care for literary niceties, since it was all to be delivered in the rather casual atmosphere of the Harvard Square Theater, ad-libs and all, to an audience so mixed (students, nonstudents, the cop on the corner, distinguished faculty, my mother, experts in music who cared little for linguistics, vice versa, scientists with no interest in poetry, vice versa) that any one precise level of diction was unthinkable. The interdisciplinary nature of the material further discouraged stylistic consistency. All in all, not exactly the recipe for an academic publication.

Yet here it all is, thanks to the persistence and inventiveness of the Harvard University Press editorial staff; the transformation has been made—not, however, without prior transformations. After each lecture had been delivered, a somewhat altered version of it was re-delivered the following night in a television studio, and committed to video tape. (That is, in a sense, another form of publication.) Then the soundtrack of those tapes was re-committed to phonograph records (under the magnificent supervision of my soundmaster, John McClure) and so the lectures exist also in that form. All these transformations, including this present book, would not have been possible without the faithful hard work of my many colleagues. Let me now praise them, and thank them, and dedicate this book to them.

In the beginning was Tom Cothran, whose musical sensibilities and poetic insights fertilized my every idea; and to him was joined Mary Ahern, whose miraculous gift for mental organization helped me give order to a sometimes chaotic mass of interdisciplinary thinking. (In both cases a considerable quantity of Irish charm enhanced the operation.) On the academic front, I give abundant and affectionate thanks to two splendid teachers: Professor Irving Singer, who guided me through some tricky terrain in the realm of Moral Philosophy (and who very gently corrected some egregious errors), and to Professor Donald C. Freeman whose combined enthusiasm and mastery of linguistic theory lifted me over more than one hurdle. Other productive conversations abounded: I remember with particular gratitude certain ones with Humphrey Burton and Elizabeth Finkler.

But none of the above would have achieved manage-ability without the tireless Grazyna Bergman, whose collating of scripts (innumerable drafts and versions, for the lectern, the piano, the teleprompter, etc.) was a wonder to behold. And I can never sufficiently thank Paul de Hueck for his collating of those collations, and for his painstaking proofreading; the same goes for Gregory Martindale, especially for his extensive proofreading of the many musi-cal examples. And I bless those eager, pretty, smiling, patient typists, Sue Knussen and Sally Jackson, who also kept the coffee and the jokes aflow. And Tony Clark. And Tom McDonald. And . . . the list is long; it begins to seem an enormous crew for the management of six little lectures. But the truth is that they were six very *big* lectures, technically complicated ones, which were moreover taped and recorded and now published. I could not have done without any

one of my helpers. And over them all, quietly presiding
and producing, sat my friend and counselor Harry Kraut,
somehow preserving our respective sanities.

Finally, I humbly thank my wife and children for bearing
with cheerful martyrdom my first year of nonstop euphoria
at my discovery of the Chomsky Connection.

Leonard Bernstein

CONTENTS

1. MUSICAL PHONOLOGY

I am delighted to be back home at Harvard. I am also somewhat petrified at the grandeur of the Poetic Chair I am occupying—a chair which over the years has grown into something more like a throne, owing to the long list of eminent persons who have occupied it. But I am comforted by the sense of having come home again, and happy to be realizing my old student fantasy of what it's like to be on "the other side of the desk." Now that I am on this side of the desk, all I seem to be able to think about is how it felt to be on *that* side. It felt good, if you want to know the truth, those thirty-odd years ago, mainly because I was very lucky in my masters: Piston and Merritt in music, Kittredge and Spencer in literature, Demos and Hocking in philosophy. But there was one master who bridged it all for me, through whom the sense of beauty, analytic method, and historical perspective all came together in one luminous revelation; and I would like to dedicate these six lectures to his memory. He was Professor David Prall, of the Philosophy Department, a brilliant scholar and a deeply sensitive aesthetician. It was in this now disdained and rather unfashionable field of aesthetics that I learned from him not only a great deal about the philosophy of beauty, but also the fact that David Prall was himself an instance of the beauty he loved—in mind and spirit. Those are terribly old-fashioned words in these days of behavioristic obsessiveness, and I hope you will pardon such ancient words as "mind" and "spirit," especially since I believe in them as strongly now as I did then.

Perhaps the principal thing I absorbed from Professor Prall, and from Harvard in general, was a sense of inter-disciplinary values—that the best way to "know" a thing is in the context of another discipline. So these lectures are

3

[1] Theme
Grave (♩ = 48)

f non legato, deliberamente

sff

*) ◇ = press down silently

4

given in that spirit of cross-disciplines; which is why I'll be speaking of music along with quixotic forays into such fields as poetry, linguistics, aesthetics, and even, heaven help us, a bit of elementary physics.

The title of this lecture series is borrowed from Charles Ives, who wrote that brief but remarkable piece of his called "The Unanswered Question" way back in 1908. Ives had a highly metaphysical question in mind; but I've always felt he was also asking another question, a purely musical one—"whither music?"—as that question must have been asked by Musical Man entering the twentieth century. Today, with that century sixty-five years older, we are still asking it; only it is not quite the same question as it was then.

And so the purpose of these six lectures is not so much to answer the question as to understand it, to redefine it. Even to guess at the answer to "whither music?" we must first ask Whence music? What music? and Whose music? It would be pretentious to assume that by the end of this series we will answer the ultimate question; but it is reasonable to assume that we will be in a better position to make some educated guesses.

Let me start with a particularly nostalgic and vivid recollection from my years with Professor Prall—the time, back in 1937, when I first heard a recording of Aaron Copland's *Piano Variations*. I fell in love with the music: it seemed so fierce and prophetic, and utterly new. [1]

This music opened up new worlds of musical possibilities to me. I wrote a raving report on it for my aesthetics course, and Professor Prall became so interested in it that he decided he wanted to learn it himself. What a man! He even bought me the sheet music. So I learned it and taught it to him; he taught it back to me; we analyzed it together. It became "our song."

[2]

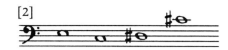

[3]

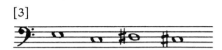

[4]

[5]

[6]

[7]

[8]

This is not just a sentimental anecdote, because as we were analyzing the Copland Variations I made a startling discovery: that the first four notes of the piece [2], which are the germ of the whole composition, are really these four notes [3], with the fourth note displaced an octave higher [4]. And I suddenly realized that these same four notes, in another order, formed the subject of Bach's C-sharp minor Fugue from the *Well-Tempered Clavichord* (Book I) [5]. Simultaneously I discovered the same four notes, transposed, with the first note repeated, germinating the variations in Stravinsky's Octet [6]. *And* the same four notes flashed through my mind, in yet another order and key, as the initial motto of Ravel's Spanish Rhapsody [7]. And on top of all *that* I suddenly recalled some Hindu music I had heard (I was a big Oriental music buff at the time)—and there were those same four notes again [8]. At that moment a notion was born in my brain: that there must be some deep, primal reason why these discrete structures of the same four notes should be at the very heart of such disparate musics as those of Bach, Copland, Stravinsky, Ravel, and the Uday Shan-kar Dance Company. All this, and more, I poured out to David Prall, and that was my first Norton lecture, to an audience of one.

From that time to this, the notion of a worldwide, inborn musical grammar has haunted me; but I would never have dreamed of basing a lecture series on a notion so ill-defined, and apparently nonverifiable, if it were not for the extraordinary materials that have appeared in recent years on the similar idea of a universal grammar underlying human speech. I have been profoundly impressed and encouraged by the burgeoning of thought in this relatively new linguistic area—an area that might be called Chomskian. By so naming it, I don't mean to restrict my observations to Noam Chomsky's work alone; it is a term of convenience, since he is the best-known, most revolutionary, and best-publicized name in that area. Along with his colleagues and disciples (many of whom are now in radical disagreement with him), he has produced a body of work that has reinvigorated linguistics to a point where it seems new light may be shed on the nature and structural functions of that elusive thing called Mind. In other words, by studying in depth why we talk the way we do—by abstracting the logical principles of language—we may be in a position to discover how we communicate in a larger sense: through music, through the arts in general, and ultimately through all our societal behavior. We may even discover how we are mentally constituted, because language is species-specific; that is, it's common to all of us who belong to the human species, and only to us. Of course, tomorrow morning cheerful new facts about dolphins or a certain chimpanzee named Sarah may throw a monkey-wrench into the works; but meanwhile this philosophical science called linguistics seems to have become our newest key to self-discovery. With each passing year it seems to substantiate ever more convincingly the hypothesis of innate grammatical compe-tence (as Chomsky calls it), a genetically endowed language faculty which is *universal*. It is a human endowment; it proclaims the unique power of the human spirit.

Well, so does music.

But how do we investigate musical universality by so scientific a means as linguistic analogy? Music is supposed to be a metaphorical phenomenon, some kind of mysterious symbolization of our innermost affective existence. It lends itself more easily to description in purple prose than in equations. Even so great a scientist as Einstein said that "the most beautiful experience we can have is the mysterious". Then why do so many of us constantly try to explain the beauty of music, thus apparently depriving it of its mystery? The fact is that music is not only a mysterious and metaphorical art; it is also born of science. It is made of mathematically measurable elements: frequencies, durations, decibels, intervals. And so any explication of music must combine mathematics with aesthetics, just as linguistics combines mathematics with philosophy, or sociology, or whatever. It is precisely for this interdisciplinary reason that I am so attracted by the new linguistics as a fresh approach to music. Why not a study of musico-linguistics, just as there already exists a psycho-linguistics and a socio-linguistics?

Now, luckily, the study of linguistics is a threefold science, and so provides us with three handy categories in which these lectures can be conceived: Phonology, Syntax, and Semantics. These are the three departments of linguistics, and they point the way for our musical investigation as well. In this first lecture we'll be oriented phonologically, examining both language and music from the most fundamental point of view—that of sound itself, the stuff of which verbal and musical utterances are made. That should give us a solid base to build on, so that in our next session we can plunge into syntax, the actual structures that arise from that phonological stuff. From then on, the remaining four lectures will confront the challenges of semantics, that is, *meaning*, both musical and extramusical meaning. Semantics can be seen as the natural result of adding phonology and syntax together—sound plus structure; and the resultant semantic inquiry will inevitably bring us around to Ives' unanswered question: whither music in our own time?

Now you can see why I became so excited when I began reading the new linguistics, which postulated the notion of innate grammatical competence. Because suddenly my old undergraduate notion of a universal *musical* grammar was reanimated. It had lain dormant for years, paralyzed, I suppose, by that deadly cliché: Music is the Universal Language of Mankind. After a thousand repetitions of that one, usually with the connotation, "Support your local symphony orchestra," the well-meant phrase becomes not only a cliché, but a misleading one. How many of you can listen to forty minutes of a Hindu raga with intelligent comprehension, to say nothing of merely staying awake? And how about certain kinds of avant-garde music? Not so universal, are they? Well, thought I, so much for the Universal Language of Mankind. But then, when I began reading the new linguistics, I thought: here is a fresh way to pursue my intuitive idea, which had grown stale and had deteriorated into a platitude. In other words, by building analogies between musical and linguistic procedures, couldn't that cliché about the Universal Language be debunked or confirmed, or at least clarified?

O.K. Let's clarify. "Universality" is a big word, and a dangerous one. At the same time that it implies likeness, it also implies diversity: remember Montaigne's remark that the most universal quality of man is his diversity. This paradox lies at the very heart of linguistic study; because at the same time that a linguist is investigating any one particular language, or even a family of languages, trying to formulate a descriptive grammar, he is also searching for the underlying similarities among different languages, or families of languages. At least the new linguists are. They construct these descriptive grammars by analyzing the mental processes of human speech, thus deriving sets of rules that (they hope) apply to all human languages, in fact, to all possible human languages, both known and unknown. Now, that's a tall order, but a magnificent goal, requiring an inspired guess, a great scientific leap of the mind. And if that goal can be attained, and the universality principle proved, it can turn out to be a timely and welcome affirmation of human kinship.

But how do linguists go about such a task? Well, one way is by seeking out what they call "substantive universals". For example, in the realm of phonology, which is our main concern in this lecture, linguists propose a substantive universal which says the following: all languages share certain _phonemes_ in common, that is, minimal speech units that arise naturally from the physiological structure of our mouths, throats, and noses. Since we all share those features, we share likewise the sound AH, for instance—a sound produced by simply opening the mouth and vocalizing. AH. Every normal human being can do this in any language; there is simply no exception, even though the vowel may vary according to the shape of the oral cavity or according to one's social background, producing such variants as clâss, and clāss, and clăss. But they are all versions of the basic phoneme AH, and so must be considered universal. Now that's a *substantive* universal for you.

Of course I'm skipping enormous numbers of other substantive universals—"distinctive features", for example. I don't want to burden you with all that. Let's say only that different linguists go about seeking universals in different ways. Etymologists, for instance, point out that the interesting thing about the Spanish word *hablar*, to speak, and the Portuguese equivalent, *falar*, to speak, is not that they seem to be totally different words, but that they are the same word, deriving from the same Latin root *fabulare*, but with phonetic deviations. Let's not go into why they deviated—though it's a fascinating study; let's agree only about the common origin.

There's the key: common origin. Because if one continues in this way, working backwards through history in search of even earlier common origins, one arrives at startling points of universality. Only such investigation has to stop short as soon as written languages run out. Obviously, the ultimate evidence of universality in speech is to be sought in the oldest languages of man, prehistoric languages which preceded, so to speak, the Tower-of-Babel moment in human evolution. But such ancient languages simply don't exist; they were spoken millions of years ago, long before written languages were developed, which was only thousands of years ago. And so, being stuck without written evidence, historical linguists are forced into speculation. Ideally, what they are seeking is a parent language, one universal tongue that may have been common to all of early mankind. And that's the tallest order of all, because it means wandering in the mists of prehistory. One tangible accomplishment at least has been to find a name for this field of inquiry, and that name is "monogenesis"—denoting the theory of all languages springing from a single source. A fine word, monogenesis, and a thrilling idea. It thrills me, anyway, to the point where I stayed up all of one night making mono-genetic speculations of my own. I tried to imagine myself a hominid, and tried to feel what a very, very ancient ancestor of mine might have felt, and might have been impelled to express verbally. I scribbled pages full of basic monosyllables which felt somehow right, which seemed to belong together, and which delighted me with their curious logic.

I began by imagining myself a hominid infant, just lying there, contentedly trying out my new-found voice. Mmmm. . . . Then I got hungry: MMM! MMM!—calling my mother's attention to my hunger. And as I opened my mouth to receive the nipple—MMM–AAA!—lo, I had invented a primal word: MA, mother. This must be one of the first proto-words ever uttered by man; still to this day most languages have a word for *mother* that employs that root, MA, or some phonetic variant of it. All the Romance languages: *mater, madre, mère,* and so on; the Germanic: *mutter, moder;* the Slavic: *mat, mattka;* Hebrew: *Ima;* Navajo: *shi-ma;* even in Swahili and Chinese and Japanese they call her *Mama.*

Well, that was a small triumph. But then I began expanding. What about MA plus L: MAL? Now there's a proto-syllable for you. My first association, of course, was with all the familiar words connoting badness: *malo, male, mauvais*—all Latin-derived languages, of course. But then, I thought, in the Slavic family of languages that same syllable connotes smallness: *maly, málenki,* etc. Sudden hypothesis: could there just possibly be a monogenetic connection, way back then, between the concepts of badness and smallness? Why not? Remember, we're being hominids now; and it's perfectly conceivable that what's small must be automatically bad. To be small is to be weak, to be only human, as against the powerful gods, as against a huge magical earth and sky; hence, weakness is undesirable, hence bad. It's bad to have a small harvest, small energy, small stature, small dinner. *Malo!*

13

Well, then, I thought—if that's true, then *big* must equal *good*; there must be a corresponding kinship between *bigness* and *goodness*. So on I went, searching through all the dictionaries I could find, and what do you think? I found it. Look: The most familiar root denoting bigness is GR; grrr, the growling of the big tiger, producing all those "big" words: GRande, GRandir, GRoss, GReat, GRow, and so on, including GRoot in Dutch, where the *G* is softened to a guttural *H*. Now these are all Latin and Germanic, but again, look at the Slavic, where again the *G* is gutturalized to *H*, and behold the glorious word *HoRóshii*, which means, so inevitably and comfortingly, GOOD! And *HRábrii* is brave, and—big, brave, good (and GOD)—somehow it all added up. Way back before and behind and beyond all these comparatively recent languages, there must lurk, I fondly hoped, one universal parent tongue, which contained the great simultaneous equation:

$$Big = Good$$
$$and$$
$$Small = Bad.$$

Triumph! But why am I burdening you with my private game-playing, this less than scientific speculation? It's hardly what a linguist would call authentic. But it interests me (and I hope you) because of what it suggests about music—the origins of music and the very nature of musical materials—the notes themselves.

Let's make a simple analogy, and return for a second to being that hominid infant who invented the proto-word MA. We quickly learn to associate that morpheme with our supplier of milk, and so we call her when we need her. MA! Now, on a purely phonological level, that sound begins with

14

an attack, an *ictus*, Maa . . . and ends in a descending
glide A

      a

        a

          a. [9] That's the way we speak: ictus plus glide.
(Of course, the glide may also be upward [10], if the
intention is interrogative: a?)

             a

          M

Maa . . . . . .

Maa . . . .

Maa . . .

But now let's feel a tremendous intensification of our need,
of our hunger, of our impatience. And so we intensify
the ictus by prolonging it: MAAA—and, lo and behold, we are
singing. Music is born. The syllable has become a note just
by eliminating the glide. MAAA [11]. Or, to use the technical
jargon of our time, the morpheme is rewritten as a pitch-
event. And what an event that must have been, way
back then.

    What we seem to be getting to is a hypothesis that would
confirm another famous cliché—namely, Music is Heightened Speech. After all, what causes such a heightening?
Intensified emotion. Hunger. Impatience. Certainly the
deepest universals we all share are emotions, or affects; we
all have the same capacity for passion, fear, anticipation,
aggression. We all display the same physiological manifesta-
tions of affect; our eyebrows go up with anticipation; our
hearts pound with passion; and fear affects us universally
with goose flesh. And in the sense that music may express
those affective goings-on, then it must indeed be a universal
language.

    Maybe even a divine one, to invoke yet another cliché.
I have often thought that if it is literally true that In The
Beginning Was The Word, then it must have been a *sung*

word. The Bible tells us the whole Creation story not only verbally, but in terms of verbal creation. God *said:* Let there be light. God *said:* Let there be a firmament. He created verbally. Now can you imagine God *saying,* just like that, "Let there be light," as if ordering lunch? Or even in the original language: *Y'hi Or?* I've always had a private fantasy of God *singing* those two blazing words: *Y'HI—O-O-O-R!* Now that could really have done it; music could have caused light to break forth. But all I've just done is to prolong the ictus again; what I've created is simply heightened speech, which would seem to corroborate yet another cliché about music beginning where language leaves off. In other words, if the theory of monogenesis is valid and speech indeed has common origins, and if the heightening of that speech produces music, then music may also be said to have common origins—and is therefore universal, whether the notes issue from the mouth of God or from that hungry infant.

But where do these notes come from? Why do our ears select certain notes and not others?

For example, why do children tease one another in a specific singsong way [12]? These are two very special notes which children also use to call one another [13] and which are often used by them in singing games [14]. Those are the same two notes, only now extended to three notes [15]. Or perhaps you once yelled, "Allee, Allee, in free!" [16]. Does that sound familiar? Well, again we must ask, why just *those* notes, in that particular order [17]?

Research seems to indicate that this exact constellation of two notes (and its three-note variant) is the same all over the world, wherever children tease each other, on every

[12]

Nya nya Nya nya

[13]

Jer – ry! Do – ris!

[14]

lit – tle Sal – ly Wa – ter

[15]

[16]

Al – lee, al – lee in free!

[17]

continent and in every culture. In short, we may have here
a clear case of a musico-linguistic *universal,* and one which
can be identified and explained in a nonvacuous way. I want
to take a little time to do this carefully, because in the
explanation lies the key to musical universality in general,
the answer to the question, "Why just those notes?" and
eventually to the question, "Why those notes in Mozart, and
why those notes in Copland or in Schönberg or in Ives?"
And in having an answer, we musicians have a singular
advantage over the linguists, who ask their question: "Why
just those sounds in human speech?" They seek their
answers by constructing a very complex hypothesis, which
is still very much in the working stage, subject to proof
or disproof, amplification or derision. But we musicians are
luckier: we have the built-in preordained universal known
as the *harmonic series.*

To those of you who know all about the harmonic series,
I beg your indulgence for a few minutes so that I can sketch
it out for those who don't.

This acoustical phenomenon called the harmonic series,
or overtone series, is not hard to understand, if you
remember the basic high school fact that all sounds are
produced by vibrating bodies, which send out waves. If such
a vibrating body is irregularly constituted, like this floor,
or this lectern, it will when struck emit waves which are
irregular, and our ears will perceive them as noise. But if the
source of vibration is of a consistent structure, like any one
of the strings in this piano, it will emit *regular* waves,
and we hear them as a musical tone. Of course, the source
doesn't have to be a string: it can be a column of air, as in a
clarinet, or a column of steel, as in a tubular bell, or a
stretched animal hide, as in a kettle drum. Whatever it is, it

17

[18]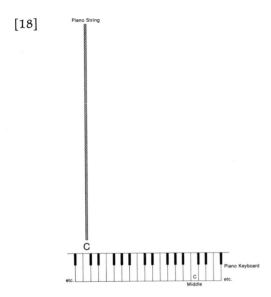

[19]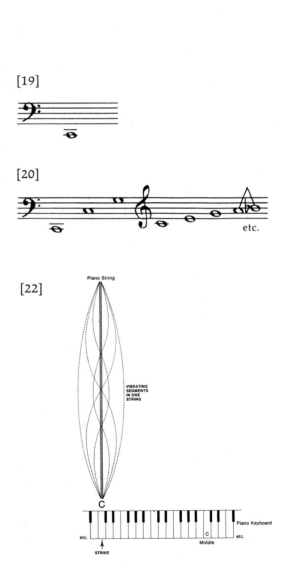

[20]

etc.

[21]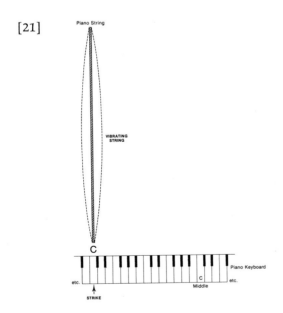

[22]

18

produces what's called "energy in vibratory motion"—
that's the official language—by being beaten, blown, plucked,
struck, or frictionized with a bow. Let's settle for a
piano string, let's say *this* one [18], which is of a particular
length, tension, thickness, and density, and when struck
by its hammer produces soundwaves at a frequency
of 64 vibrations per second, and is known to the world as
the note C [19].

Now comes the interesting part. If I sit at the piano and
play that low C, you may think you're hearing only that one
tone—a dark, rich bass note—but you're not; you are
simultaneously hearing a whole series of higher tones that
are sounding at the same time [20]. These are arranged in
an order preordained by nature and ruled by universal
physical laws. If this is news to you, I hope it's good news.

All these upper notes of which you may be unaware
result from a phenomenon of nature whereby any sound-
producing source, or I should say "pitch-producing source",
such as that piano string, vibrates not only as the whole
string, in all its whatever-inch glory, sounding that low C
[21], but also in fractional segments of that string [22]—
each vibrating separately. It's as though the string were
infinitely divisible, into two halves, into three thirds, four
quarters, and so on. And the smaller those segments are, the
faster they vibrate, producing higher and higher frequencies
and therefore higher and higher tones—OVERtones. And
these overtones, or harmonics, as they're also called, are all
sounding together with the fundamental sound of the full
string. This is the basic principle by which the entire
harmonic series is generated, starting on any fundamental
tone.

Now if you already knew all that from high school

[23]

[24]

[25]

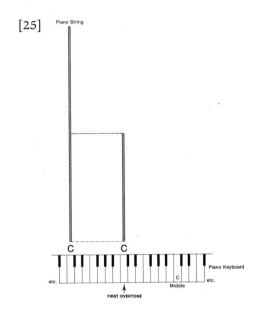

[26]   [27]   [28]

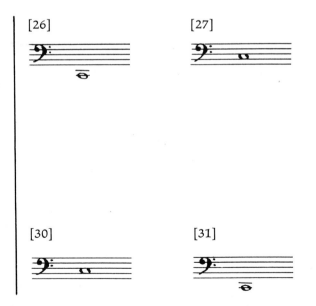

[29]

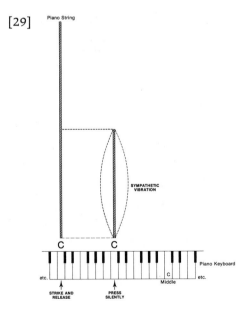

[30]   [31]

physics, you will also know that these overtones are naturally less apparent to the ear than the fundamental, which is in this case low C [23], and in fact they sound more and more faintly as they go higher. Any note I strike [24] will contain its own series of overtones, but the lower the note I strike, the more abundantly audible will be its harmonic series, which accounts in part for the comparative richness of that low C.

Disc
Side 1
band 1

Now remember, I spoke of a preordained order in which the overtones appear. Let's see if I can make you actually hear some of those overtones in that order.

The first overtone of the series [25], according to the laws of physics, has to be exactly an octave higher than the fundamental C we have been hearing [26]. In other words, it's going to be this C [27], an octave higher. Now if I silently press down the key of this higher C and hold it so that the string is free to vibrate, and then abruptly strike the fundamental C an octave lower [28], what do you hear? You are clearly hearing the first overtone vibrating symphathetically an octave above its fundamental [29]. So, obviously, this upper C [30] is an integral part of the C an octave below [31]. It's a built-in harmonic, sounded by the two halves of that lower string vibrating independently [32].

The next overtone of this preordained order results from that same fundamental string vibrating in three parts: and this one will be the first *different* overtone—that is, the first one you'll hear other than a C. It's going to be a G [33]. And now, let's repeat our experiment: I press this new one down silently, then again strike the fundamental C [34]. And what do we hear now? That G, right? A new tone, again clear as a bell. Now we've just reached a very

[32]

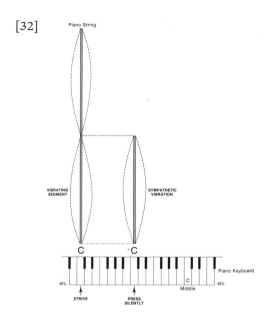

[33]

[34]

21

[35]

[36]

[37] octave
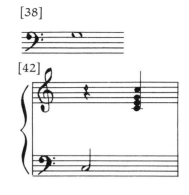
C   G

Tonic Dominant

[38]

[39] 5th

[40]

[41]

[42]
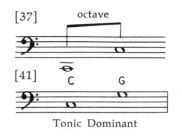

[43]
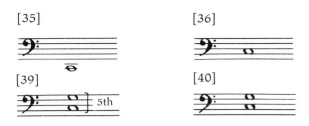

[44]
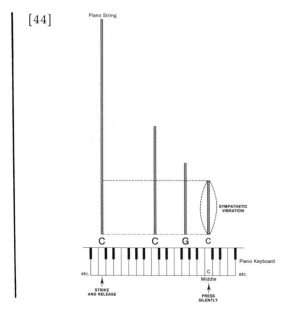

[45]

[46] 4th

[47]
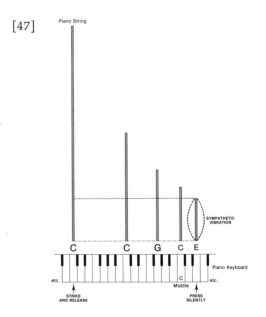

[48]
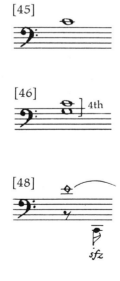
sfz

22

significant point. Have you noticed that the fundamental tone [35] and its first overtone [36] are really the same note, C, but an octave apart [37]? But this new overtone, G [38] is a fifth away from C [39]. So we now have two *different* tones; and once they are established in our ears [40], we are in possession of the key to the whole tonal system—a system based on the concept of tonic and dominant [41]. The C represents the idea of tonic, which has the function of establishing the tonal basis of any given key [42]. The function of the dominant (G) is to aid and abet in the establishment of that tonality through a special relationship it enjoys with the tonic, owing to their proximity in the harmonic series [43].

But more of that later. Right now on to the next overtone [44], which is again a C [45], a fourth higher than the G we just heard [46]. But the next one is again a new pitch, this time a third higher than its predecessor [47]—(notice that the intervals are getting progressively smaller as we ascend the series—which began with an octave, then a fifth, a fourth, and now a third), and this new overtone will be this note E [48]. Listen. It's a bit fainter, but it's there for all to hear.

And there you have the first four overtones of the series: the fundamental, plus one, two, three, four [49 and 50], three of which are *different* pitches [51]. Now it must be obvious to you that these three notes, rearranged in scalar order [52], constitute what is known as the *major* triad [53], which is the very nucleus, the cornerstone of most of the music we hear from day to day, whether it's a symphony or a hymn or a blues. This triad—with its tonic-dominant relationship [54], plus the third sandwiched in between [55]—this triad is the foundation of Western tonal music as

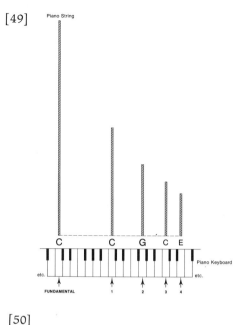

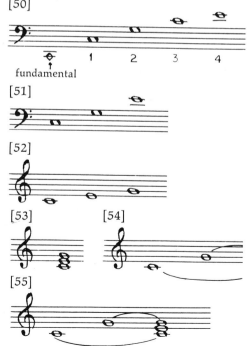

Videotaping a lecture, WGBH studio

24

it has developed over the last three centuries or so, along with the development of our Western culture in general.

But let's not make the mistake so many people make of regarding this triad as a basic universal: that is a misapprehension that is far too common, in that it fails to recognize that our Occidental culture is only one of many world cultures, in spite of its current prevalence and worldwide influence. A perfect example of this misconception arises with the very next overtone in the series, which is a stranger to Western tonal culture. In fact, this next overtone does not even appear on the piano, which means that I can't demonstrate it for you as I have all the preceding ones. More exactly stated, it is not to be found on the piano in its natural, or pure form, as it derives by physical law from that fundamental C string.

Let me digress for a moment to tell you why. You see, this piano, like all keyboard instruments, is a *tempered* instrument, which means simply that its notes have been tempered, or tampered with, so that each one of them can serve its function in all twelve keys at once. This readjustment in tuning became inevitable when music reached its tonal adulthood, around 1700, and found that it didn't have to remain in one key from the beginning to the end of a piece, but could modulate from one key to another in the course of it. But the notes deriving naturally from the harmonic series will work in only one key at a time. That is, what's in tune in one key is likely to be out of tune in another. Would you believe that if this piano were to encompass only natural, untempered tones, this single octave space [56] would have to contain seventy-seven different keys? Well, you can understand that a compromise had to be made somewhere, and that somewhere was the

[56]

[57]

[58]

[59]

[60]

[61]

[62]

[63]

Nya nya   Nya nya   Al – lee, al – lee   in   free!

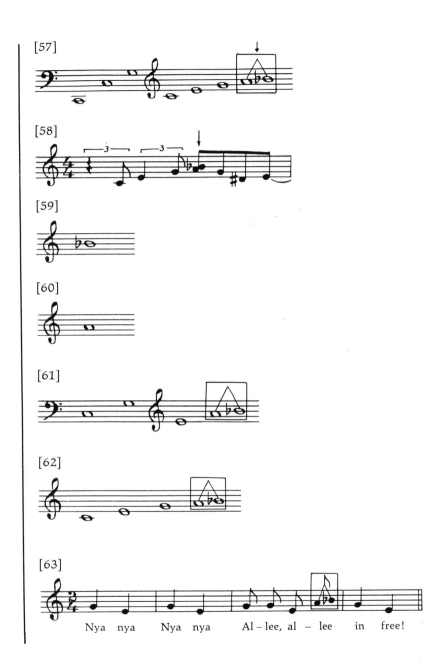

moment in history when the rapid development of tonal harmony coincided with the equally rapid development of keyboard instruments with their fixed unchangeable tones.

Disc
Side 1
band 2

And that's how the tempered clavichord came to be, to say nothing of this Baldwin grand. And that's why I can't play you this next overtone. Actually, if we approach it pianistically in our ascent of the harmonic series we find it somewhere around here [57], lying in the crack between this B flat and the A. It's one of those blue notes [58]. That blue note can be construed by the human ear as either the higher version of the note, B flat [59], or the lower version, A [60]. In either case, it requires a little push up or down to be accommodated on a piano.

But, whichever way we construe it, it becomes our newest overtone. So we are now equipped with four different overtones [61]: the C *plus* G plus the E plus that blue note, that dubious A. Or, rearranged in scalar order [62], C, E, G, and sort-of-A. And here we hit a real musico-linguistic universal: because now we can understand and explain that famous worldwide teasing chant [63]. Because all it is, is a constellation of those first four different overtones [64] with the tonic omitted, or rather, implied. You see, this *tonic* C [65], which is the same note as the *fundamental* C [66], is heard in the mind's ear; and only the three *new* overtones are sung [67]. Those three universal notes are handed to us by Nature on a silver platter [68]. But why are they in this different order—G, E, and sort-of-A? Because that is the very order in which they appear in the harmonic series: G, E, and sort-of-A [69]. Q.E.D.

Now this is a *substantive universal*—the sort of thing

[64]

C   E   G   A+

[65]

[66]

[67]

E   G   A+

[68]

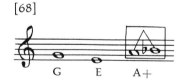

G   E   A+

[69]

28

linguists hunger for, but the likes of which are simply not available to them. Indeed, as we ascend further in our harmonic series, more and more fascinating and incontrovertible universals keep appearing. For instance, this next

Disc
Side 1
band 3

new overtone is D [70]. And so, we now have five different tones to play with [71], which we again put into scalar order [72], and presto, a new universal is given us—the five-note, or pentatonic scale. Now because of that dubious last note [73], the scale can take either of two forms, one culminating in B flat [74] and the other in A [75]. Let's opt for the second of these, the lower one, which is by far the more common of the two [76]. This is humanity's favorite pentatonic scale, and by the way, this is the scale you can find so easily on your own piano by playing only the black notes [77]. In fact, the universality of this scale is so well known that I'm sure you could give *me* examples of it, from all corners of the earth, as from Scotland [78], or from China [79], or from Africa [80], and from American Indian cultures, from East Indian cultures, from Central and South America, Australia, Finland . . . now, *that* is a true musico-linguistic universal.

But let's be careful about making linguistic analogies: we *could* conceivably equate a fundamental tone such as this C [81], with the basic morpheme MA, which we discovered before, and extend the parallel by equating the overtones of that fundamental C with a set of words evolving from that MA syllable—maybe; it's all still speculation. But what appears to be much more convincing is the analogy between Chomsky's innate grammatical competence and the innate musical-grammatical competence which we may all possess universally. This competence would be our in-built capacity to construe those naturally serialized overtones, and to

construe them *in different ways,* just as the various cultures
of the world may have construed basic monogenetic materials and constructed out of them thousands of particular
grammars or languages, all different from one another.

Analogously, varied human cultures can construe this
pentatonic scale in different ways, depending, for example,
on which of the five notes is taken to be the tonal center,
for example this one [82]. That's one way. Or this one
[83], if we shift the center of gravity. You see how it makes
it a whole different pentatonic? But they are the same five
notes, only with a different tonic.

Here's yet another [84]. Obviously there are five different
Disc
Side 2
band 1
pentatonic scales available depending on the tonic. And
to add to the diversity, there is always that "blue note" to be
considered [85]. If the ear construes it as the upper B flat
instead of the lower A, it would give us a whole other
pentatonic scale [86], which produces some beautiful
African music. And there are even more complex processes
which we won't go into, but which account for the existence
of the highly differentiated Japanese pentatonic scale [87],
or the unique pentatonic of Balinese music [88]. But
enough of pentatonics. I think we've seen enough of the
way the harmonic series operates to recognize the fact that
as we ascend the series [89], always finding new tones to
be added to our collection, we can eventually account for six-
and seven-note scales (including Greek modes and church
modes) and the diatonic scales (both major and minor) and
eventually all twelve tones of our so-called chromatic
scale [90].

And you may well ask, why just twelve tones? Patience.
You'll find out in a minute. But even these twelve tones
don't exhaust the potential of the harmonic series. The

upper reaches of the series continue to furnish us with intervals even smaller than the half tones that make up our chromatic scale—intervals such as quarter tones, or even thirds and fifths of tones, all of which still inhabit areas of experimentation and electronic research; to say nothing of microtones, which are such an essential part of much Oriental music.

But the overriding fact that emerges from all this is that *all* music—whether folk, pop, symphonic, modal, tonal, atonal, polytonal, microtonal, well-tempered or ill-tempered, music from the distant past or the imminent future—all of it has a common origin in the universal phenomenon of the harmonic series. And that is our case for musical monogenesis, to say nothing of innateness.

But is it necessarily a case for universality? Think—what about those Hindu ragas that so many people find difficult to comprehend? I suggest a simple answer, in the light of our linguistic analogies. Just as the grammars of human languages (even mutually unintelligible ones) may have sprung from the same monogenetic sources, so in the same way highly varied musical tongues (which are also strangers to one another) can be said to have developed out of their common origins. In purely phonological terms, these tongues are tonal languages that have developed out of a universal, naturally ordered tonal structure.

I trust you realize that all of this has been enormously compressed and undocumented by historical musical examples. That would take all night. But this is not a linguistics course, nor is it a History of Music course. What we're trying for is a high overview of musical development in terms of a vocabulary constantly being enriched by more and more remote and chromatic overtones. It's as if we

[91] Fair Har – vard thy sons to thy Ju – bi – lee throng

[92] And with bless – ings sur – ren – der thee o'er

[93] octave

[94] octave

[95] 5th

[96] By these fes – ti – val rites from the Age that is past

[97] 4th

[98]

[99]

[100]

[101] Maestoso

34

could see the whole of music developing from prehistory to the present, in two minutes.

Disc
Side 2
band 2

Let's again pretend we're hominids, and that the smash hit of the moment is, say, "Fair Harvard." Here we are, in our hominid hut, crooning [91]. Now maybe our wives, and maybe our prepubescent sons, join in, and automatically we're singing not in unison but in octaves, since men's and women's voices are naturally an octave apart [92]. Now that octave interval [93] happens to be the first interval of the harmonic series [94], if you remember. Do you?

Centuries pass, and inevitably the *next* interval of the harmonic series is assimilated by humanity, namely the fifth [95]. And now we can be singing: "By these festival rites from the Age that is past . . ." [96] Of course, this little change brings us forward a mere ten million years, into the tenth century A.D., and into a fairly sophisticated musical culture. But now we admit the next interval of the series—the fourth [97]—so that we can *mix* intervals of the octave and the fifth and the fourth [98]. That's beginning to sound like polyphony.

Again comes a great leap, as music absorbs the next overtone, acquiring the interval of the third. Just listen to the difference [99]. It's a whole new music, richer, mellower, with a new coloristic warmth. (I must admit I like the older sound better.) As we know, this new interval of the third introduces into music the phenomenon of the triad [100], so that now "Fair Harvard" can begin to sound more like its Victorian self [101]. And so there is born what we now call tonal music, a stable tonal language firmly rooted in the basic notes of the harmonic series, the fundamental [102] and its first different overtone, the fifth [103]—now and forevermore to be known as the tonic [104] and the dominant [105].

[102]

[103]

[104]

[105]

35

tonic   dominant   subdominant   supertonic   new dominant   new tonic

36

And that fifth interval really does dominate; because once
this tonic-dominant relationship is established, it is a
field day for composers. There can now be fifths of fifths of
fifths [106], each one of them a new tonic producing a new
dominant—a whole circle of fifths—twelve of them, in fact,
always winding up with the starting tone, whether
proceeding upwards, let's say from the low C [106], or
preceding downwards [107] back to C. That's a circle of
twelve fifths: and that's the answer I promised you; that's
how we get the twelve different tones of our chromatic
scale. If you take all twelve tones of the circle of fifths and
put them together in scalar order you get this [108]. And
those twelve notes generate a circle of twelve *keys* through
which, thanks to the perfecting of the tempered system,
composers can now go free-wheeling at their own chromatic
pleasure [109].

Disc
Side 2
band 3 Ultimately "Fair Harvard" can sound like this [110].
That's chromatic porridge; and in our own century it's going
to become goulash. How does music contain this loose,
runny chromaticism? By the basic principle of *diatonicism*
—that stable relationship of tonics and dominants, subdominants and supertonics, new dominants and new tonics
[111]. We can now modulate as freely as we want, as
chromatically as we want, and still have complete tonal
control.

This great system of tonal controls was perfected and
codified by Johann Sebastian Bach, whose genius was to
balance so delicately, and so justly, these two forces of
chromaticism and diatonicism, forces that were equally
powerful and presumably contradictory in nature. This
point of delicate balance is like the still center in the flux of
musical history—a condition of such stability that it was

able to continue without remarkable changes for almost a century, a century which became a Golden Age.

This is not to say that there were not drastic changes in style and form during those hundred years. After all, this Golden Age saw the emergence of a whole new Rococo style, to say nothing of the phenomenal rise of sonata form in the hands of such giants as Carl Philipp Emanuel Bach, Haydn, Mozart, and Beethoven himself. But these changes are syntactic and semantic changes, which we'll be examining and enjoying in future lectures. Right now we're limiting our investigation to phonology, and in these specific terms we can see the peak attained by Bach continuing as a kind of plateau, level and lofty, right into the music of Beethoven.

At this point I would like to invite you to listen with me to one of the supreme examples of this Golden Age, Mozart's G Minor Symphony, a work of utmost passion utterly controlled, and of free chromaticism elegantly contained. I'll try to prepare you a bit with a few illustrations of this control and containment in the hope that you can then hear the symphony with fresh, phonological ears. Remember: what we're looking for is the wonderfully creative ways in which chromatic flexibility can be systematically contained within the framework of tonic-dominant relationships.

It's a curious thing, and a crucial one, that through this perfect combination of opposites, chromaticism and diatonicism, there is distilled the essence of ambiguity. Now this word "ambiguity" may seem the most unlikely word to use in speaking of a Golden Age composer like Mozart, a master of clarity and precision. But ambiguity has always inhabited musical art (indeed, all the arts), because it is one of art's most potent aesthetic functions. The more

ambiguous, the more expressive, up to a certain point.
Of course, there's a limit, which we're going to run into in
the course of these lectures. We're eventually going to
arrive at a state of such increased ambiguity that problems
of musical clarity are bound to arise. That's when we'll
be confronted head on by Ives' Unanswered Question—
whither?

But, meanwhile, we're still in the Golden Age, with
ambiguity classically contained in the Augustan balances and
proportions inherent in this Mozart symphony. Let's look
at it very briefly.

You all remember the opening of the first movement
[112]. Now this whole section moves quite easily and
diatonically from its G-minor tonic to its first cadence, which
is, naturally enough, on the dominant [113], and just as
easily slips back into the tonic [114]. (You remember that
this tonic-dominant relationship arises from the adjacency
of the fundamental tone, in this case G [115], with its
first overtone [116], that basic interval of a fifth.) From this
point the music proceeds by the circle of fifths in a downward progression [117], to its relative major, B flat, which is
exactly where it's supposed to be (according to sonata-form
principles), for the appearance of the second thematic section
[118]. But notice that Mozart's new theme is already
chromatically formed [119], and it gets more so as it goes
on [120]; and even more so when it repeats [121].

[119]

[120]

[121]

41

What's this? A-flat major, a sudden new key, unrelated to either B flat or G minor. How did we get *here?* By the well-known circle of fifths [122]. Do you hear those stable consecutive fifths striding inexorably from dominant to tonic in the bass? [123] And each dominant leads to a tonic which instantly becomes itself a dominant, leading in turn to *its* tonic. While above, the melodic line descends by chromatic half-steps into the nether regions of A-flat major! There's that classical balance we were talking about—chromatic wandering on top [124] but firmly supported by the inverted tonic-dominant structure underneath [125].

Do you see now what I mean by the beauty of ambiguity? It's the combination of those two contradictory forces, chromaticism and diatonicism, operating at the same time, that makes this passage so expressive.

So, we're in the midst of a chromatic adventure. How do we get out of this strange A-flat territory? [126] By a simple chromatic shift, like side-slipping on skis [127]—and there we are back safely in B-flat major, where we belong.

Now, if you could follow that, you can follow any number of similar adventures—for instance, the way Mozart starts his development section. He has established us firmly in B-flat major [128]; but, no [129], off he goes on another chromatic adventure [130] which lands us in the impossible key of F-sharp minor! Now, this was done by absolute whim—arbitrarily. It's a bit of chromatic acrobatics, if you will, startling us into a development section, which is just what a development section should be—startling new looks at old material. But, eventually, he must get us back to a recapitulation in G minor, the original home soil. And he's completely free to make this journey as chromatically as he wishes; his fantasy is totally released. After all, it's a

44

development section, free-wheeling time. But even here, the
basic diatonic laws contain and control that free-wheeling,
the passion, the fantasy. And all by those progressions
of fifths—the dominant seeking its tonic and each tonic
turning into a dominant seeking its tonic, over and over
again. We were in F-sharp minor, right? [131] Now, through
a sequence of such progressions, he changes that F-sharp
tonality from a tonic function to a dominant function [132],
which is seeking its tonic, B natural, and here we are! [133]
But now B natural is a dominant seeking its tonic, E, and
so into E we go [134]—and by the same chain of fifths, E
seeks A [135]. And A seeks D [136], and so on through the
circle until we're finally led back home to G minor. But
even this lead-in to the home key is highly chromatic, only
firmly held in place by a dominant pedal. (Listen to this
creepy, crawly chromaticism . . .) [137]. And we're back to our
oh-so-gratifying and welcome recapitulation in G minor.

   Now, I must point out that these adventures are much
more complex and subtle than I made them sound. The
procedure is not always exactly by fifths; there are twists
and turns which would take hours to describe accurately,
even to a classroom of Harvard music students. The best I
can do is to give you some insight into this marvel of
ambiguity, the diatonic containment of chromaticism, so that
when you hear—for instance, in the second movement—
this extraordinary chromatic passage [138], you can also be

[138]   Andante

aware of the strong diatonic underpinnings, those fifths in
the bass again striding inexorably from tonic to dominant
[139]. Even in the third movement, the minuet (which is
extremely diatonic, hardly chromatic at all [140]), Mozart
cannot resist, just before the end, one of his charming
chromatic excursions [141]. But, instantly, it all rights itself
in a classical dominant-tonic cadence [142].

The most breathtaking chromatic trip of all occurs in
the final movement, which begins innocently enough, and
isn't too eventful tonally throughout the whole exposition
[143]. But then, again comes the development section,
and all hell breaks loose [144]. Do you realize that that wild,
atonal-sounding passage contains every one of the twelve
chromatic tones except the tonic note G? What an inspired
idea—all the notes except the tonic! It could easily pass
for twentieth-century music, if we didn't already know it
was Mozart. But even that explosion of chromaticism is
explainable in terms of the circle of fifths, not that I'd dream
of burdening you with it. Take my word for it, that out-
burst of chromatic rage is classically contained, and so is the

[144]

climax of this development section, which finds itself in the unlikely key of C-sharp minor [145], which is as far away as you can get from the home key of G minor. And, again, believe me: all these phonological arrivals and departures to and from the most distantly related areas operate in the smoothest, Mozartian way, under perfect diatonic control.

What does this all add up to? Let's find out by hearing the whole work, and I hope we'll be listening to it with fresh ears.

(At this point, Mozart's Symphony No. 40 in G Minor K. 550, is performed.)

What a piece! No amount of analysis or explanation can prepare one for the overwhelming surprise of its existence when it is actually heard in performance. It is hard to think of another work that so perfectly marries form and passion.

Finally, a short word about our subject next time, which will be syntax—you remember, the second of the three linguistic departments—musical and linguistic syntax. We will be examining some of the structural formations of these phonological elements we've discussed tonight. Then we'll be ready to understand the *semantic* problems of music from Mozart to the present, and I hope come closer to understanding, and maybe even answering, Ives' Unanswered Question.

2. MUSICAL SYNTAX

Every once in a while during the preparation of these lectures, I find myself asking—and others asking me— what's the relevance of all this musico-linguistics? Can it lead us to an answer of Charles Ives' Unanswered Question —whither music?—and even if it eventually can, does it matter? The world totters, governments crumble, and we are poring over musical phonology, and now syntax. Isn't it a flagrant case of elitism?

Well, in a way it is; certainly not elitism of class— economic, social, or ethnic—but of curiosity, that special, inquiring quality of the intelligence. And it was ever thus. But these days, the search for meaning-through-beauty and vice versa becomes even more important as each day mediocrity and art-mongering increasingly uglify our lives; and the day when this search for John Keats' truth-beauty ideal becomes irrelevant, then we can all shut up and go back to our caves. Meanwhile, to use that unfortunate word again, it is thoroughly relevant; and I as a musician feel that there has to be a way of speaking about music with intelligent but nonprofessional music lovers who don't know a stretto from a diminished fifth; and the best way I have found so far is by setting up a working analogy with language, since language is something everyone shares and uses and knows about.

Last week we went rather extensively into phonological aspects of both language and music, seeking analogies between linguistic universals and the natural musical universals that arise out of the harmonic series. It is time now to investigate analogies from a new point of view, that of syntax, which is the study of the actual structures by which those sonic universals have evolved into words, and words into sentences. And here is where the name of

Chomsky assumes a critical importance. For Noam Chomsky, like most linguists, is not primarily interested in historical inquiry such as monogenesis, or theories of the Origin of Language, but rather in analytical inquiry— seeking universal rules of syntax *and* phonology which can apply to the 4,000 or so particular languages that exist in the world today.

Now I am obviously in no position to present a critical analysis of Chomsky's work, nor would time permit me to even if I were. What interests us here is not the rationalist Cartesian philosophy to which Chomsky has returned to seek his roots. But we are interested in why he returned to those roots, because it is from them that his ideas of a "universal grammar" have grown. In brief, he believes along with Descartes that there are human phenomena which cannot be explained by any purely corporeal theory; that the physical theories of body must be supplemented by the postulation of another substance, to be called Mind. This philosophical proposal, of course, is in frequent conflict with empiricist thought, as exemplified by a Locke or a Berkeley, and currently by the behaviorists, who demand perceived evidence at all costs. But the Cartesians insist, and say further that the theory of corporeal body cannot account for the most obvious facts of human action, the basic properties of thought, and in particular the normal use of human language.

Amen, says Noam Chomsky to all that; there must exist in all of us an innate language faculty, or as he calls it, a linguistic competence. He starts with a simple but riveting question: How else, he asks, can we account for brand-new utterances by two-and-a-half-year-old children—grammatical sentences which they can produce without ever having heard them before? What rules enable them to do this amazingly creative thing—to say for instance, "I like the green ice cream" (in whatever language—Zulu, French or Eskimo) a sentence which neither has been taught them, nor is an imitation of that sentence previously uttered by someone else, but is a sentence newly invented on the basis of very skimpy grammatical data gleaned from the child's immediate environment? It is an amazing question. Just think about it for a second.

Chomsky arrived at this concept of universal grammar by steadily refining a theory in which he postulates what he calls "formal universals"—that is, genetically inherited types of rules that operate on the most profound level in all languages. I believe that in seeking these rules he was driven by a need to see the world whole, to understand the human mind rather than the American or Zulu or French or Eskimo mind. He has always stressed the importance of the latent similarities among languages rather than the patent differences among them. The differences are indeed more obvious, but they are also more superficial, whereas the similarities are more profound, and at least as striking as the differences. With time, in fact, the similarities grow increasingly more striking, and infinitely more exciting because they reinforce our feelings about a single united human race. And I believe it is this almost Beethovenian impulse that has impelled him through his own developments.

I suppose what Chomsky is really after is a system that can describe the miracles that enable us to form intelligible verbalizations of our primal need to share what we know and feel. And what this system does is to provide us with a new way of looking at the miraculous process by which we structure even the simplest sentences; and the study of these structures is known as *syntax*.

But what does syntactic investigation have to do with music? All musical thinkers agree that there is such a thing as a musical syntax, comparable to a descriptive grammar of speech. Using the terms of this syntax they are able, in one way or another, to analyze and account for most musical phenomena—except, of course, the main one: talent. No one can explain that. But what of you, untrained and unprofessional music lovers? How can I make syntactic musical analysis comprehensible to you? I could try, by using a musical equivalent of grammatical description; but imagine how tedious it would be. For example, I could take the opening phrase of Mozart's G Minor Symphony, which we heard last week, and parse it, as we used to be taught in school to parse a phrase or a clause [1]. Now I could say that this is in G minor and in a duple meter of half notes; that the melodic material begins with the two eighth-note upbeats [2], which are respectively the sixth and fifth notes of the G-minor scale, leading by repetition to a quarter-note downbeat on that same fifth tone—and so on, and so on—unbearable, and purely gratuitous information. It would be an endless description, and it would wind up telling you very little more about the music than you would know from just hearing it. But you may argue, that was only a description and not a grammatical explanation; that is, I have not pointed out to you the functions and interactions of these eighth notes and quarter notes and downbeats. Right; only that would bring

[1]

[2]

56

us back to musical syntax again, and you would have to own a great deal of technical terminology. But you could understand the inner syntactic functions of that Mozart, or any other music, for that matter, by analogy with similar functions in language. And there *are* similar functions, cognate processes operating in both music and language which are discoverable by linguistic method. All we need is to have analogous terms in which to articulate them.

So let's pull up our socks, and make a stab at constructing a quasi-scientific analogy between verbal and musical terms. I say *quasi*-scientific because in using linguistic analogy I should, strictly speaking, be committed to "scientific method." But I am not a scientist. I will inevitably make certain statements in one context which would be false in another. Even scientists freely admit that they do this, especially philosophical scientists; so did Nietzsche, so did Kierkegaard, and so does Chomsky, by his own say-so. How much truer of me. Therefore, I am restricted to hypothesizing and speculation; if I am lucky, I may strike a nugget or two. And if I am really lucky, I may suggest some hints that will stimulate further thought among those of you who are scientifically well-grounded.

O.K., let's examine one of many attempts that have been made to establish consistent correspondences between verbal and musical elements. How about starting with this simple equation: a note equals a letter [3]. Now, by extension, that equation would yield this one: a scale equals an alphabet. That is, all the notes we use equal all the letters we use. But whose notes, and whose alphabet? The twelve notes of our Western chromatic scale, or the five notes of the Chinese pentatonic scale? And which alphabet —the German, the Russian, the Arabic? Well, so much for

[3]

MUSIC   LANGUAGE
1) note = letter
2) scale = alphabet

[4] **1)** **MUSIC**   **LANGUAGE**

       note = **phoneme**

MUSIC   **LANGUAGE**

1)   **note** = **phoneme**

[5] **2)**   **motive** = **morpheme**

MUSIC   **LANGUAGE**

1)   **note** = **phoneme**

2)   **motive** = **morpheme**

[6] **3)**   **phrase** = **word**

MUSIC   **LANGUAGE**

1)   **note** = **phoneme**

2)   **motive** = **morpheme**

3)   **phrase** = **word**

[7] **4)**   **section** = **clause**

5) movement = **sentence**

6)   **piece** = **piece**

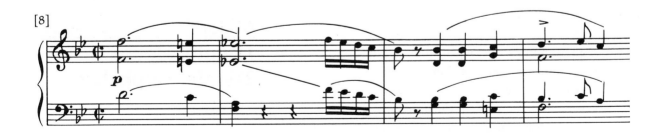

[8]

58

that one. We have arrived at chaos. We obviously need a better system.

All right; let's try another one, more scientifically oriented in that it employs a phonetic terminology, so that one isn't stuck with loose terms like "alphabet". Here goes: a note equals a phoneme [4], which is a minimal sound unit such as *Mmm* or *Sss* or *Eee*. Then, a motive, or motto, or even a theme, would equal a morpheme, that is, a minimal meaningful sound unit, like *ma,* or *see,* or *me* [5]. In that case, a *phrase* of music [6] would have to correspond to a word (uh-o, we are getting into trouble here); and a musical *section* would then equal a clause, and a whole *movement* would be a sentence, and a complete *piece* would equal a complete piece [7].

Well, that finally looks a little better (piece = piece), but it still has its problems. If we accept that a phrase of music equals a word of language we are closer to understanding Mozart's music. For instance, take the second theme of this same G Minor Symphony [8]. Those first three notes sound like a word [9]; that's a fairly convincing isolated unit. So is the next unit [10]. A fine word. But here again the analogy breaks down, because the last note of the first word, as played by the strings [11], also functions as the first note of the second word, as played by the woodwinds [12], which is linguistically impossible. It's as though one said the words "dead duck" with the final "d" of "dead" serving as the initial "d" of "duck": deaduck. Impossible. Then there is the further confusion in the use of the term *phrase.* All one's instincts cry out for *phrase* to equal *phrase* instead of *word* or whatever else.

Why am I taking your time to show you analogies that don't work? For this very important reason: to get your

[13]

[14]

Cadence

[15]

End   Beginning

minds into the swing of thinking about music in the same way you think about language. These failed attempts I've been showing are not in vain. And curiously enough, the best thing about this particular attempt [see 7] you are looking at now is the equation that seems offhand to be weakest: namely, *movement* equals *sentence*. It seems at first like total confusion; try, for instance, to think of the whole first movement of that Mozart symphony as one sentence. And yet there is truth in it. I believe it is no accident that the German word *Satz* means both "sentence" and "symphonic movement".

But the fact is there *are* no sentences in music, as there are in prose, since most continuous pieces of music do not reach a full stop until they end. And if we define "full stop" (in tonal music, at least) as a full cadence [13] and take that to be the equivalent of a period at the end of a prose sentence, then we can find dozens of them in the course of a movement such as Mozart's, but in every case that cadence coincides with the beginning of the next episode, or "sentence," so to speak. In other words, there is no pause for the period such as I make now to end this sentence. Period. Pause. Next sentence. It is in the nature of music to be *ongoing,* so that as we approach a full cadence in Mozart [14], we seem to be arriving at the end of a sentence, but no: on it goes [15], no period; and the cadence turns out to be the beginning of a new episode. I'm afraid it's "dead duck" time again. It seems as if all music is made up of relative clauses, all interdependently linked by conjunctions and relative pronouns; and therefore, it seems that the closest we can get to a prose sentence in music is an entire movement.

Well, then, given all this terminological chaos, what

[16]

[17]

[18]

[19]

[20]

Cruel Fate

[21]

Kind Fate

[22]

Tricky Fate

[23] Waltz Tempo

mf

interdisciplinary terms *can* we use (without cheating)? I think there are some equations that will stand the test. For one, we can confidently equate a musical motive, or motto, with a grammatical substantive or noun (or "noun phrase", as they say in linguistics). For example, the Fate motive in Wagner's Ring Operas [16]. Now those three melodic notes [17] are like three letters (or phonemes or morphemes, whichever you prefer) that make up a word which is a noun, a substantive, a self-naming entity. (I don't mean that it names "Fate", either; it is a *musical* noun all by itself no matter what it stands for in the opera. That Wagner intended it to signify "Fate" is the sort of semantic consideration we will consider in our next lecture.)

Secondly, we can equate a chord, a harmonic entity [18], with a grammatical modifier, such as an adjective, because obviously the chord *modifies* by descriptive coloration the noun to which it is attached. So those three notes [19] of Wagner's Fate motive acquire a specific added meaning because of the chords that modify them; for instance: Cruel Fate [20], or Kind Fate [21], or Tricky Fate [22].

I think it follows that if we can identify musical analogues of nouns and adjectives, we can do the same with verbs, the analogue here being obviously with rhythm, with material which activates or motorizes the substantive just as a verb does. Here is the same Wagner motive activated by rhythm [23]. What has happened is simply that I have added a verb function in the form of a waltz rhythm to the noun-plus-adjective functions already present. It is as though I had made a musical equivalent of the sentence *Cruel Fate waltzes.* One could go further, and show a combined verb-adjective function, as in a Chopin Nocturne, where the arpeggio accompaniment is at the same time

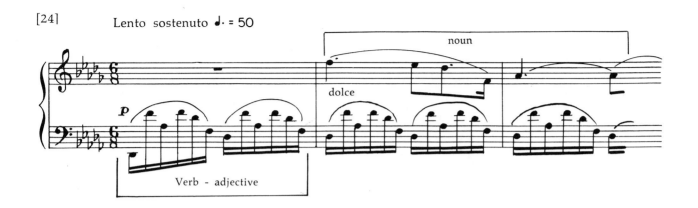

both a rhythmic activator *and* a chordal modifier of the noun which appears as a melody [24]. The possible extensions of this idea are innumerable: what I am hinting at here is that convincing musical analogues might be found for *all* parts of speech. Now there is a fascinating subject for an honors thesis. I wish I were back here at school: I would try it myself.

In any case, now that we have seen some of the ways in which we can think comparatively about music and language, and maybe even have some terminology in common, we are ready to return to Chomsky and see how his principles can be applied to music.

But first—what are these principles? It would take all of our six lectures to explain them: but briefly stated, his work has been, and continues to be, a steady progression of insights into what he calls "transformational grammar". He found in his early work that the existing concepts of grammatical analysis were inadequate, because they could account for certain linguistic relationships, but not for others. For instance, they were adequate to explain a sentence such as *The man hit the ball*, but not to explain how that sentence relates to more complex ones like *The ball was hit by the man*; or, *It was the man who hit the ball*; or, *It was the ball that was hit by the man*—all of which are basically synonymous.

I can remember in the old days back at the Boston Latin School, we were taught to analyze sentences by parsing, and that seemed perfectly adequate. We could take a sentence like *Jack loves Jill*, and analyze it very simply by breaking it down into its components [25]: *Jack*, subject of the transitive verb *loves*; *Jill*, object of the same. There doesn't seem to be anything more to say about that diagram. Just a subject and a predicate.

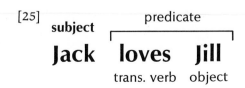

[25]

subject   predicate

Jack loves Jill

trans. verb object

Videotaping a lecture, WGBH studio

In the same way we would parse the passive version of that sentence: *Jill is loved by Jack* [26], where now *Jill* is the subject of the sentence, the subject of the *passive* verb *is loved*, leaving *by Jack* in the lowly position of an adverbial phrase.

Perfectly clear parsing. Nothing wrong with it, except that it doesn't explain the relationship between the two sentences—that is, it provides no means of exemplifying the subconscious processes by which the first sentence has been turned into the second.

Transformational grammar, on the other hand, does provide such means. Let me give you a tiny example. Here is the way a transformational grammarian would diagram *Jack loves Jill* [27]. (Don't let it throw you. I am not going to explain all those NP's and VP's; I just want you to get the main point.) As you can see, this is not radically different from my Boston Latin School version, except in the method of diagramming. This "tree diagram", as they call it, shows Jack on the bottom still in the subject position, on the left hand side, while Jill is on the right, just as in my Latin School diagram. Right? But it also shows us something else, and this is important: it shows us how transformational linguists approach language. They organize it on two levels—a surface level and a deep level. What you see at the top is the sentence as it is spoken: *Jack loves Jill*. This is called the "surface structure". What you see at the bottom *resembles* that surface structure; but it also reveals the sentence on a deeper level, and is therefore called the "deep structure". *Jack love Jill*. There is obviously one little difference between the deep structure and the surface structure: the addition of the letter *s* to the verb *love*, which obeys a rule of English regarding the

[26]

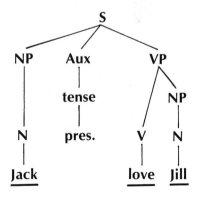

subject | predicate
Jill | **is loved** | **by Jack**
         | passive verb | adv. phrase

[27]

Jack loves Jill.

S

NP   Aux   VP

tense   NP

N   pres.   V   N

Jack   love   Jill

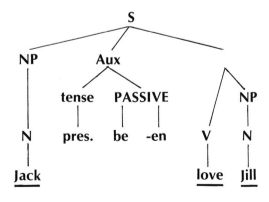

[28]

Jill is loved by Jack.

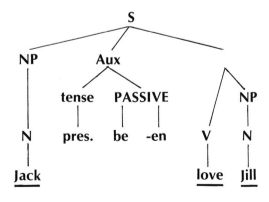

present tense. That already represents a transformation, albeit a trivial one; and to that extent it shows us a difference between deep and surface structure.

But now think of that sentence transformed into the passive: *Jill is loved by Jack.* If we were to make a tree diagram of the *surface structure* of this new sentence, it again wouldn't differ significantly from my Boston Latin School version, except in the diagramming. Jill would still be in the left-hand position and Jack on the right. But (and here is the point) we all have the intuitive knowledge that even in this passive form of the sentence, it is still *Jack* who is doing the loving and *Jill* who is getting loved. How to explain this paradox? What's Jill doing in the subject position when she is the object of Jack's love? The transformational linguist explains it by a *deep-structure* diagram [28], which captures our intuitions about the real meaning of that sentence. And what do we find at the bottom of this diagram? The *deep* structure: *Jack LOVE Jill.* Exactly the same as the active version. Eureka.

Since this is not a linguistics class, I have avoided the technical jargon and the complex diagrams which are essential to a real explanation of the transformational process, that is, the process by which the deep structure is converted into the surface structure. But we know enough so that we can now see two utterly different sentences, active and passive, and realize that they both have exactly the same deep structure: *Jack love Jill,* in both cases. Only the second sentence has undergone a passive transformation. You see that big word "passive", there in the diagram? That is the transformation. *Transformation:* that's the key word.

What exactly is a transformation? O.K., Chomsky says,

look: here are two sentences that are obviously related, in fact, mean the same thing but have completely different structures. How do we get from one to the other? Obviously one has been *transformed* into the other, the active into the passive, and that power to transform, he says, is a genetic endowment we all share. If it weren't, and had to be learned laboriously over the years, how come that any child can do it, in any language? A child is born with the capacity to learn sentences. Right? Let's say he learns three basic ones: "The man hit the ball"; "I like green ice cream"; and "Chomsky loves Skinner". That won't get him very far. What does get him far is his equally innate capacity to learn certain types of rules that will transform those sentences into exponentially greater numbers of them. These rule types are called "transformations", and they are the combustion engines of language.

Take the passive transformation, for instance. Once the child grasps that, very early on, he can already say: "The ball was hit by the man". Then once he learns the *negative* transformation, he can say: "The ball was not hit by the man" and "I don't like green ice cream"; to say nothing of, "The man did not hit the ball", and "Green ice cream is not liked by me". Then he learns the interrogative trans-formation, and now he can say: "Wasn't the ball hit by the man?" and "Doesn't Skinner like green ice cream?" and "Am I loved by Chomsky?" It is a breathtaking explosion: the sentences multiply like rabbits: "Does Skinner like to hit Chomsky?" "Doesn't the green ball love ice cream?" I'm going mad, but only out of excitement. And what excites me is that the transformational process is a *creative* one which is responsible for all the varieties of natural human speech, from a child's sentence to the most intricate word patterns of Henry James.

70

This process is made clear to us by the crucial invention called transformational grammar, through which we can see how the tiniest basic concepts, or units of information, buried in the depths of the mind, are selected, combined, connected, and refined, and make their way up through the "neural net" to a mental surface where they are expressible. So, in a larger sense, transformational grammar can provide us with a model of how we think, not only in developing speech formations, but in all kinds of creative expression. I guess that's what I meant in my last lecture by saying that this Chomskian area of investigation might eventually enlighten us on the nature of Mind itself.

Well, it hasn't brought us there quite yet; but you can see why this theoretical system Chomsky has evolved over the last decade or two has been called revolutionary, and at the very least a breakthrough. It is a breakthrough for us, anyway, because for our purposes it offers at last both terminology and procedures that are directly applicable to music.

Even with the tiny amount of linguistic knowledge we have acquired, I think we are ready for the experiment of making musical analogies with a whole prose sentence, not just a word or a phrase. Any simple sentence will do. For instance: *Harvard beat Yale*, with all the possible transformations: *Harvard did not beat Yale. Did Harvard beat Yale? Didn't Harvard beat Yale? Will Harvard beat Yale? . . .* But I think we would do better if we stick with Jack and Jill so as to avoid emotional involvement. These names, you see, are merely linguistic symbols not unlike *x* and *y* in algebra. So Jack and Jill will do as well as any.

O.K. We've got our sentence, *Jack loves Jill*. Now every experiment has to start with certain assumptions, and our basic assumption here would have to be the simple equation, *note = word*, even though we know it to be scientifically shaky. On this basis, let's construct a musical equation that goes: *Jack loves Jill* [29]. Not exactly breath-taking music, nor is it a musical sentence; but it serves our purpose by presenting three notes as deep-structure units linked together to form a triadic surface structure [30], which makes syntactic sense.

Now just as those three notes are linked together, so are the three basic components of the sentence, *Jack*, *love*, and *Jill*, which have also gotten linked together in a kind of chain—in what Chomsky called an "underlying string", borrowing a term from mathematics. The string looks like this: *Jack* plus present tense plus *love* plus *Jill* [31]. This string tells us all we need to know about the situation *except* how it gets structured to form a sentence. That is why it is called an *underlying* string; it underlies the final product, the surface structure.

Now by applying transformational rules, we find that there are at least eight basic sentences that can be derived from that one underlying string:

1. *Jack loves Jill* (which we already know about). Then,
2. *Does Jack love Jill?* (Interrogative transformation.)
3. *Jack does not love Jill.* (Negative transformation.)
4. *Doesn't Jack love Jill?* (Interrogative plus negative transformation.)
5. *Jill is loved by Jack.* (Passive transformation.)
6. *Is Jill loved by Jack?* (Passive plus interrogative transformation.)
7. *Jill is not loved by Jack.* (Passive plus negative transformation.)
8. *Isn't Jill loved by Jack?* (Passive plus negative plus interrogative transformations.)

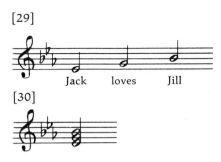

[29]

Jack   loves   Jill

[30]

[31]

Jack + Present + Love + Jill

Disc
Side 2
band 6

All these sentences represent surface structures, as distinct from, but deriving from the same deep structure.

Now, let's go back to our three little notes, this triad [32], and see if similar musical transformations can yield us musical equivalents. For example, the interrogative transformation, *Does Jack love Jill?* How do we turn that triad of notes into a question? One possible way would be to use our modifier principle, that is, chord = adjective, which will provide the Jill-note with an adjectival chord that is questioning and unresolved. And that would give us: *Jack loves Jill, (maybe)* [33]. Or, *Jack loves Jill?* [34] Or, *Jack loves Jill: (I wonder)* [35]. In any case the irresolute last chord functions as a question mark, changing a declarative sentence into an interrogative one [36]. *Does Jack love Jill? (Question mark).*

Now what about the negative transformation? Easy: syntactical change of the verb-note "love" [37] from the major third to the minor third [38], thus plunging the whole triadic structure into the minor mode, and yielding the sad sentence: *Jack doesn't love Jill* [39]. And to make the combined transformation of negative plus interrogative, we simply combine the two musical transformations, and it comes out: *Doesn't Jack love Jill? (Question mark)* [40]. And so we could go on with similar triadic variants through all eight derivations, but I am sure you get the point.

Now we are ready to take our next little step into a slightly more complex sentence. Let's forget Jack and Jill for a while and turn to Harry and John, two favorite characters of the Chomskian school. Here is a Chomsky classic: *Harry persuaded John to take up golf.* Isn't that beautiful?

[32]

[33]

[34]   Jack   loves   Jill, (maybe)

[35]   Jack   loves   Jill?

     Jack   loves   Jill: (I wonder)

[36]

     Does   Jack   love   Jill?

                       (Question mark)

[37]

[38]

[39]

     Jack   doesn't love   Jill.

[40]

     Doesn't Jack   love   Jill?

                       (Question mark)

This little sentence has a massive deep structure which I won't go into, except to point out that among the possible underlying strings involving persuasion and taking up golf are other implied substructures—such as *I say to you; there is a man named Harry; there is a man named John*—plus other implications based on the notions that Harry likes John, and also likes golf, but that John doesn't like golf, and that if he did like golf Harry could be seeing a great deal more of him, especially on Sundays, which is when golf is usually played, which is why Harry has persuaded him, and so on. Now the point of all this is that the final surface structure arrived at, namely that sentence *(Harry persuaded John to take up golf)* is the result of many transformations, not the least of which is the deletion of all those other implications. I press this point a bit too hard, perhaps, but only because I want to emphasize this principle of *deletion,* a key word in our inquiry, as you will see when we apply it to music. Deletion is probably the most striking transformational process in all language. For instance, that same sentence actually consists of two structural segments:

> 1. *Harry persuaded John* and
> 2. *John (to) take up golf.*

(That second string must be written as it is, since it tells us *who* is to take up golf—not Harry, but John.) Putting these two segments together, we get:

Harry persuaded John/John to take up golf.

Now obviously there is one John too many in the deep structure, and he must be eliminated, by the transformational rule called *deletion.* So out he goes, and we wind up with our cherished Chomskian utterance: *Harry persuaded*

John to take up golf, which—and mark this well—has been derived by rules we have never been taught, and of which we are not even aware.

Now I want to take you only one step further into the Wonderful World of Harry and John: *John was glad that Harry persuaded him to take up golf*. There are three different structural entities underlying this sentence, embedded one within the other:

1. John was glad (that)
2. Harry persuaded John
3. John (to) take up golf

These three strings are knotted together into a sentence, by the process of *embedding:* that is, number 3 is embedded in number 2, and the resulting combination is then embedded in number one. Remember this concept of embedding; it is going to bear fruit when we apply it to music.

But in order to accomplish the embedding two important transformational actions must first take place, the importance of which you will again recognize when we apply them to music. The first of these you already know about—deletion. You recall that in our last example there was one John too many and he had to go [41]. But now there is still one John too many, up there in the second string, and he is causing trouble. *John was glad that Harry persuaded JOHN to take up golf*. And that is clearly an impermissible sentence. You would never say it, although perhaps you could not cite a rule that forbids it. Yet such a rule does exist in the human mind, a transformational rule called pronominal substitution, or pronominalization, which is much easier to understand than to pronounce: it

[41]
1) John was glad (that)
2) Harry persuaded John
3) . . . (to) take up golf.

simply means the substitution of the correct and relevant pronoun for the repeated name. And so the second John is rewritten as the pronoun "him", and a grammatical sentence is born. This transformation is extremely important: imagine our having to go around saying things like *John promised that John would do John's homework the minute John finished John's dinner.*

Well, transformation, deletion, embedding, pronominalization: what, I ask again, has all this to do with music? A great deal. If we revert for a brief moment to our old friends Jack and Jill and complicate their relationship by this utterance: *Jack does not love Jill or Mary or Gertrude,* it would seem easy enough to make a further musical analogue by using our minor version of the negative transformation [42] and simply adding arbitrary new notes representing Mary and Gertrude [43]. (Remember, we are still using our convention of word equals note.) All together, the five notes make a lovely phrase, which is, in fact, the subject of a famous Bach fugue [44]. But the achieving of this phrase linguistically is not so simple. Consider the deep structure [45].

Disc
Side 2
band 7

[42]

Jack   doesn't love Jill

[43]

Jack   doesn't love   Jill   Mary   Gertrude

[44]

[45]

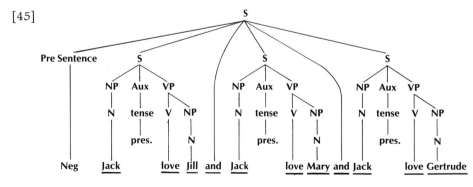

Isn't that impressive? Don't panic, I'm not going to analyze it. But to reproduce that deep structure musically, we would have to play something like this [46]: *Jack doesn't love Jill*, and *Jack doesn't love Mary*, and *Jack doesn't love Gertrude*—all of which is repetitious, and considerably less lovely than the subject of Bach's fugue.

Now this is exactly where the transformational process becomes operative; by deleting and condensing those underlying strings, we evolve out of that burdensome deep structure a clean, natural sentence, *and* a fine musical phrase [see 44], both of them *surface structures*. I am sure I don't have to trouble Jack and Jill any further to demonstrate that similar musical results can be achieved by other transformations such as permutation, pronominal- ization, and the rest, nor shall I trouble you.

But what have we really achieved with all this transforming? An interesting analogy between a sentence and a musical phrase. Then I must object to my own line of reasoning, and so should you. Is it a true analogy? No, not quite, because that sentence about Jack and Jill belongs to the world of prose, of literal meaning; whereas the corresponding musical phrase inhabits a world of poetry— sensuous, aural poetry. This series of notes has already led us into an aesthetic domain; but that series of words about Jack not loving whoever-it-was leaves us grounded in the world of prosaic fact.

[46]

Jack doesn't love Jill + Jack doesn't love Mary + Jack doesn't love Gertrude

You see, language leads a double life; it has a communi-
cative function *and* an aesthetic function. Music has an
aesthetic function only. For that reason, musical surface
structure is not equatable with linguistic surface structure. In
other words, a prose sentence may or may not be part of a
work of art. But with music there is no such either-or; a
phrase of music is a phrase of art. It may be good or bad art,
lofty or pop art, or even commercial art, but it can never be
prose in the sense of a weather report, or merely a statement
about Jack or Jill or Harry or John. To put it as clearly as
possible, there is no musical equivalent for the sentence
I am now speaking. Language must therefore reach even
higher than its linguistic surface structure, the prose
sentence, to find the true equivalent of musical surface
structure. And that equivalent must of course be *poetry.*
I hope I have made that point clearly, because everything
from here on depends on it.

Here I go with another rash hypothesis; and
remember that I am only suggesting hints to stimulate your
own thinking. But this is a hint-and-a-half. Isn't it just
possible that by reapplying those same transformational
rules of deletion, embedding, and so on, to a linguistic
surface structure, or sentence, we can transform it into a
new super-surface, an *aesthetic* surface, namely poetry?
And once we have established this aesthetic surface
structure, above and beyond the prose Chomskian surface,
then we can have a true parallel with music—poetry. It
means making an extra push, or better, taking a leap—a
metaphorical leap into the super-surface structure of art.
Super-surface structure! Talk about the traps of
terminology! Let's see if I can say it differently, avoiding
the trap.

[47]

etc.

[48]

(amo)   (amas)   (amat)

etc.

[49]

f

[50]

f

rall.

p

80

We are speaking of surface structures, musical and verbal. They are unlike, for the following reason: A verbal surface structure, or prose sentence, can be converted into verbal art by certain transformational processes; whereas musical surface structure already is musical art, has already been converted by those same processes. But converted from what? From musical prose? What is musical prose?

I have asked myself that question for a long time, and I have a short answer. Does the name Hanon mean anything to you? Hanon was the author, if you can call it that, of those horrible, endless five-finger piano exercises we all had to practice when we were very young [47]. On and on. Now that is some kind of musical prose, I guess. Yes, I know: it isn't really, because it's not grammatical; but then it is grammatical material in that it is like conjugating a verb (*amo, amas, amat,* etc.) [48]. Yes, but that's not a sentence. Ah, but it is an underlying string, or more exactly, a string of strings. But that's precisely the point. Musical prose, if it can be described at all, *is* underlying elements combined into strings, raw material waiting to be transformed into art. I suppose I could make a kind of sentence out of those Hanon strings by applying one transformational rule— permutation—to give us a cadence. It would be something like this [49]. That example more nearly resembles verbal prose: at least it stops. It's got a period. Now if I transform it further by applying the permutation a bar earlier, and immediately following it with another transformation, namely deletion, then it will begin to sound like *music* [50]. That's almost poetry, isn't it? You can see that the more those strings are transformed, the less prosy they become and the closer they arrive at a poetic surface structure. I became so fascinated by this idea that I even began to write

Fuga a 3

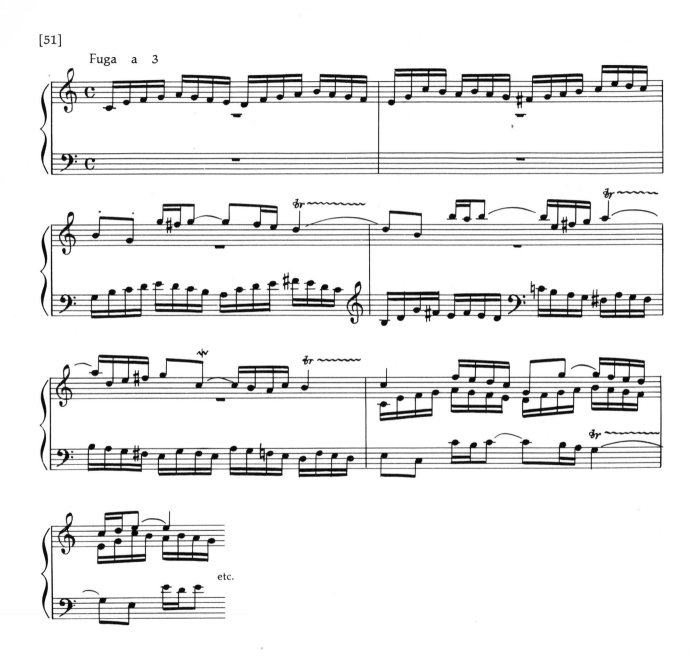

etc.

a fugue on this material, using all sorts of transformational devices, not just to prove to myself that Hanon Can Be Beautiful but to demonstrate a clear musical analogy with my new-found hypothesis about converting prose into poetry [51].

This hypothesis of reapplying transformational rules does not seem to me farfetched, even by the scientific standards of linguistic theory. I refer you back to Chomsky's own word "creativity," which he uses to characterize a child's ability to utter original sentences he has never heard. Now let's extend the concept of creativity, and reapply those same tranformational rules to prose sentences, re-create them, so to speak, and then we may be able to account for the otherwise unaccountable creative utterances of poets.

One such utterance, for example, is the formidable opening line of that Shakespeare sonnet:

Tired with / all these, / for rest / ful death / I cry,

Now there is a super-surface structure whose beauty derives from all kinds of transformations. The most immediately apparent are the inversions—permutations of the word order, which, rearranged into its more normal, less poetic state, is obviously

I, tired with all these, cry for restful death.

And in fact the poetic beauty of this line results from transformations which are not even syntactic. For instance, its metrical structure of iambic pentameter with the typically Shakespearean irregularity of inverting the first foot into a trochee, *Tired with,* and that marvelously heavy spondee in the second foot, *all these.* Those are also transformations, of another order. But let's not be seduced into the delights of poetic analysis; we are trying to be as scientific as we can. Obviously, this line must be syntactically derived from a substructure of prose—a sentence which doesn't exist, but which one could extrapolate on the basis of Shakespeare's single line. Let me try; something like this: "I am tired of life, so many aspects of life, that I would like to die—in fact, I cry for death—because death is restful, and would bring me release from all of life's woes and injustices, which I shall now enumerate". That's a long drink of water, at least forty words, but it is, like it or not, a grammatically valid sentence.

In other words, it is already in itself a surface structure. Imagine what some of the underlying strings might be:

I am tired
many things tire me
I am crying
I long for death
death is restful
death would end my tiredness,

and so forth. All of these strings, and more, have been transformed by deletion, conjoining, permutation, and other devices, into my extrapolated sentence, and then retransformed by the very same rules of deletion, et cetera (plus Shakespeare's genius), into one single line:

Tired with all these, for restful death I cry.

The whole process is one of creativity: the big push, the metaphorical leap.

We might try to visualize this process by a chart, a sort of double ladder of ascending hierarchy in language and in music. At the bottom of the language ladder [52] lie (A), all

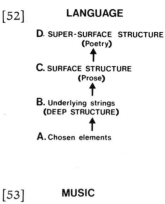

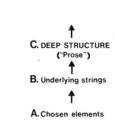

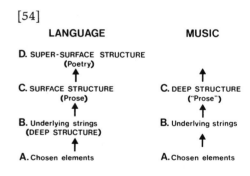

those basic elements, units of information, including everything from a morpheme to a word. Certain of these elements are then chosen by the creative will to express a concept, and out of these arise (B), the deep structure, those underlying strings we know so well, which by transformational rules generate (C), a surface structure, such as a prose sentence. And then finally, taking the metaphorical leap (by reapplying transformational rules) we attain (D), our aesthetic surface, or poetic utterance.

Now let's see how the musical ladder chart matches up with the language one [53]. Down on the bottom rung (A) lie the musical elements to be chosen by the creative will: pitches; tonalities, with the scales and chords peculiar to them; and meter with all its motoric implications, such as tempo, et cetera. Out of these arise (B), certain combinations: melodic motives and phrases, chordal progressions, rhythmic figures, and so on. These are the "underlying strings", so to speak (matching those of the language chart), which can be manipulated by transformations such as repositioning and permutation, into (C) what we have called musical prose. And here is where our charts don't quite match [54] since, as you can see, the prose sentence in language is a *surface* structure, whereas musical prose can be construed only as *deep* structure. But we've been expecting this disparity, haven't we? We are already aware that music cannot be prose. Therefore, onward with our leap, and our retransformational process will produce (D), the aesthetic surface we know as music [55].

Now this double chart is an eye opener in yet another respect [56]. Because of that disparity in the relative positions of deep structure and surface structure, we can now understand why it has been so difficult to establish all

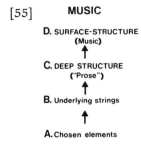

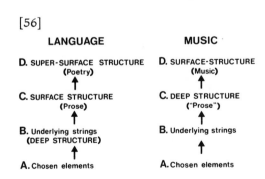

those other charts of equivalencies that we attempted in the beginning: note = letter, note = word, or note = anything. It may not only be difficult but virtually impossible ever to arrive at a list of consistent correspondences because of that built-in discrepancy between language and music. But basic as that discrepancy may be, the overall parallelism is at least as basic and important, as we are about to see.

Now that we finally have a reasonable parallel pair of ladders, it remains for us only to test the strength of the musical ladder by the same method we applied to Shakespeare's line—that is, by trying to extrapolate the deep structure of an equally beautiful line of music. Our victim this time will be Mozart, and for the equivalent musical line we will turn again to the opening statement of his G Minor Symphony.

But first, I think we are due for a breather. I know I am. We have been concentrating hard on difficult material for almost an hour, and I think a short break will refresh us for our attack on Mozart.

II

Mozart's G Minor Symphony is such a revered treasure of our heritage that it seems almost sacrilegious to lay linguistic hands on it; but if we are to understand the nature of its deep structure, even one aspect of it, some sort of extrapolation is necessary, similar to the prosy substructure we found beneath Shakespeare's line. So let's take the musical equivalent of that line, the first twenty-one bars of this symphony, and try to seek out one possible deep structure for it. But let's first hear those twenty-one bars as Mozart actually wrote them, just to refresh our ears. And remember: this is the *surface structure* we are about to hear,

Disc
Side 3
band 1

the top of that ladder, the actual music Mozart wrote.

(*At this point, Mozart's* Symphony No. 40 in G Minor, *K. 550, is performed for approximately 30 seconds showing the "surface structure".*)

Now our job is to invent, or discover, a deep structure out of which that marvelous surface structure has been generated. According to our hierarchical chart [see 56], this deep structure must result from a chain of possible and desirable combinations of elements, chosen from that mass of basic materials at the bottom of the ladder: the key of G minor, for example, with all its constituent factors of scale [57], its tonic [58], its dominant [59], related triads [60], its relative major [61], and all the rest. This choice of G minor automatically presents certain notes as consonant, and others as dissonant, so that certain relationships of tension and resolution are already implicit. What's more, the choice of G minor brings with it those inevitable associations we tend to have with a minor key, like melancholy, or uneasiness, dark colors, introspection. (But this much-discussed associative phenomenon is really a semantic consideration, and we will go into that sad–glad/minor–major syndrome in our next lecture.) Now, going on with our basic chosen elements, there remains the choice of duple meter, two beats to a bar, which establishes such absolutes as upbeats and downbeats, strong beats and weak beats. Then there is the tempo, *allegro molto*, plus other choices: the orchestral medium of wind and string instruments, the datum of sonata form, stylistic features of the late eighteenth century, and so forth. Out of all these choices will arise (B) [see 56] the melodic, harmonic, and rhythmic combinations, which constitute the "underlying strings"— the specific entities that are to be recombined into the deep

[57]

[58]

[59]

[60]

[61]

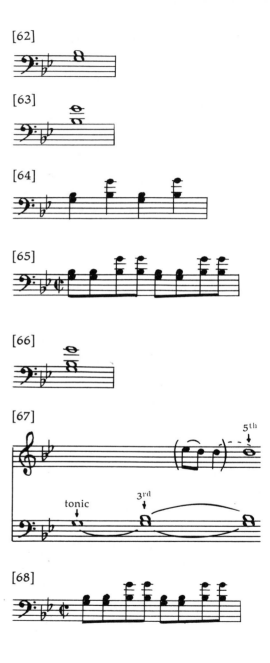

structure of those first twenty-one bars. Among them for instance are the motor rhythm of the accompaniment, based on the alternation of a minor-third interval [62] with its inversion, the major sixth [63]. Not only do those two intervals alternate [64], but each one is repeated before alternating [65].

That introductory accompaniment, or "vamp" as they call it in the entertainment industry, is not only a rhythmic motor—or "verb", if you remember—but also a harmonic modifier, or "adjective", which sets up the key of G minor by outlining its tonic triad [66], giving us the tonic and the third, but conspicuously omitting the fifth, which, when it does appear later in the melody, will complete the triad [67]. So we find that this motor [68] is both a verb and an adjective, a kind of participle that is both a rhythmic activator and a chordal modifier.

Now over this participial vamp comes the "noun" [69], the initial seed of the main melodic string. And what is it made of? Two notes, E flat and D [70], with the D repeated [71]. So obviously, the D is the principal constituent of the three-note figure, owing to the emphasis on it by repetition, to say nothing of its prominent position on the downbeat [72]. If you remember, I was doing something like this description about an hour ago—we called it parsing then— and you remember how fruitless it seemed. But what I am doing now will be fruitful, because we have a syntactic background against which to view it.

What does this three-note design mean syntactically? Simply that the D [73], the main constituent, is the fifth degree of the G-minor scale [74], that very note we were missing in the "almost-triad" of the vamp [75]. So, the D completes the triad [76]; but more than that, it appears as a

resolution of the non-triadic note E flat [77], a relatively
dissonant note which carries a weight and tension that must
be resolved to the consonant note D [78]. That noncon-
sonant E flat is called in the trade an *appogiatura, a leaning
tone* (meaning that it "leans" on its consequent resolution)
[79]; and in the stylistic terms of Mozart's period such a
dissonant note must be relieved. (I am trying as hard as I
can to use words like "weight" and "tension" in a precise,
syntactic way, avoiding any connotations of "feeling" or
"emotion." I am trying: but, believe me, it's not easy.) To
continue this syntactic chain, Mozart takes his initial three-
note unit [80], repeats it twice [81], and concludes his chain
with an upward leap of a sixth [82]. And there is the first
phrase of his melody [83].

You can see that at this rate of analysis it would take us
hours to get through all the syntactic factors and structures
operating in all twenty-one bars. But you can also see, I
hope, what some of these syntactic elements are like; and so,
with that in mind, we can now race forward toward devising
a putative deep structure for these opening bars.

To save time, let's limit ourselves to extrapolating our
deep structure from one point of view only, that of
symmetry. The reason I pick symmetry as our starting point
is that it is a *universal* concept, based on our innate
symmetrical instincts, which arise from the very structure of
our bodies. We are symmetrically constituted, dualistically
constituted, in the systole and diastole of our heartbeats, the
left-rightness of our walking, the in-and-outness of our
breathing, in our maleness and femaleness. This dualism
invades our whole life, on all levels; in our actions
(preparation/attack, tension/release) and in our thinking
(Good and Evil, Yin and Yang, Lingam and Yoni, progress

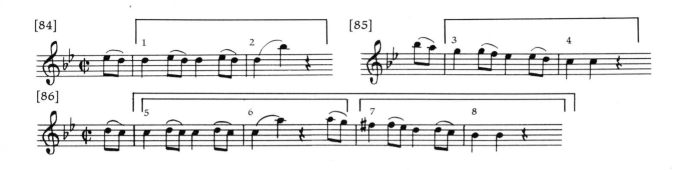

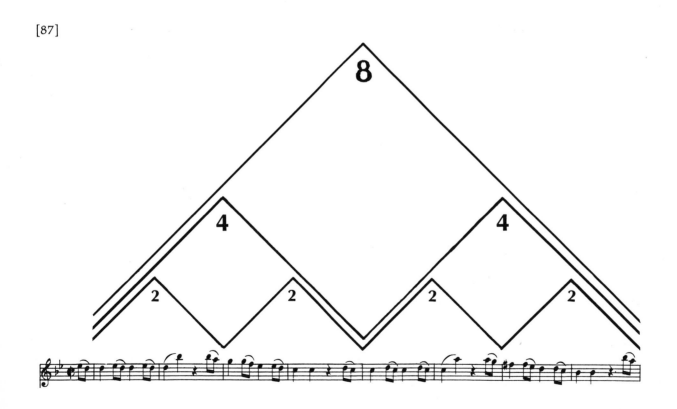

and reaction). And all these find musical expression in such oppositions as downbeat versus upbeat, half note versus quarter note, and especially in the elementary musical structure principle of $2 + 2 = 4, + 4 = 8, + 8 = 16$, et cetera ad infinitum. That's why the clue to our deep-structure project is to be found in the highly symmetrical formation of Mozart's main theme.

The theme begins with the chain we've already discovered [84]; and this phrase, which is two bars long, is immediately countered, or answered, or mirrored if you will, by a complementary two-bar phrase [85]; thus producing a symmetrical four-bar structure. But this double phrase is clearly incomplete, and so we find it followed by its counterpart—another four-bar phrase which is reducible to a similar pair of two-bar phrases [86]. The theme is now balanced [87], as you can see in the accompanying diagram, but as you can *hear* it's still incomplete. But even incomplete those eight bars present the main material: four symmetrical strings of two-bar phrases, perfectly balanced, and comprising in themselves a string of dualities: two within four within eight.

Now from this point on we're inventing—just as we did with the Shakespeare line—dreaming up a prose structure based on the absolute symmetry of these eight bars of music. If we really stick to that symmetrical principal, the introductory vamp-accompaniment preceding the theme should also be eight bars long, or at least four, or at the very least two. And in the same way the new material *following* the eight-bar melody should also proceed in sections of four or eight bars each, always in multiples of two, always aiming at the absolute symmetry posed by the theme itself. Of course we know that Mozart did nothing of the sort. But I

Delivering a lecture, WGBH studio

have. I have been secretly working out an extrapolation on
my own, and I have come up with something that could be
construed as a *prose* equivalent of the first twenty-one bars
of Mozart's symphony. It happens to be thirty-six bars long,
as might be expected of a deep structure; just as the single
Shakespeare line produced a substructural sentence of
forty-odd words. And if I were more pedantic (and more
cruel), I could have made this musical deep structure even
longer. In any case, here it is, a perfect nightmare of
symmetry [88].

Disc
Side 3
band 2

[cont'd]

[88 cont'd]   4 bars

4 bars

4 bars

4 bars

4 bars

96

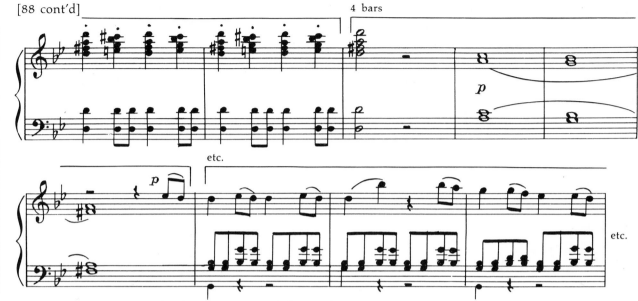

[88 cont'd]   4 bars

etc.

etc.

And once again, we're back to our principal theme. But
what a drag it's been to get there: so much academicism, so
many unnecessary schoolboy repeats, such a lack of deletion.
This is "prose," or else music by a bad composer. It's
stalling for time, the way people do while they're thinking of
an answer to a question. "Uh, how old is Mildred?" "Oh,
Mildred—must be—— uh——Mildred is 69."

Of course my musical repeats were made in the name of
symmetry. But symmetry is not necessarily balance: that's
a precept we all learned long ago, and it's worth saying again.
What Mozart has done—as any great master does—is to
make the leap from prosy symmetry into poetic balance, that
is, into art. And he accomplishes this leap through those
very principles of transformation so deftly enunciated by
Chomsky; only Mozart achieves thereby not the mere
grammar of a sentence, but the *super*-grammar of an
aesthetic surface.

By far the chief transformational principle employed by
Mozart is that of *deletion*, just as we have seen it to be in the
deep structure of language. The most obvious use of deletion
occurs right at the beginning of the symphony, where *my*
prosy four-bar vamp is reduced to one bar only—not even
two bars, but one [89]. What is Mozart telling us through
this deletion? Two things: first, that we are not to expect
constant duple symmetry throughout this movement, as
conventional procedures might lead us to expect. And

[89]

[90] Poco moto

[91]

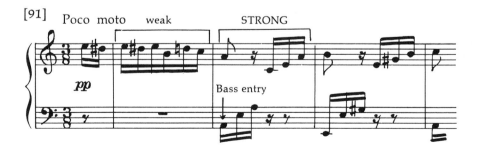

secondly, and far more important: that the bar in which the melodic material appears, bar two, is not automatically a strong bar, as the first bar of a melody is usually expected to be, but a weak bar; that is, it functions as an *upbeat bar*. What is an upbeat bar? Well, for instance, you know that little Beethoven piece all kids have to learn, called "Für Elise"? There is a perfect example of a weak bar used in the sense of an upbeat [90]. Do you notice how clearly the *strong* bar is indicated by the entrance of the accompaniment in the bass [91]?

But we're not so lucky in the Mozart, where there is no bass entrance to guide us, since the accompaniment is already there, having been there since the beginning [see 89]. So how do we know which is a strong bar, and which is weak?

We are now confronted by one of the great failings of our notational system in music: its vagueness in regard to this question of bar-by-bar accentuation. We're fairly clear about what beats a composer means to stress within any one given bar—for example, the first beat, or downbeat, tends to be stronger than the others, while the last beat of a bar tends to be the weakest, a so-called upbeat [92]. Downbeat strong, upbeat weak. But music is not made of isolated bars; instead, the bars group themselves together into aggregations of bars, or *phrases*; and it is these bar-phrases that provide the real articulations of musical flow. A performer gauges these articulations in various ways: according to the *dupleness* (two-, four-, and eight-bar structures arising out

[92]

99

[93]

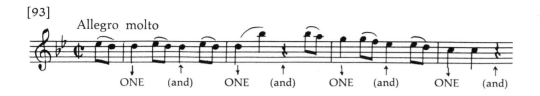

Allegro molto

ONE   (and)   ONE   (and)   ONE   (and)   ONE   (and)

[94]

2 bar phrase   2 bar phrase

STRONG   weak   STRONG   weak

[95]

up-beat bar   down-beat bar

[96]

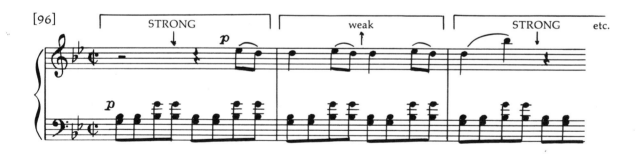

STRONG   weak   STRONG   etc.

100

of our innate sense of duple meter), or by relying on printed accents, or phrase marks provided by the composer. But even these marks can be misleading—for example, when the composer wishes to indicate syncopations, or irregular stresses, and similar surprises. This is especially true when the tempo of a piece is so fast that one feels a single beat per bar. And in this Mozart symphony, the tempo is fast enough so that it *approaches* the feeling of one beat per bar [93]. And here is where we run into trouble: instead of dealing with down*beats* and up*beats* (*one*-two, *one*-two) within a bar, we are now dealing with down-*bars* and up-*bars*. So how do we know which is a down-bar and which an up-bar, since they all look alike? Every bar is mainly one beat, a downbeat. Then how do we differentiate the strong bars from the weak?

Most people hearing Mozart's opening theme for the first time will hear it in groups of two-bar phrases, which is correct; but they naturally tend to hear the first bar of the pair as strong and the second as weak [94]. But there's the rub: it's not so at all. The syntactic truth is that within this pair of melodic bars it is the *first* bar which is weak, and the *second* which is strong. That is, the first bar works as an upbeat bar to the second; and it is the second which is actually the down-bar [95]. Just the opposite. And what makes us so sure of this? Well, for one thing, that very deletion in the vamp-accompaniment, by which Mozart gives us only one single introductory bar—a strong one of course, being the first one, thus automatically causing the melody to enter on a *weak* bar [96]. You can easily see that this deletion of Mozart's knocks the whole symmetrical structure of my pedantic prose version into a cocked hat.

Instead of a shape that looks like this [97] (a single
introductory bar followed by four pairs of bars), the true

[97]

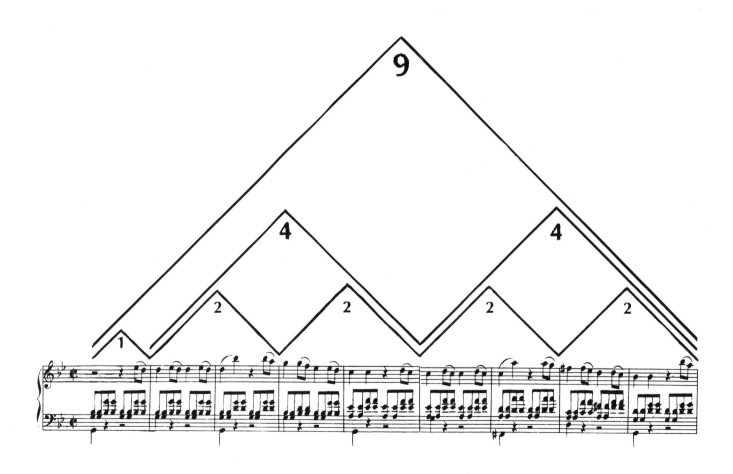

shape turns out to be a symmetrical pyramid built of four
pairs of bars right from the start [98]. And if you think this

[98]

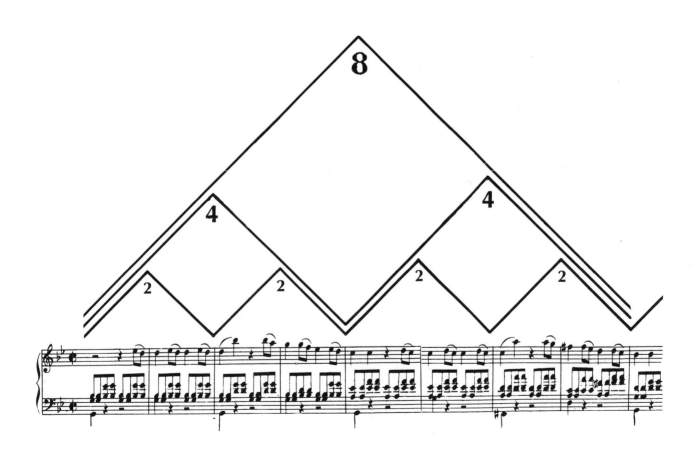

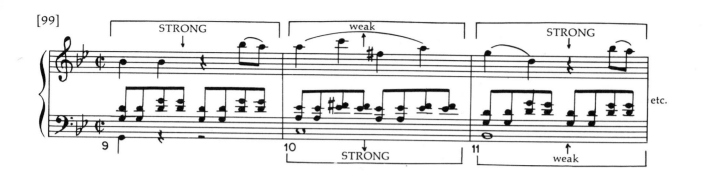

analysis is complicated, it gets even more so on the tenth bar [99], which is both strong *and* weak. This is a new ambiguity, setting up a new order of strong-weak pairs of bars.

So what? you ask. Why burden us with all this pedantic hair-splitting? Isn't this all stuff for the musicologists? Not at all; it's of major importance to the performer, and therefore to you, the listener. For if the conductor fails to grasp the significance of that one-bar vamp, his performance of the succeeding pairs of bars will automatically be reversed, hence wrong, and so will the hearer's perception of them. And that misconception will distort not only these few opening bars, but inevitably the shape and flow of the entire movement.

So the performer must understand what Mozart has done —that he takes our universal instinct of symmetry and plays with it, violates it, *ambiguifies* it, by using the equally universal process of deletion to operate counter to those instinctive symmetrical forces that operate in us. And therein lies the creativity; that's what makes it art.

If any of you still find this point debatable, or arbitrary on my part, Mozart corroborates it in no uncertain terms by the way he positions his bass notes on the downbeat of each bar. These bass notes are all G's—the tonic fundamental of G minor [100], but they alternate bar by bar an octave apart. Obviously, the lower G, with which he begins, is stronger than the upper one [101], and this clearly indicates the strong-weak progression of each pair of bars. And this progression happens to coincide exactly with the bar-phrasing we have already discovered to be true [102]. And

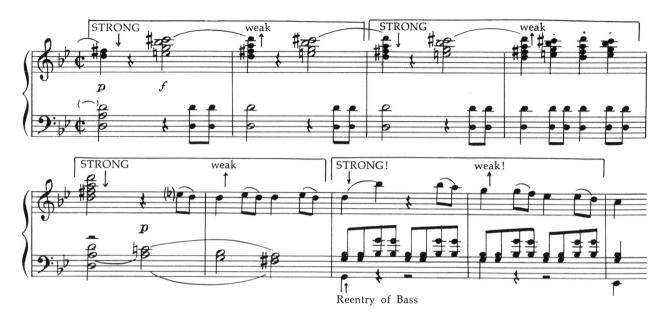

if you're *still* not convinced of Mozart's intentions, there is incontrovertible proof waiting in bar 21, where Mozart returns to this principal theme. And here (just as we saw how the bass entry articulated the phrase structure in "Für Elise",) it is now the re-entry of Mozart's bass accompaniment that pinpoints, like a ray of light, the exact position of the strong bar [103]. There can be no further doubt of Mozart's intentions; the purpose of his deletion is now perfectly clear.

But, you now ask, why did we need Chomsky to reveal all this to us? Couldn't we have discovered Mozart's intentions without recourse to transformational rules of deletion and what-not? Certainly we could have (I am sure a lot of musicians among us knew it anyway), but it is in the parallel with language that such difficult analysis as bar-phrasing becomes possible for *laymen* to understand. Language is our common property, and therefore our universal area of syntactic reference—for musicians and laymen alike.

What is really being clarified here, I hope, is a new kind of ambiguity—a structural ambiguity, distinguishable from the phonological or chromatic ambiguity we were discussing in our last session. It must be clear by now that the surface structure we have just been examining is dramatically at variance with the boringly symmetrical deep structure I devised as underlying it; and that this discrepancy produces a syntactic ambiguity in Mozart's musical phrase structure— an ambiguity arising from nonsymmetrical operations, but an ambiguity which is under perfect control, classically contained by the balanced proportions of Mozart's sonata form. It is a *controlled ambiguity,* of the same kind we considered last week from a phonological point of view: chromaticism contained within diatonicism. In fact, the

[104]

[105]

[106]

[107]

Clarinet   Bassoon

[108]

108

nonsymmetricality that makes us feel the ambiguous quality of the phrase structure can be regarded in itself as a kind of chromaticism—a sort of *rhythmic* chromaticism. It is another order of ambiguity.

These ambiguities, I must emphasize even at the expense of repeating myself—these ambiguities are beautiful. They are germane to all artistic creation. They enrich our aesthetic response, whether in music, poetry, painting or whatever, by providing more than one way of perceiving the aesthetic surface. Why are we so moved by Othello when he says, "It is the cause, it is the cause, my soul", or, "Put out the light, and then put out the light"? Ambiguities, which you have all debated in your Shakespeare courses. (And why is the Mona Lisa the world's most famous painting?)

But there is one form of ambiguity that only music can offer us—and that is *contrapuntal syntax.* Don't be put off by this grand-sounding term. I mean by it simply the miracle of being able to perceive simultaneously two different syntactic versions of the same idea. This miracle is made possible by *counterpoint*, the interweaving of two or more melodic lines, or "musical strings," as the linguists might say. Hence, the term "contrapuntal syntax".

For instance, in this same first movement of Mozart's symphony, he is developing the initial motive of his principal theme [104]—developing it by transposing it to a new key [105], isolating and repeating it [106], and then tossing it back and forth between the clarinet and bassoon [107]. Now that's one syntactic form of the motive. But at the very same time, in those same few bars, there is another form of the same motive being tossed back and forth between high and low strings [108]. This is simply another

[109]

[110]

[111]

[112]

high Strings

p

Clarinet   Bassoon

p

low Strings

p

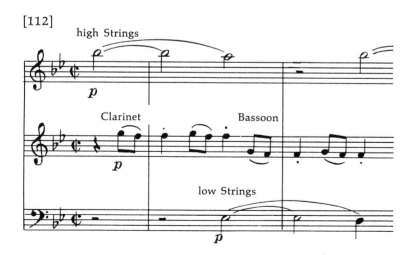

110

syntactic statement of the same material—the same initial two notes very much slowed down, transformed by what musicians call "augmentation." In other words, those two notes we have been recognizing as quick eighth notes [109], now appear augmented eightfold, as if whole notes, eight times as slow [110]. This is a syntactic transformation in the true Chomskian sense—a structural permutation. And what is more, it is a perfect equivalent of yet another transformational procedure known as "conjoining"; these augmented two-note motives are so composed that the second note of each coincides or *conjoins* with the first note of the other. Listen [111]. Do you hear the conjoining? And even that's not all. In between those conjoined high and low strings are *embedded* the woodwind figurations we heard before [112]. That's a perfect example of the embedding process.

So all these syntactic transformations of the *same* material are happening together: transposition, permutation through augmentation, conjoining, and embedding—all combined to produce that special musical wonder, contrapuntal syntax.

I sense the logical objection you want to make: why is contrapuntal syntax peculiar only to music? Don't we all know about so-called "double syntax" in poetry, where a phrase can conjoin with either the preceding or succeeding phrase? For instance, the famous example in Shakespeare's ninety-third sonnet which is quoted by William Empson in that marvelous book (which, if you haven't read it, I highly recommend), called *Seven Types of Ambiguity*. He talks specifically about these four lines:

[113]

[114]

[115]

[116]

But heaven in thy creation did decree
That in thy face sweet love should ever dwell,
Whate'er thy thoughts or thy heart's workings be,
Thy looks should nothing thence, but sweetness tell.

These lines work equally well whether you put a period at the end of line two or at the end of line three, as you can immediately see when you read them in those different ways. Well, then doesn't this "double grammar" or "double syntax" belong within the same mode of aesthetic ambiguity as contrapuntal grammar in music? No, it doesn't, for the simple reason that the doubleness of that third line of Shakespeare's is not a *simultaneous* doubleness: it is either the end of a sentence or the start of another one. The resulting sense of ambiguity may occupy a given moment in time, but the line itself, the actual *aesthetic surface*, does not. The musical lines in Mozart, on the other hand, all occupy the same momentary span in time—they literally *move together* [see 112]. Of course, one more second of thought on this matter, and we'll be trapped in a discussion of Aesthetic Time—of "virtual time" versus "clock time"— and clock time is what we don't have for this particular digression.

But now it's time to hear that whole Mozart movement again; only now I keenly want you to hear it in a *structural* way, along with the delights of listening to its chromatic adventures as we did last week. I want you to listen for the syntactic transformations that make it the great poetry it is: for instance, deletions [113]. Did you hear the deletion of one figuration in the contrapuntal imitation? It makes the difference between this [114]; and this [115]. And listen for conjoinings, as in this famous phrase [116]—do you hear how the two pieces of material conjoin? And listen for embeddings, such as the one we heard before.

[117]

[118]

[119]

If these aren't enough for the eagerest beavers among you, you can also hear examples of linguistic repositioning, where the three-note motive [117] is transformed by *inversion* [118], that is, simply turned upside down. A clear example of permutation [119]. Even pronominalization is to be found in this music, but I'll spare you that. Anyone who really wants to investigate Mozart's use of pronominalization may consult the score, bars 114 and 115 of the first movement.

Well, that's a smattering of syntax. And even so, I've gone more deeply into musical structure than I've ever dared before with a lay audience. But that's the lure of this university: one is always tempted by the standard of intelligence to try a little more than one would ordinarily. It has something to do with those "elitist" inquiring minds I spoke of earlier. I believe your minds can take it: last week, phonology; this week, syntax. And next week, semantics, the embedding of both. Until then, good night, and thank you for listening with such concentration, patience, and intelligence to a long, long lecture.

3. MUSICAL SEMANTICS

The other day an undergraduate cornered me in Harvard Yard and asked what all this was leading up to—all these musico-linguistical meditations of the last two lectures. What am I getting at, she asked; do I really believe in the analogies I suggest between "transformational grammar" and musical transformations?

I was brave and stoutly responded: yes, I deeply believe in the analogies. I've found that this linguistic approach to poetry illuminates musical analysis and vice versa, and, to my delight, so have some linguists and other scholars I've run into between lectures. As to what I am getting at, it's a broad, dispassionate look at the musical crisis of our own century, as dramatized by Charles Ives' *Unanswered Question*, and analogously, how poetry shares in that crisis.

But my bright new friend was only warming up to her inquisition. I follow your linguistics, she said, but you begin to lose me when you start crossing Chomsky with aesthetics. How does transformational grammar lead you to the beauty of ambiguity and to increased aesthetic response? Aren't you being somewhat ambiguous yourself? I was suddenly not so facile in my response, and found myself defensively trying to recall my original enthusiastic impulses when I first conceived these lectures. Phonology. Syntax. Semantics . . . Meaning. Ah, *Meaning*. There's the rub. I began, to her distress, by spewing out, as well as I could remember it, an analysis of a classical Chomskian ambig- uous sentence: *The whole town was populated by old men and women.* We're now dealing with a third kind of ambiguity, I told her, neither phonological nor syntactic, but both: a new, semantic ambiguity. I gave her a hasty run- down on why that sentence is ambiguous, without diagrams

120

of course, being in the wilds of Harvard Yard, and unfortunately too, because this area of ambiguity is where Chomsky's tree-diagrams are so particularly helpful.

The whole town was populated by old men and women is an ambiguous sentence because it has two different deep structures. The first would show us one meaning: that the town was populated by old men and *old women*, possibly because all the young people had gone off to the Big City, leaving only the old folks behind. But there is a second meaning, arising from the other deep structure, and based on the idea that the young men had all gone off to war, leaving behind old men and *women of all ages.* You see the difference? But through our well-known transformational processes, mainly *deletion,* those two deep structures have been combined and condensed, yielding the one ambiguous phrase *old men and women.* That's a famous example of the figure of speech known as "zeugma", meaning in this case two nouns yoked to one adjective—as the nouns *men* and *women* are both yoked to the single adjective *old,* which may or may not modify both nouns.

There is a fascinating and helpful musical analogy to be made here, which I naturally could not demonstrate to my charming young inquisitor, there being no piano in Harvard Yard. But I *can* demonstrate it to you.

Think of this famous passage in Stravinsky's *Petrouchka* [1]. You all know that "Dance of the Coachmen"? Now, recalling analogies from our very first lecture, try to think of all that melodic material on top as a series of nouns [2]. Now think of the harmonic support underneath as a verbal adjective: (remember those correlations we made?) [3]. Put it all together, and what have we got? A zeugma; with the same unchanging adjective modifying all those different nouns [see 1].

Meanwhile, back in Harvard Yard, my blond inquisitor was getting impatient. Zeugma, shmeugma, she said; get to the point; what has all this got to do with poetry? Patience, I said; I'm just coming to the point—The Big Leap. By *re*applying the transformational rule of deletion to that sentence, or prose surface structure, *the whole town was populated by old men and women*, we can turn an already ambiguous sentence into an even *more* ambiguous one, a *super*surface structure: *The whole town was old men and women*. And that, for better or worse, is a line of poetry: The whole town *was* old men and women. A poetic statement. In fact, *old men and women* is all by itself a quasi-poetic phrase, resulting from the previous deletion of one "old" from the prosy phrase *old men and old women*. But now we've also deleted "populated by", making it even more poetic *because* it is more ambiguous. The sentence can now be said to be supercharged with possible meanings; and that is one definition of poetry.

Maybe, said my charming inquisitor; maybe it is poetry, but can you prove it? No, I can't; I can't *prove* anything. I *could* possibly explain it, again by borrowing methodology from linguistics. A linguist would say: Look, when you are confronted by a sentence like that one (*The whole town was old men and women*) which is syntactically correct but semantically incorrect (since a town is a *place* and men and women are *people*, and a place can't be people)— when you are confronted by a sentence like that your mind automatically goes through a series of decision-making steps: first, it seeks some grammatical justification of the semantic conflict, and finding none, can then decide one of two things: to reject it as illogical, hence impermissible speech, or to find another level on which it may be acceptable—a *poetic* level. In other words, something in the mind intuits a *metaphorical* meaning, and can then accept the semantic ambiguity on that level.

Did that word "metaphorical" register with you? I hope so, because metaphor is our key to understanding. In fact, I just used a metaphor, when I said "metaphor *is* a key." In other words, I have made an equation between a figurative way of speaking called a metaphor and a small metal object called a key. What I have said, in effect, is "this equals that", where *this* and *that* belong to two completely different and incompatible orders, exactly like the town and its aged inhabitants. In other words, I've broken a semantic rule. But it is precisely this linguistic misdemeanor, Breaking the Rules, by which metaphor is achieved. "Juliet is the sun"—there's a classic example of "this is that", equating two incompatible orders—one human, the other sidereal. Juliet is a human organism, the sun is a star. How do they get to be equal? How does the copulative verb "is" apply equally to both? (How indeed? said my pretty new friend.)

Well, I replied, Chomsky would say that there are certain syntactic rules associated with "lexical" meanings—that is, we all possess a learned lexicon that has its own rules and classifications. Our mental dictionary in English, for instance, permits us to say such things as "Trilling lectured on sincerity", which he did, in the last Norton lectures, but forbids us to say "Sincerity lectured on Trilling". There are certain things we know about the lexical items *sincerity* and *lecture on* that prevent our saying that sincerity lectures on anything or anyone.

Of course, Chomsky is not concerned with poetry; his inquiry is into normal human speech. And "Juliet is the

sun" is abnormal human speech; it is, so to speak, illogical.
But we can find the logic in it—the poetic logic—by using,
ironically enough, Chomsky's own transformational
principles.

What if we were to construct a logical progression that
would "normalize" Shakespeare's metaphor? We could
say:

There is a human being called Juliet
There is a star called the Sun
The human being called Juliet is radiant
A Star called the sun is radiant

[hence:]

The human being called Juliet is like a star called the Sun
in respect to radiance.

Perfectly logical. Now come the transformations, which are
all deletions, as you might have known; we delete all those
logical but unnecessary steps that are built into the deep
structure of any comparison, and wind up with our
conclusive simile, *Juliet is like the sun*, which is true in one
respect only, that they are both *radiant*. We then make the
final, supreme deletion of the word *like*, and behold, our
simile is transformed into a metaphor. Juliet *is* the sun.
This *is* that.

Of course, that last metaphorical leap makes it false
logic, as in that invalid syllogism they always throw at you
in Elementary Logic courses: *my dog is brown, your dog is
brown*, hence, *my dog is your dog*. Wrong! My dog is *like*
your dog, in terms of brown-ness, and only of brown-ness.
Right!—But it's not poetry. It's not a metaphor but a
simile, which belongs to the realm of literal discourse;
whereas the "false-logical" version, *my dog is your dog*,
has its own nonliteral, metaphorical logic. Are you

124

beginning to see what I mean? And there in a nutshell is the difference between art and what we loosely call "reality".

What must be clear by now is that a metaphor—or any comparative statement, even a simile—must function in terms of the two compared items being related to a third item, which is common to both. That is, we are comparing A and B, whether they are my dog and your dog, or Juliet and the sun—A and B, both of which must relate to a third factor, X, which is abstractable from both. If A is Juliet and B is the sun, then X is *radiance* (or any number of other things, but let's say *radiance*); A has X, and B has X, therefore A is like B. Juliet is like the sun. We then delete the *like* and Juliet *is* the sun. And what a deletion is there! Of such transformations are metaphors made, and of such metaphors is beauty born.

Terrific, said my beautiful blonde inquisitor, I think I understand you. What I don't understand is how you relate all this stuff to *music*. You will, I said; come to the next lecture. Well, this is it, and I hope she's here, because we've just reached the crucial point.

You remember I spoke of the mind having to go through a series of decision-making steps when confronted by a semantic incongruity—first seeking justification, and then either rejecting it or accepting it on a poetic level? Well, add to that a whole other series of steps, these very ones we've been describing—namely, the finding of an X-factor to which A and B can both relate. (My dog is your dog because they're both brown. But that can't be, says the mind; oh, I see, it *can* be, *in a poetic sense*.) Now all of that complex mental process takes place in a millisecond, a flash of time: such is the wonder of our cerebral computer. But the moment we come to deal with *musical* metaphor,

126

even that millisecond is eliminated—because we don't have
to deal with the problems of *A* and *B* being incompatible.
Why not? Because the *A*'s and *B*'s of music are not
burdened by literal semantic weights like my dog or your
dog or even Juliet. If we call the first two bars of Brahms'
Fourth Symphony *A* [4], and the second two *B* [5], we
instantly perceive the musical transformation, with no time
or effort needed to explain that relationship in terms of
semantic meanings; the only time required is the time it
takes to play the music.

In fact, when you think of the number of transformations
taking place in the short space of those few bars of Brahms,
it becomes almost incredible that all of them can be
instantaneously perceived. What we've called *A* in itself
involves a transformation [6]: the descending major third
transformed to its exact inversion, an ascending minor
sixth. So *A* already contains a metaphor; and so does *B* [7].
But in addition to that, B is itself a metaphor of *A*, being a
comparative transformation of *A* [4], one degree of the
scale lower [5]. And add to that the *harmonic* metaphor
accompanying the melodic one [8]: the *A* progression
is tonic/subdominant, and the *B* progression is dominant/
tonic; a beautiful parallelism, and a luminous example of
this-is-that.

So in music as well as in poetry, the *A* and *B* of a
metaphor must both relate to some *X*-factor—not radiance
or brownness, but a common factor such as the rhythm
[see 4 and 5] or those harmonic progressions [see 8]. You
see there is still that triangular formation of *A*, *B*, and *X*
to be reckoned with. And yet, with all this to be perceived,
all these metaphors-within-metaphors, we still don't
require even that one millisecond before perceiving it. There

is no need to go through "that-can't-be—oh,-I-see-it-can-be-in-a-poetic-sense"; because the music *already exists in the poetic sense*. It's all art from the first note on. And there, my lovely Inquisitor, you have your introduction to musical semantics.

But what is musical semantics, as related and opposed to verbal semantics?

Let's first look briefly at the verbal side. I think most linguists will agree that semantics, the study of pure meaning, has always been the weakest of the three linguistic departments because it's the least studied. And that's because it's the hardest discipline to render in scientific fashion. As a result, linguists have usually left semantic considerations to other disciplines such as philology, etymology, lexicography, aesthetics, or literary criticism; and this fact has spawned some of the sharpest criticisms of Chomsky, mostly by his own disciples, the Young Turks, many of whom are now busily engaged in an effort to evolve a theory of semantic structures which can be as scientifically sound as the syntactic one. In fact, Chomsky himself is said to be working in this area, trying to head off the Young Turks at the pass. But it's not easy—especially for us old Turks.

Do you recall from the opening lecture our experiment in monogenesis—how we prolonged the ictus of the proto-syllable MA, and heightened it into a musical tone, MAAA? That was a fairly pure scientific attempt, but not so pure that we could for one second ignore the semantic resonance of *motherhood* in that one syllable, MA. Nor could we avoid amorous inferences in the syntactic entanglements of Jack and Jill during our last lecture, no more than Chomsky himself can avoid similar inferences when he speaks of Harry and John and golf and persuasion. There is a semantic trap that no linguist can totally escape.

In the same way, as we have been discussing the musical equivalents of these linguistic areas, we too have been semantically entrapped. Willy-nilly, we've been dealing with semantics all along. In the first lecture on phonology, we dealt with the ordering of phonemic elements out of the harmonic series so as to produce meaningful tonal relationships; *meaningful,* ergo *semantic.* In the second lecture, on syntax, we were dealing with the ordering of those tonal relationships so as to produce meaningful structures. So now that we come to consider musical semantics in general, what meanings are there left to deal with? Obviously, the musical meanings that result from the combination of both, of what we might call phono-semantics plus morpho-semantics—meanings derived by the various transformational procedures with which we've been playing.

"Playing": that's the word that leapt out, and precisely the word I want to use. It sounds frivolous, I know, but it is on the contrary essentially related to our semantic thinking. "Play" is the very stuff and activity of music; we *play* music on our instruments just as the composer *plays* with notes in the act of inventing it. He *juggles* sound-formations, he *toys* with dynamics, he *glides* and *skips* and *somersaults* through rhythms and colors—in short, he indulges in what Stravinsky called "Le Jeu de Notes". The Game of Notes: a striking concept of what music is.

And why not? All music, even the most serious, thrives on its puns and anagrams. Where would Richard Strauss be without his musical puns, or Bach and Beethoven without their musical anagrams? One can almost think of a given piece of music as a continuing game of anagrams, in which there are, as it were, twelve "letters" [9] that can be juggled and rejuggled. The constant rearrangement and transformation of these "letters" is made particularly rich by the combined possibilities of horizontal and vertical structures —melodic, harmonic, and contrapuntal anagrams—which of course language cannot do, even with twenty-six letters. Music is further enriched by the extension of these possibilities to near-infinity, through the extraordinary variety of high and low registers, durations, dynamics, meters, rhythms, tempi, colorations. It's as if all music were one supergame of sonic anagrams.

But does this Stravinskian game concept of music really cover the subject? A game may serve a number of purposes: to release energy, to exercise the mind or body, to while away the time. A game may also have more affective functions: to compete, to show off, to establish a shared intimacy with the opponent. All these may well be functions of music too, and frequently are; but nobody is going to assert that music stops there. There's got to be more to it than those merely pleasurable functions, even if they do go so far as to constitute a refreshment of the spirit. Music does more than that, says more, *means* more.

"Means": there's the problem. Means what? Sad? Glad?

[9]

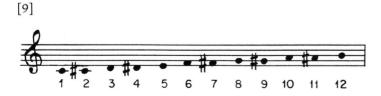

"Moonlight" Sonata? "Revolutionary" Etude? Bi-units of Information? Significational sensory effects? Cybernetic feedback? What do we mean by "mean"?

Well, the very first Young Peoples' program I ever gave on television, about fifteen years ago, was entitled "What Does Music Mean?" Here I am still asking that question, and my answers haven't changed very much. But I think I can now present a more mature formulation of them, particularly since I have a more mature audience to tell it to.

As concisely as possible, this is it: <u>music has intrinsic meanings of its own</u>, which are not to be confused with specific feelings or moods, and certainly not with pictorial impressions or stories. These intrinsic musical meanings are generated by a constant stream of metaphors, all of which are forms of poetic transformations. This is our thesis.

I believe this thesis can be demonstrated, and in fact has already been partly demonstrated, even if not scientifically proved. The problem of proof stems, no doubt, from that very unscientific word "metaphor", which I have already been using in a highly metaphorical way, and will no doubt continue so to do. But I should clarify this broad use of the term at least to the extent that we can distinguish one use from another.

There are three specific ways in which I want to use the term "metaphor". First, those <u>intrinsic musical metaphors</u> I have already mentioned, which are of a purely musical order, and operate rather like those puns-and-anagram games we were speaking of. All these metaphors derive from transformations of musical material—those very *Chomskian* transformations we investigated last week. By transforming any given musical material from one state to

another, as I showed earlier with that bit of Brahms, we automatically arrive at the test equation of any metaphor: this-is-that; Juliet is the sun.

Secondly, we must define *extrinsic* metaphors, by which musical meanings relate to nonmusical meanings. In other words, certain semantic meanings belonging to the so-called "real world", the "world out there"—the *non*musical world—are assigned to musical art in terms of literal semantic values, namely extramusical ones. This form of this-equals-that is typified in Beethoven's *Pastorale* Symphony (which we will be hearing after the intermission), in which certain notes are *meant* to be associated in the listener's mind with certain images, such as merry peasants, brooks, and birds. In other words, these notes equal those birds; *these are those.* It is a variation of the old formula.

And finally, we must think of metaphor in an *analogical* way, as we compare those intrinsic musical metaphors with their counterparts in speech, strictly verbal ones; and this comparison is in itself a metaphorical operation. It says: this musical transformation is like that verbal one; this is like that. Delete "like", and you have the metaphor.

Now, having defined my usages of "metaphor", I suppose I am committed to plunging into the perennial æsthetic debate. It's a debate I don't particularly wish to prolong. So many excellent and sensitive minds have wrestled with this problem of the Meaning of Music, to say nothing of the Meaning of Meaning: Santayana and Croce, Prall and Pratt, I. A. Richards, Suzanne Langer, Bergson, Beardsley, Birkoff, and Babbitt—and Stravinsky himself. One thing they have always agreed on, in one way or another, is that musical meaning *does* exist, whether

133

Rehearsing at Symphony Hall, Boston

rational or affective or both. As hard as they have all tried to be logical, to avoid romantic generalizing or philosophical maundering, they have all had to bow eventually to some nagging truth which insists that those innocent F sharps and B flats, however sportively juggled or played with, do emerge from a composer's mind meaning something, nay, expressing something—and expressing what may otherwise be inexpressible.

But wait: isn't there a difference between "meaning" and "expressing"? There is, if we are to be at all accurate. When a piece of music "means" something to me, it is a meaning conveyed by the sounding notes themselves—what Eduard Hanslick called "sonorous forms in motion" (a wonderful phrase), and I can report those meanings back to you precisely in terms of those forms. But when music "expresses" something to me, it is something I am feeling, and the same is true of you and of every listener. We feel passion, we feel glory, we feel mystery, we *feel something*. And here we are in trouble; because we cannot report our precise feelings in scientific terms; we can report them only subjectively. If we could collect sample "feelings" from a concert audience, lay them slide by slide on a lab table, compare them and find them consistent, *then* we'd know something, then science would smile on our endeavors. But alas, "feelings", whatever they are, slither past the scientific laboratory, and we are left asking such pseudo-scientific questions as, "Where does *affect* come into all this? Is it those intrinsic musical meanings that move us so deeply, or is there a transference of affect, via the notes, from the composer to the performer to the listener?"

Disc
Side 3
band 3
When we hear the opening notes of this Beethoven Piano Sonata [10], are we feeling what Beethoven supposedly felt when he wrote them? I could try to verbalize what *I* am feeling [11]:

135

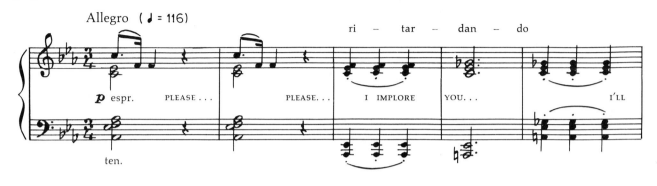

IF YOU DO . . .

(We receive the same answer)

(New pleading methods)

leggiero

scherzando

(coy . . .)

(wheedling . . .)

etc.

and so on through the whole movement, eventually invoking tears, passion, temper, bribery . . . I could go on building a whole drama of pleading and refusal—nothing specific, you understand—but a drama nonetheless, ending up in the last few bars, with yielding, compromise, and a firm agreement [12]. Settled. But, did Beethoven feel all that, or anything like it? Did I just make up these feelings, out of the blue, or are they to some degree related to Beethoven's feelings transferred to me through his notes?

[12]

We'll never know, we can't phone him up; but the probability is that *both* are true. And if so, we have just discovered a major ambiguity—a beautiful new semantic ambiguity to add to our fast-growing list.

But whichever is true, the basic point remains: music does possess the power of expressivity, and the human being does innately possess the capacity to respond to it. Everyone agrees on that, in one way or another—even William James, who regarded our reaction to music as nothing but a nervous tic. Where they disagree is in making the distinction between what music expresses and how it expresses it. The "what" is very hard to pin down, as we've seen; but the "how" we do know about: and that is Metaphor. In any sense in which music can be considered a language (and there are some senses in which it cannot be so considered) it is a totally *metaphorical* language. Consider the etymology of the word "metaphor": *meta-*, beyond: *pherein,* to carry—carrying meaning beyond the literal, the tangible, beyond the grossly semantic, to the self-contained *Ding-an-sich* of musical meaning. Metaphor is the generator, the power-plant of music, just as it is of poetry. Aristotle puts metaphor "midway between the unintelligible and the commonplace . . . " (a marvelous remark). "It is metaphor," he says, "which most produces knowledge." The artist cannot help but agree, nor can the lover of art. Quintilian says, even more strikingly, that metaphor accomplishes "the supremely difficult task of providing a name for everything". By "everything" he

"Juliet is the sun" has more meaning than saying Juliet is radiant.

139

obviously meant our interior lives, our psychic landscapes
and actions, where names elude us. It is thus that poetry
and music—but especially music, because of its specific and
far-reaching metaphorical powers—can name the
unnamable, and communicate the unknowable.

If we accept this general idea of music as a metalanguage
—and I can see no reason why we shouldn't—and if we
relate it back to our investigation of transformational
linguistics, then a remarkable and exciting hypothesis
presents itself: is it not conceivable that there exists an
innate universal grammar of musical metaphor? Think of
it; just let your mind reprise what has led up to this point:
the original idea of universality, that all grammars evolve
from basically similar principles; that out of these formal
universals arise cognate deep structures within the various
particular languages; that via transformational paths these
deep structures then rise to the surface as normal speech,
and that via a further transformational leap those surface
structures in turn re-evolve into what we call "poetry".
Given this chain of ideas, hasn't everything we've been
saying for three weeks led us inexorably to the hypothesis
that all transformational processes ultimately yield
metaphoric results? That is, if you recall the parallel ladder
charts from the syntax lecture (see p. 85), these processes
can produce such results in language but *must* produce
them in music. In other words, don't all metaphors, verbal
or musical, derive from transformational processes?

I suggest that the answer is an overwhelming yes.

In our last lecture we saw how some of these transformational processes might operate analogously in Shakespeare and in Mozart. It was a sort of game (that's really what we musicians do best, play games); and I now propose to continue playing that game in a more detailed way: to find musical equivalents for smaller, more specific metaphorical operations in language—namely, simple figures of speech, such as antithesis, alliteration, and the like.

And here my pretty young inquisitor might well interrupt again: how can you include simple figures of speech in the category of metaphor? Aren't they simply rhetorical devices, stylistic embellishments of language? No, because they can also contribute to metaphoric utterance, particularly when they occur in series. The proliferation of any given figure of speech sets up an array of *A's* and *B's*, all of them alike in deriving from some aesthetic principle of design. And it is this very principle which now serves as the *X*-factor.

Take antithesis, for example, which we all recognize when we read a Biblical psalm:

> The dead praise not the Lord, neither any that go
> down into silence.
> But we will bless the Lord from this time forth
> and for ever more.

Antithesis, *A* versus *B*, "they" versus "we". But in these lines, we recognize much more than the figure of speech: in fact, through that figure of speech we perceive a large poetic meaning. Why set up the dead at all in opposition to us, the living; isn't it enough to say, "We will bless the Lord"? No, it is not enough, not for making this particular

Delivering a lecture, WGBH studio

poetic statement. These verses are a microcosm, a poetic essence, of the entire psalm which is all established on antithesis, beginning, "Not unto us, O Lord, not unto us, but unto Thy name give glory," and continuing that antithetical design by setting up the polar extremes of idols made of silver and gold ("eyes have they, but they see not", etc.), and on the other hand, "But our God is in the heavens", which in turn leads to further antitheses, until we are finally ready to understand those last lines distinguishing between the dead, who praise not, and us, who do. We now perceive, through that continuing antithesis, that by "the dead" the psalmist is speaking metaphorically of the idolatrous nations, who worship the work of their own hands. Now that's an example of how a simple figure of speech can be extended to permeate and qualify a whole poetic structure. Can this also happen in music?

It can and it does. Examples abound; I pounce on one at random—Mozart's great C Minor Piano Sonata, which presents itself at the very outset in a striking antithesis: *A* countered by *B* [13]. But you may argue: yes, maybe, but is it really the equivalent of verbal antithesis, of a heavenly God versus a man-made idol, a clear, tangible opposition? Isn't the Mozart rather an example of contrast than of antithesis? Yes, it does involve contrast, loud versus soft, rising intervals versus falling ones, rough hammer-blows

[13] Allegro

[14]

A   B

[15]

[16]

144

versus tender entreaty, and so on. It is not a literary figure
of speech, as in the psalm, but it *is* a figure of musical
speech; and because of the abstract nature of music, the
pure, nonrepresentational nature of music, such a figure
can affect us with even greater directness and force than
a verbal one.

And again, as in the psalm, but even more than in the
psalm, this figure of Mozart's musical speech is extended
to condition and characterize the whole poetic structure.
Look at this marvel: that four-bar opening statement, in
itself so abundant in its antithetical meanings [see 13], is
immediately answered by a counterstatement [14]. This is
not only a *thematic* answer to the first statement, but a
harmonic opposition to it, since the first one proceeded from
the tonic to the dominant [15], while the counterstatement
does the opposite, starting with the dominant [16] and
ending up with the tonic. So we now have not one but
three antitheses [17]—two of equal length conjoined to
form yet a third, twice the length of either. And we could
go on through the whole movement finding constantly new
sets of antitheses—but enough. I have taken more time
than I meant to with this one figure of speech, antithesis,
but I did want you to understand what I meant by such a
figurative device as antithesis becoming a basic structural
principle, the metaphoric fountainhead, so to speak, of a
Davidic psalm or a Mozart sonata.

To pursue the matter, antithesis itself is founded on an
even more basic structural principle—that of *repetition*.
Where would these Biblical or Mozartian antitheses be
without the previous assumption of repetition, which can
then be varied by applying to it the principle of opposition?
Indeed, all figures of speech, and all metaphors, in speech

[17]

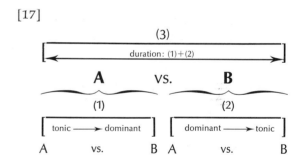

146

and music alike, depend ultimately on repetition, which is
then subjected to variation, or as the linguists say,
transformation.

I cannot stress this point strongly enough. In fact, it has
been authoritatively suggested that the main reason a
serious theory of musical syntax has been so slow to
develop is the refusal of musical theorists to recognize
repetition as the key factor. I think it was Nicholas Ruwet,
a distinguished musicologist as well as linguist, who
proposed this suggestion. And his argument grows out of a
proposition by Roman Jakobson, the great linguistic thinker
and one of Chomsky's most influential teachers. Jakobson,
speaking of poetry, said (and I reduce this quote): "It is
only . . . by the regular reiteration of equivalent units that
poetry provides an experience of time . . . comparable to
that of musical time." Now that would seem a gross
oversimplification, especially if he is referring to the
regular reiteration of metrical units. *Da-dá, da-dá, da-dá,
da-dá* hardly produces poetry; it's more like doggerel. But
the moment we apply to that mechanical regularity the
processes of transformation and variation, we immediately
see what he's getting at, and we can extend Jakobson's
reiterative principle to include all facets of poetic diction,
not only meter.

For example, the repetition of elementary sounds—
vowels, consonants, phonemes—which gives us the whole
range of poetic assonance, from the simple alliteration of
Shakespeare's "full fathom five" to the complex and
mysterious resonances of Milton in *Paradise Lost*, "fragrant
the fertile earth after soft showers"; or of Gerard Manley
Hopkins' sonorous hymn of praise for "dappled things"
"for skies of couple-colour as a brinded cow"; to say

148

nothing of the fascinating auditory correlatives that resonate in the poetry of Dylan Thomas, "And green and golden I was huntsman and herdsman"; or the so-called prose of James Joyce, which is really poetry: "Beside the rivering waters of, hither and thithering waters of. Night!" Even more, we can see poetry born of the repetition of actual words, not just sounds, but whole words: only think of the five consecutive "never's" uttered by King Lear in his death scene. We can expand the idea further to include the repetition of whole images, as in T. S. Eliot's *Four Quartets*; or even the repetition of whole lines—a device so commonly found in the Bible, or in poetic drama: "Brutus is an honorable man", over and over again. Not to mention Gertrude Stein, who made a whole career out of repetition.

The point must be clear by now: that it is repetition, modified in one way or another, that gives poetry its musical qualities, because repetition is so essential to music itself. And that is true of all metaphorical phenomena down to the last little figure of speech. Take alliteration, perhaps the simplest of all. Shelley writes: "Wild west wind", for example. All right, back to our game: where is such alliteration to be found in music? Everywhere. In Beethoven's Eighth Symphony [18], in Schubert's *Rosamunde* [19], in Shostakovich's Fifth Symphony [20], in the César Franck Symphony [21], and even in *William Tell* [22]. But that's all too easy: the game becomes really *pro* when we move from identical initial notes to identical initial *groups* of notes. And here the term "alliteration" is not enough; we must use the far grander term "anaphora", which in rhetorical circles names the device of beginning lines or stanzas with identical words or phrases, such as Tennyson's famous sequence:

Ring out, wild bells, to the wild sky . . .
Ring out the old, ring in the new . . .
Ring out the grief that saps the mind . . .

One can find anaphora in almost any religious litany, such
as in The Beatitudes, as well as throughout the Old
Testament, as in Isaiah 5:18-22:

Woe unto them that draw iniquity
    with cords of vanity . . .
Woe unto them that call evil good,
    and good evil . . .
Woe unto them that are wise in their
    own eyes . . .
Woe unto them that are mighty to
    drink wine . . .

Disc
Side 3
band 5 And, lo, we find anaphora in Mahler's Fifth Symphony
[23], and in Beethoven's Second Symphony [24], and . . .
but *basta* Anaphora. Onwards.

What do you suppose is the rhetorical figure operating in
this most unrhetorical Schubert melody [25]? It is a device
that bears the proud name "chiasmus", a fancy word that
means simply reversing the order of elements midway
through a statement: "What's Hecuba to him, or he to
Hecuba?" Or John Kennedy's: "Ask not what your country
can do for you, but what you can do for your country."
Notice again how this figure is based on repetition, as they
all are—repetition subjected to reversal, AB:BA. And
Schubert, blissfully unaware of chiasmus, just went ahead
and created one in his B Minor Symphony [26]. That
melody is so obviously dependent on repetition that it

barely needs mentioning; what's important is the variation of those *A's* and *B's,* which has transformed them into a musical metaphor—AB:BA.

Disc
Side 3
band 6
I was astonished one day suddenly to discover a huge chiasmus just squatting there, in so unpretentious a piece as Chabrier's rhapsody *España.* This chiasmus involves two different consecutive *tunes,* not just bars but whole tunes, one a chiastic version of the other. The first one [27] goes: $A + B$, which is then repeated. And *then* the chiasmus breaks open, $B + A$ [28]. It's an exact and perfect reversal. AB:BA.

Incredible, I find it, and much more than just an amusing game. I have discovered rhopalism in Beethoven's First Symphony, polysyndeton in *Petrouchka,* and asyndeton in Bruckner—but fun is fun.

What's seriously striking about all this is that these figures of speech, be they poetic or rhetorical devices, are transformations in our old familiar Chomskian sense. And, as I've proposed, all musical transformations lead to metaphorical results. A piece of music is a constant metamorphosis of given material, involving such trans-formational operations as inversion, augmentation, retrograde, diminution, modulation, the opposition of consonance and dissonance, the various forms of imitation (such as canon and fugue), the varieties of rhythm and meter, harmonic progressions, coloristic and dynamic changes, plus the infinite interrelations of all these with one another. These *are* the meanings of music. And that is as close as I can come to a definition of musical semantics.

After a brief pause we are going to see and hear a filmed performance of Beethoven's Symphony Number 6 in F. Why this particular symphony in this particular lecture?

153

Beethoven's Sixth would seem to be the least likely piece on earth to illustrate purely musical meanings, since it is encumbered from start to finish with nonmusical meanings. It even bears the subtitle *Pastorale*, which instantly places the work in an area of extramusical meaning, namely the area of the countryside. And as if that weren't enough, each of its five movements bears its own subtitle: "The Awakening of Cheerful Feelings on Arriving in the Country", "Scene by the Brook", "Happy Gathering of Peasant Folk", "Storm", and finally, "A Shepherd's Song of Joy and Thankfulness After the Storm". That alone would be enough to distract any listener's attention from such things as inversions and subdominants, to say nothing of deletions and permutations—but no, Beethoven goes even further, and injects actual onomatopoeic references to country life: bird calls and village bands, lightning and thunder and shepherd's pipes. It's as close to program music as Beethoven ever came. So why the *Pastorale* in this lecture, where we are concerned not with the birds and bees, but with the F's and the C's, the notes themselves which form the intrinsic metaphors of music, metaphors that evolve out of syntactic and phonological transformations? But that's precisely the reason: to clarify and distinguish between one kind of metaphor and another, between the intrinsic and the extrinsic, the musical and the verbal. I will try to help by preparing you somewhat at the piano; and then we can go on playing our game: testing whether it's possible for us to listen to this piece as pure music—not as a pastoral symphony but purely as Beethoven's *Symphony Number 6 in F major*, opus 68. Do you think it is possible? That is what we are going to find out after this pause.

156

II

Where were we? Oh, yes; we had just come face to face
with a most intriguing question: is it possible to hear
Beethoven's *Pastorale* Symphony as pure music, divorced
from all its extrinsic, nonmusical metaphors? Well, it should
be possible, since Beethoven himself said that his subtitles
and cuckoo calls and thunderclaps were to be taken only as
suggestion—"not as tone-painting" (to use his own words)
"but as *Empfindungen*, feelings"—and therefore not too
literally. But still those extramusical references *are* there;
Beethoven put them there with his own hand, and it's not
easy to ignore them.

What they do, actually, is to form a kind of visual
curtain of nonmusical ideas, a semi-transparent curtain, so
to speak, that interposes itself between the listener and the
music per se. What I propose to do is to change the lighting
on that curtain, using a light strong enough to render it
wholly transparent, to turn it into a "scrim", as they say in
the theater, through which we can look directly into the
music, in all its intrinsic meanings, clearly, freed from the
bondage of so-called "music appreciation" or of flowery
program notes or of those Disney nymphs and centaurs
which have also gotten painted onto our scrim. Away with
all that. I am presenting you with a challenge: to rid your
mind of all nonmusical notions, all birds and brooks and
rustic pleasures, and to concentrate only on the music in all
its *own* metaphorical pleasures. I want you to hear it as if for
the first time.

Let's begin at the beginning [29]. These first four bars
are the material out of which the whole first movement is
going to grow, and it's not just the main material but the
only material. Every bar and phrase to come—and I mean

every one, without exception—will be some kind of
transformation, some metaphorical rendering, of the
elements present in these four little bars. And what are
those elements? On the face of it, they seem to comprise a
blithe little tune in F major, beginning on the tonic and
ending on the dominant with a pause, or as we say,
a *fermata*.

But is that really all? By no means. Just look at the bass
line, which you'd hardly notice as a line, although it is:
tonic F to dominant C [30]. And this F-C, or *fa-do* [31]
turns out to be the real motto of the whole movement (and
by extension, the whole symphony); it's as much the motto
of the Sixth Symphony as this [32] is the motto of the
Fifth. And it will keep reappearing, over and over, in the
bass [33], or up on top [34], or hidden in between [35], or
transposed [36], or transformed [37], or speeded up [38],
or whatever, as a constant running metaphor throughout,
like the "Figure in the Carpet" in Henry James' great story.
The whole piece is virtually an essay on the subject of *fa-do*.

But what of the more obvious melodic material in these
opening bars, the tune on top [39]? What Beethoven does
with that, in true Beethovenian style, is immediately to
develop it, to vary it, to *transform* it [40]. Right away we
can spot one obvious transformation: what was this [41]
has now become this [42]. And so we already have a
metaphor: this-is-that, in disguise. What went down [43]
now goes up [44]. That's an elementary permutation:
simple inversion; but there is a far subtler transformation
involved here, namely a linguistic deletion of the kind we
found last time in the Mozart symphony. Look again at the
opening four-bar phrase ending on the dominant [see 30].
Now according to the symmetrical demands of the deep

159

[45]

[46]

etc.

[47]   [48]   [49]

cresc.

[50]

[cont'd]

structure, there *should* follow a complementary four-bar phrase ending in the tonic [45]. How dull. The symphony would have died a-borning. Imagine then trying to go on with the next section [46]—sheer agony. The remedy, of course, is deletion: just lose that second complementary phrase, and eliminate the agony. The opening material is now free to develop.

But to develop how? Like this [47] and repeat [48]; then new material [49] and repeat [50], and *repeat* [51], and *repeat, repeat, repeat* . . . how many times have I repeated the word "repeat" in this short development? I've lost count. What *is* all this repetition business? Here we were just a moment ago shouting praises for *deletion*, for the omission of repeats, and that was our leading metaphor in the *Pastorale*. Now we suddenly find Beethoven repeating as if obsessed. What is this new paradox? It's actually not a paradox at all; it needs only a few words of clarification.

First of all, not one of those repeats is an exact or literal repeat. Each one contains some variation or other—a slight elaboration, or an added voice, or a structural ambiguity, or a change in the dynamics of loud and soft. And second, what *is* variation, anyway? It's always, in one way or another, a manifestation of the mighty dramatic principle known as the Violation of Expectation. What is expected is, of course, repetition—either literal or in the form of an answer, a counterstatement, or whatever; and when those expectations are violated, you've got a variation. The violation is the variation.

In other words, variation cannot exist without the previously assumed idea of repetition. This assumption explains the deletion we heard at the beginning of the symphony; what was deleted was the instinctive expectation of a symmetrical counterpart to the first four-bar phrase [see 45], and that deletion is in itself a kind of variation. Do you see what I mean? It is the conspicuous absence of the expected repetition which makes that particular musical surface structure what it is.

If I've succeeded in making that point clearly, then I'm sure you will be able to follow this, the topper: the *idea* of repetition is inherent in music even when the repetition itself is not there at all. In other words, the repetitive principle is at the very source of musical art (and of poetry), as we learned from Jakobson's reiterative   p 147 principle.

Now we have an insight into repetitive functions that enable us to view this *Pastorale* Symphony (sorry, I mean the *Sixth* Symphony in F; we have to be careful in this metaphorical territory), to view all this Beethovenian repeating with new comprehension, and to see exactly how Beethoven transforms garden-variety repetition into metaphor. In other words, we are now in a position to examine how he prevents garden-variety repetition from becoming garden-variety boredom, by the magic of transformation.

In the interest of clarity let's reduce that opening melodic material to its component parts: bar one which we might call the "head" of the theme [52]; then bar two, a jaunty, rhythmic motive which we'll call—well, let's just call it the "jaunty motive" [53]; and finally bars three and four, which being all scalewise can be called the "scalewise motive" [54]. Now, if you remember, Beethoven began at this point to develop that material, in what seemed to be mere repetition of the thematic head and jaunty motives [55]. We immediately found a transformation of the

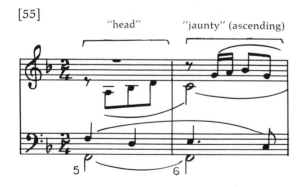

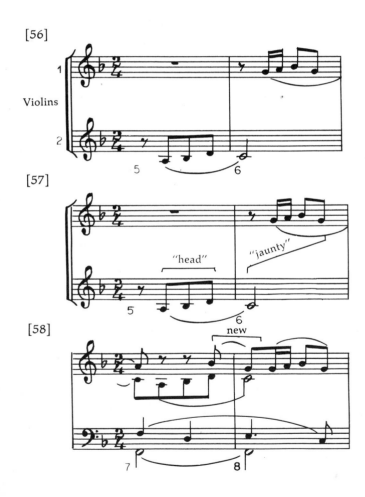

164

originally descending jaunty motive [see 52] into an ascending one—a simple figure of musical speech called inversion (just as the phrase "roses are red" can be inverted to "red are roses", resulting in a more "poetic" structure). But there is also another figure of speech at work here— a device called "fragmentation"—which transforms the repetition even further. These first two developmental bars are split up, and shared by two different instrumental voices: the second violins play the head motive, and the first violins answer with the already transformed jaunty motive [56], thus making it a double transformation.

But wait: Beethoven carries the fragmentation even further. The two parts of this split-up are not just a neat division into head motive and jaunty motive; that would be too simpleminded. What actually happens is that the second violins play the head *plus* the first note of the jaunty [57], whereupon the first violins respond with the remainder —namely, the jaunty minus its first note. This is no mere whim of Beethoven's; it exemplifies the incredibly on-going nature of his music, that molecular growth-process of his, whereby motives, or parts of motives, can become attached or detached in infinite numbers of ways by constant repositioning, conjoining, and embedding. This process is so intense and diversified that even so apparently destructive an activity as fragmentation contributes profusely to the growth of this living organism.

Obviously the study of these two little bars is endlessly fascinating; but let's move on to the next two bars [58], which are an almost literal repeat of those we've just examined. But only *almost* literal. Do you notice the two added notes in the first violin part? A B-flat and a G—just enough elaboration to avoid a strictly literal repeat.

[59]

[60]

[61]

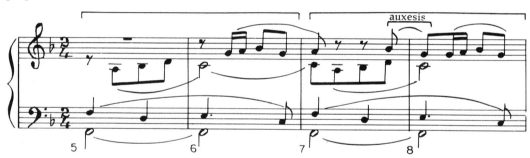

[62]

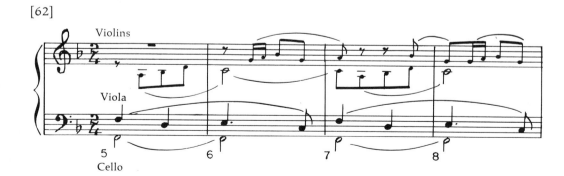

166

That transformation is also a nameable figure of speech; it is called "auxesis"—an increase in density. But why were just *those* two notes added, that B-flat and that G [59]? Because they form an interval of the third—a descending interval which mirrors the rising interval of the third, B-flat to D, in the head motive [60]. The auxesis is simply the addition of this descending third to the repetition in the upper voice, and a metaphor has been created between the two pairs of *almost* identical developmental bars [61].

Well, inversion, fragmentation, auxesis—that's a lot of transformation in the short space of four little bars, especially when you know that they are really only *two* bars, almost literally repeated. But the big news is that we still haven't uncovered the most striking and beautiful metaphor of all in these same four bars, and that is to be found in the viola part. Did you know that under all that head-and-jaunty exchange in the violins the violas are solemnly playing this tune [62]? Unless you are an experienced listener, such inner voices are the hardest to perceive, sandwiched in as they are between the sky above and the mud below. You may have missed it. But now that you know it's there, are you going to ask why it's there, where it came from—*or*, do you sense something inherently relevant about it, a family resemblance, a familiar resonance? If you do, then you have perceived the metaphor, whether you can explain it or not. But that's not your job; it's mine, and I will try to explain it.

This metaphor arises out of *three* different and simultaneous transformations: inversion, retrograde, and augmentation. Inversion we already know about; and in this case what is being inverted is that very moment of fragmentary conjoining when the head motive latches on

167

168

to the first note of the jaunty motive [63]. You can see those conjoined intervals of an ascending third followed by a descending second [64]. Now our metaphorical viola line simply inverts those intervals, to a *descending* third followed by an *ascending* second [65]. This metaphor is further enhanced by the fact that its intervals, a third followed by a second, are the direct reversal of the head motive itself, whose intervals are a second followed by a third [66]. Hence the term "retrograde", or going backwards. As for "augmentation", we simply mean an increase of note length. In other words, the viola tune proceeds in quarter notes, whereas the head motive from which it derives moves in eighth notes, twice as fast [67]. Thus the viola tune is twice as slow, its notes *augmented* to double duration. And so through these three devices, this triple transformation, a rich metaphor is created, a particularly strong example of this-is-that. If you think of the viola line as the "this", and the violin music on top as the "that", and then hear them together, the whole complex metaphorical structure will come clear [68]. Do you now hear what goes on in those four bars? They are a striking model of the human brain in action and as such, a model of how we think. For this reason, music (especially music by a genius such as Beethoven) provides what is probably the clearest linguistic model you can find. That's the unique miracle of music: that it enables us to perceive This and That *simultaneously;* there can be no stronger or richer presentation of metaphor.

But now, in the ensuing four bars, we discover a new musical wonder: a metaphor of a metaphor. This new material [69] is not new material at all, but again a transformation, by inversion, of that same viola line we

were just examining, which went, as you know, like this
[70]. Beethoven just turns those three notes upside down
[71], and lo, there is his "new material" [see 69]. It's
miraculous; and, of course, therein lies the secret of the
inevitability one always feels in Beethoven's music: it is a
constant metaphorical growth, self-generating, always on
its own track.

For example, those last four bars of "new material" are
immediately subjected to a repetition, but again Beethoven
avoids literalness—by two transformative devices. First,
there is a dynamic transformation; that is, the four bars are
first stated *piano, crescendo* to *forte* [72], but they are
restated *forte*, with a sudden drop to *piano* in the third bar
[73].

Did you hear that peculiar last note of the melody [74]?
That note introduces the second transformation, and
through it we come upon a beautiful new ambiguity—a
structural ambiguity. Because that last bar [75] initiates a
whole string of repetitions—eight of them, in fact—and
literal repetitions at that [76]. But are they literal? Not on
closer inspection. They are also subjected to a dynamic
transformation, this time *crescendo* to *forte*, and *diminuendo*
back to *pianissimo*, which creates the metaphor of
approaching and receding. But even that's not the main
event; the master stroke is that bar 16 (the fourth bar of
the earlier four-bar phrase [77]), which was the initiator of

[77]

171

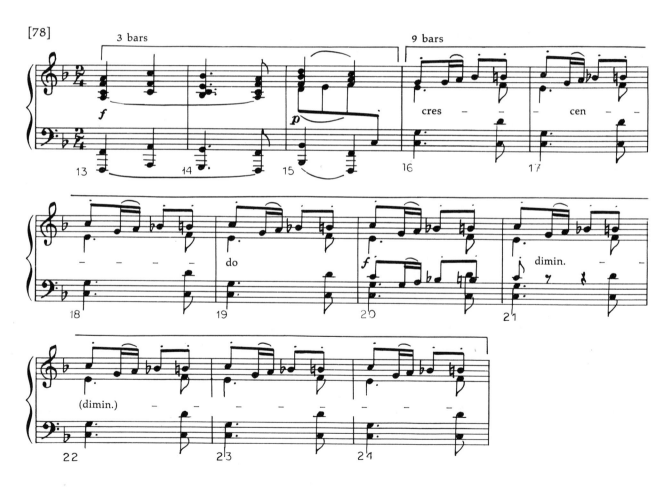

this repetitive string, is *also* the first bar of the string itself. We know this to be so because Beethoven marks the beginning of his crescendo on that very bar. What does this mean? Clearly that the four-bar phrase was really a *three*-bar phrase, and that the eight-bar repetitive string is really a nine-bar string [78]. Three plus nine. But we know this only in hindsight, after we've already heard it; what we heard, or thought we heard, was four bars followed by eight [79]. Then which is true, three plus nine or four plus

[79]

173

eight? The answer is that *both* are true; and the tension that results from that contradiction is what makes this ambiguity so beautiful and exciting. And then, as if nine repetitions weren't enough, Beethoven pretends to go on repeating [80], only he drops out the accompaniment in bar 25 (another transformation), and then in bar 26 raises each repetition by one degree of the scale (yet another transformation), returning us in blissful satisfaction to our opening theme (bar 29).

Well, that's the beginning of the *Pastorale* Symphony —only the beginning, mind you, of only one movement. We've been analyzing approximately thirty seconds of music, music that continues for over thirty minutes. And even so, this has been a very limited analysis, showing only one aspect of the music: how a metaphorical language is created by transformations, all of which are some kind of varied repetition.

This one aspect, however, is probably the most germinal and rewarding one in all musical analysis. Consider, for instance, another form of varied repetition, the practice of sequences. A sequence is simply a series of repetitions of the same phrase on different degrees of the scale. Here's a famous one from the development section of this same first movement [81], based on a multiple transformation of the material we analyzed back in bars 9 through 12. The sequence takes shape through a rising repeat [82], and then

[82]

251   252   253   254

another [83]—but what's this new wrinkle? We've hit the
minor mode—but only for a moment [84], and we're safely
back in the major.

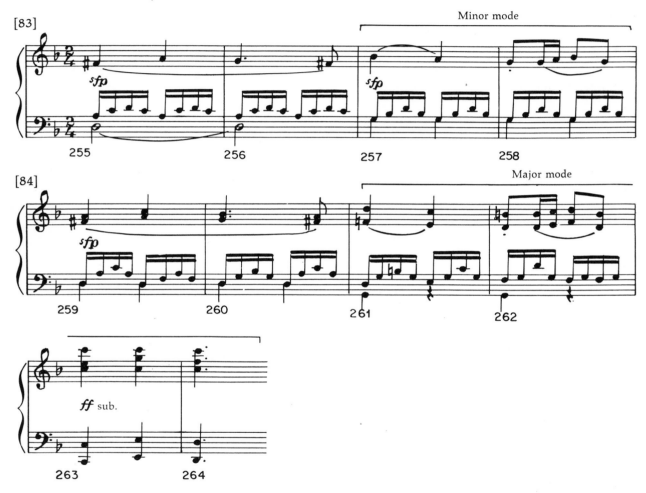

What happened? Why was that brief excursion into the minor so terribly moving? Do you realize that this is the only minor moment in the entire movement? It's as though suddenly, in the midst of all this cheerful, sunny music, for a second, one little cloud darkened the sun. Now there *I* go using an extrinsic metaphor. Haven't I contradicted myself? What has *minor* to do with darkness or light or clouds or sun?

That's one of the questions I'm most frequently asked by nonmusicians: why is the minor "sad" and the major "glad"? Isn't this proof of the "affective" theory of musical expression? The answer is no; whatever darkness, or sadness, or passion you feel when you hear music in the minor mode is perfectly explainable in purely phonological terms. If you think back to our first lecture when we discussed the harmonic series, or overtones, you'll recall that one of the earliest overtones of any fundamental is the major third [85]—a strong, consonant overtone which is clearly heard as part of its fundamental. Along with its neighboring overtone, the interval of the fifth, it contributes to the basic triad [86]. Now the *minor* third, which would turn that triad into a minor one [87], is a very late and remote overtone way up here in the series [88]—overtone number 18. So that when *it* is employed to create music in

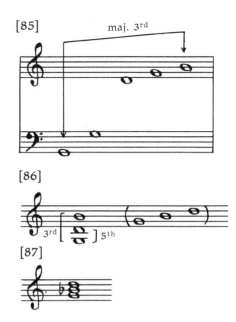

177

[89]

[90]

[91]

178

the minor mode, it is at variance with the major third which is implicitly present in the fundamental. This creates what is called in acoustics "interference", meaning that we are, so to speak, hearing both the major and the minor thirds at once [89].

This interference of the two frequencies causes a phonological disturbance, which we hear as a "disturbed" quality, a troubled, unstable sound. And so we call minor music "troubled", "sad", "unstable", "dark", "passionate", or whatever. In other words, we translate a phonological disturbance into an affective one. We are *affected* by it, as in this Chopin *Ballade* [90]. Now whatever subjective feelings we're going to report about that, they're going to be somewhere in the area of "passionate", "dark", "yearning", "not satisfied"—the very opposite of our Beethoven symphony [91], which is as major as can be.

But now we can explain this opposition in completely phonological terms. So we come to realize that this so-called "affective" phenomenon of the minor mode is not an extrinsic metaphorical operation at all; it is intrinsic to music, and its meaning is a purely musical one. As exemplified in that sequential passage of the Beethoven symphony, it is simply another metaphorical way of varying a repetition. Of course, it's a very expressive way; we're curiously moved by it; but the *meaning* of it—do you remember the distinction I made earlier between meaning and expression?—the meaning of it is an intrinsically musical one.

But what are we to say of the long strings of *unvaried* repetitions that inhabit this same development section? Like

this one, which seems interminable [92]. Simply unbelievable in its dogged insistence. Yet this is one of the most exciting passages in all music. How can it be exciting if there is so much literal repetition? Why is there so much repetition in this symphony anyway? Granted that we know repetition to be a fundamental principle of all music, even possibly the key to musical syntax—even so, why such an obsession with it in this particular work? It could be suggested that this compulsive repeating on Beethoven's part is related to the programmatic nature of this pastoral piece, and the profuse repetition could be seen as a metaphor for the profuse repetitiveness of Nature herself, the infinite reduplication of species, of jonquils and daisies, of sparrows and poplars and mosquitoes. To say nothing of the regular movements of sun, stars, and moon. But these are not the kinds of metaphor we are seeking; they are again extrinsic, extramusical, and we are after purely musical semantics. Then what is the *musical* metaphor to be discovered in that famous long passage of literal repeats?

It is to be found in the large design that is ultimately formed out of these bar-by-bar repeats. We've been dealing so far with small patterns, two-bar and four-bar phrases, or maybe eight- or nine-bar phrases. But what we now see is a pattern of *ninety-two* bars [93], all to be comprehended together as one immense metaphorical design: twenty-four plus twenty-two, which makes forty-six, and again twenty-four plus twenty-two—another forty-six—which already reveals a large inner repetition. Now don't panic: we're not going to slog through all those ninety-two bars, but we can look briefly at the design of the first twenty-four. What are they, and what is their metaphorical meaning—not in terms of jonquils and daisies, but of notes and rhythms? To begin

[93]

181

with, we know that these notes come from our well-known "jaunty" motive [94], now transformed and transposed to B-flat [95], and played four times by the first violins [96]. This is then literally repeated by the second violins, doubled by a woodwind an octave higher [97]. That makes eight bars, right? Now that eight-bar segment is itself repeated and re-repeated, with slight transformations we won't discuss right now, but always with the same alternation of first violins as against second violins plus the high woodwind; and it's played three times in all—three times eight bars, making twenty-four bars [98].

98

Now that's one way of looking at this episode, from an orchestral point of view. We perceive *one* of Beethoven's intentions via his instrumental texture, the alternating high and low registers, and the twenty-four bar *crescendo* to a climax. But now let's view the same twenty-four bars *harmonically*, and we find a very different story. Four bars of B-flat in the first violins [99], as before, repeated as before in the second violins with the higher woodwind octave. Then again the first violins—that's now twelve bars; and *now* a sudden switch of key to D major (bar 163) for twelve more bars. We're still following the same instrumental pattern, mind you, but in this new key of D, which is maintained for two more repeats, and finally, climax. Now this has been a totally different construction of those same twenty-four bars—it's two times twelve: twelve bars in B-flat and twelve bars in D. Not at all three times eight, as we saw at first. In other words, there are two different orders of articulation, two different substructures functioning simultaneously within this single span of twenty-four bars. One order [100] articulates the orchestral texture, three times eight; and the other one

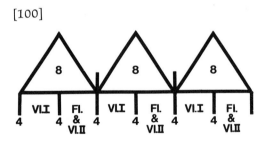

[100]

184

99

[101] articulates what Walter Piston called the "harmonic rhythm", two times twelve. And the simultaneous contradiction of the two creates [102] one glorious ambiguity: this-is-that, or better in this case, this-*but*-that. Thus is born a great musical metaphor, out of what seemed to be merely twenty-four stupefying repetitions.

At this point I think any further analysis would involve us in truly stupefying repetitions. It's time now to hear the music performed, not in bits by me at the piano, but in its entirety, by the Boston Symphony. And I hope it's time for you to listen to this music purely *as* music, as a magnificent utterance in a metaphorical language, a language of creative transformations. I hope you are somewhat prepared for this, prepared to renounce the whole pastoral paraphernalia, jonquils and daisies included. It's not easy; but it is possible. It's even possible to get over such challenging hurdles as those bird calls toward the end of the second movement, which Beethoven has specifically named in the score: Nightingale, Quail, and Cuckoo. Think of them instead as a little cadenza for three woodwinds before the final bars. (There is plenty of precedent for that in the symphonies of Haydn, and don't forget that Haydn was a great model for Beethoven.) And then, of course, the storm in the fourth movement: even that blasted storm can be conceived structurally as a huge transition from the scherzo to the finale (which, in a way, it is)—rather like the corresponding passage in Beethoven's Fifth Symphony, which is indeed a transition from the scherzo to the finale. (And don't forget that Beethoven was writing his Fifth and Sixth symphonies practically simultaneously.)

[101]

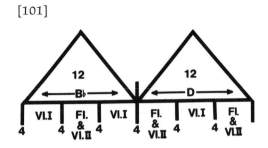

[102]

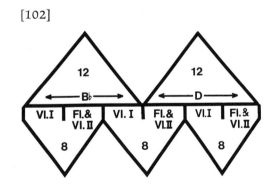

Even if you *can* succeed in disregarding all these programmatic elements, and substituting structural and transformational ones, you're still going to have a hard time ridding yourself of associations, including *un*pastoral ones. This challenge I'm offering invites you to discard your customary listening habits of letting the music nudge you into pleasant, passive associations with your personal memories, with images, colors, random emotional states—all those experiences of synaesthesia. I am rashly suggesting that you change your habits on the spot, that you dump the whole synaesthetic baggage, including Beethoven's own suggestive titles, and hear this marvelous example of symphonic metamorphosis as just that.

I know how hard it is to do this; I, too, often have difficulty in shedding extramusical associations. It's like that old mental exercise: don't think of an elephant for the next five seconds. Can you do it? Don't think of an elephant: one . . . two . . . three . . . four . . . five. Did you succeed? Well, maybe. It's the same with listening to the *Pastorale* Symphony: only here it's a matter of not thinking of those birds and those storms and those shepherds' pipes. Some of you may resist this challenge; some of you may even rebel. Some may say, I *like* those centaurs and fauns and Walt Disney, and I *want* to think of them when I hear this music. But do give it a chance. At the very least it's splendid self-discipline, good for the character. And at best, if you do succeed, you may be hearing a whole new piece by Beethoven.

(*At this point Beethoven's* Symphony No. 6 in F Major, *Opus 68, is played.*)

I don't know to what extent you've succeeded in avoiding

the elephant, or the birds and the bees. I doubt that any of you succeeded one hundred percent because, as I warned you, it's almost impossible to divorce your minds from the associations that insist upon being there. But even if you succeeded only partly, even *one* percent, you've accomplished a lot, because you've taken at least a first step toward new listening habits; and once you've begun to hear music as music only, then you're already over the toughest hurdle, and well on your way toward a whole new way of listening to music. And to that extent, I congratulate you.

This glorious piece we've been listening to is, as I said before, as close to program music as Beethoven ever came, and it placed him squarely in the vanguard of the surging programmatic movement that was to engage with increasing force the minds of romantic and impressionist composers for a whole century to come. This intense preoccupation with literary and pictorial association, with its inevitable set of new ambiguities, is going to be the area of our investigation in the next lecture. And now that we have a fairly comprehensive grounding in the three linguistic departments (phonology, syntax, and semantics), we should be able to subsume that knowledge, and concentrate in the next three lectures less on linguistics and more on musical poetics.

When I first wrote down the title of this lecture, *The Delights and Dangers of Ambiguity*, I had no idea that the word *dangers* would itself acquire an ambiguous meaning by the time the lecture was delivered. I had had in mind *aesthetic* delights and dangers only; but a few days ago (Friday, October 26, 1973, to be exact), a formidable new danger was thrust upon us, when our Secretary of State announced that the armed forces of the United States had been put on worldwide alert in response to what he called "the ambiguity of some of the actions and communications", regarding respectively movements of Soviet troops and statements of Russian diplomats. Now that is dangerous ambiguity, dramatizing the dangers that accompany a lack of clarity in human communication. Those are clear and present dangers; failure of communication can lead to a complete breakdown, and to disastrous consequences. Then why this persistent emphasis on the "beauty of ambiguity", as I have put it, and on which I was challenged last week by my blonde inquisitor? The answer must be obvious: ambiguity *may* be a useful tool in diplomacy, as it is in art; but it can be catastrophic when diplomacy turns into hard fact, just as it can be perfectly glorious in an actual work of art. Aesthetics, sí; politics, no!

Part of the danger is that "ambiguity" is in itself an ambiguous word—that is, it has more than one meaning. And I think that before we go one step further into our inquiry we would do well to have a solid dictionary definition or two. *Or two;* that's the problem. There are two distinct definitions, arising from the dual meaning of the prefix *ambi-*, which can signify "bothness" (that is, being on two sides at once) and also "aroundness" (or being on all sides at once). The first connotation, *bothness,* yields such

4. THE DELIGHTS AND DANGERS OF AMBIGUITY

[1]

etc.

[2]

chromatic line

diatonic bass

194

words as "ambidextrous" and "ambivalent", which imply duality. Whereas the second connotation, *aroundness*, conditions such words as "ambience", "ambit", and so on, which relate to the general surround, thus implying vagueness. Webster gives these two definitions of "ambiguous": (1) "doubtful or uncertain" and (2) "capable of being understood in two or more possible senses." But that "two *or more*" presents an ambiguity of its own; so let's delete "or more" for our purposes of the moment, so that *we* at least can be clear in our human communication. Our definition now reads: "capable of being understood in *two* possible senses." Now we can make sense. Everything we've been saying about puns, antithesis, zeugma, symmetry, chiasmus, Yang and Yin, Lingam and Yoni, upbeat and downbeat, strong and weak—all this has involved duality, and at some point we've always arrived, if you recall, at a manifestation of ambiguity which arose from the basic concept of two-ness.

This idea of duple ambiguity has been an underlying string running through all three lectures so far, but only lightly touched on, and only intermittently plucked. In our first lecture, for instance, we traced a growing chromaticism in musical history, based on the accretion of more and more remote overtones of the harmonic series as they were gradually accepted into common practice [1]. With that growing chromaticism we found a corresponding growth of ambiguity, and a resulting need to contain that chromaticism, to control it through the basic powers of diatonicism [2], the tonic-dominant structure of tonal music. We found that this containment of chromaticism-within-diatonicism reached a state of perfect equilibrium in the music of Bach, initiating a Golden Age of roughly one hundred years, an

196

age of imperturbable tonal stability. But we also realized that this perfectly controlled containment is in itself an ambiguity, in that it presents two simultaneous ways in which to hear music, via the contained chromaticism and via the containing diatonicism.

Similarly, in our second lecture on syntax, we found new ambiguities in Mozart's G-minor Symphony, if you recall, arising from violated symmetry, deep-structure symmetries which were converted by linguistic transformational procedures into beautifully ambiguous surface structures. We were then in a position to recognize, and even account for, certain musical phenomena whose beauty *depends* on ambiguous procedures. For instance, do you recognize these bars [3]? The whole world has been swooning to this Adagietto from Mahler's Fifth Symphony ever since "Death in Venice" invaded the silver screen. Why the swooning? After all, it's nothing but a dominant leading to a tonic— three conventional upbeats in F major [4] leading to an appoggiatura downbeat which then resolves [5], again in the most conventional way. (Do you remember about appoggiaturas from our Mozart analysis—those "leaning notes", dissonant tones that bear a special weight and tension which must be resolved, notes that lean on their resolutions? Well, this is one of them; and it does resolve just as conventionally as in Mozart.) Then what's the magic secret? Ambiguity, as if you didn't know—and more than just dualistic ambiguity. You see, all that preliminary vamping on the harp [6] is first of all *syntactically* vague; we have no idea what beat we're on or what meter we're in. What's more, the harp is setting up the key of the piece, F major, by suggesting its tonic triad [7], but only *suggesting* it, because the fundamental note, the root of that triad, F itself, is missing. Only two-thirds of the triad is given us, the

197

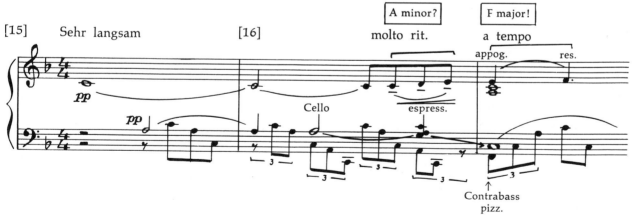

A and the C, reduplicated in several octaves, it's true, but
still only *two* different notes. So we're not yet *really* sure
that our key is going to be F major. It's exactly like that
children's teasing chant that we examined for its universality
in our first lecture. You remember [8]? Those same two
notes. And do you remember how we found that the tonic
fundamental of those two overtones [9] is not sung but is
present by implication only? Well, that omission, the absence
of that tonic makes us only *possibly* aware of F major, in
this Mahler piece as well as in the teasing-tune; because the
two notes we hear [10] *could* turn out to be two-thirds of a
whole other triad, namely A minor [11]. Automatically we
are facing another ambiguity: which of the two keys *are* we
in, A minor [12] or F major [13]? In the case of the teasing-
tune, that ambiguity lends a certain poignancy, almost
hurtful, because of the implication of something else [14],
something which could be rather nasty. Of course,
Mahler isn't being nasty; quite the contrary. But the
principle is identical, because again, which of the two keys
are we in [15]? As the three upbeats begin, we'd almost
vote for A minor [16] because there's that A in the cello
part which seems to predominate; but no, it sneakily descends to G, and then when the basses confirm the descent
to F—oh, it feels so good. We're home, in F major; but
there's still an unresolved tug-at-the-heart in that appoggiatura up there in the melody, and when *it* resolves we
just melt away, with the pleasure of fulfillment.

Enough of ambiguity? We've barely begun. Because last
week we ran into yet a new ambiguity, neither phonological
nor syntactic, but a third one, a *semantic* ambiguity, a real
problem in *meaning*. There we were, if you remember, chin-

200

to-chin with Beethoven's *Pastorale* Symphony, a piece
brimming with nonmusical birds and bees, and defying it to
mean anything other than its own intrinsic musical metaphors. But to whatever extent we succeeded in avoiding the
peasants and the cuckoos, one thing remained brightly
unambiguous: that this Beethovenian experiment in semantic conflict, namely program music, was still under perfect
classical control; all its ambiguities—chromatic, structural,
or metaphorical—were classically contained in Augustan
fashion. Remember that Beethoven himself said he was
trying only to suggest feelings of country life; he was not
indulging in "tone-painting", as he put it. The *Pastorale* is
still a monument of the Golden Age.

But now, as we move forward through the nineteenth
century, we're going to find all three strains of ambiguity
increasing sharply in both quantity and intensity. By the
time the century is finished this epidemic increase will have
brought us to Webster's other definition of ambiguity—
sheer vagueness. And that's where the aesthetic delights of
ambiguity start turning into dangers.

The irony of all this is that it was Beethoven himself who
started the ambiguity-inflation. He was a walking, living
ambiguity in himself—at once the last great classicist and
the first great Romantic. Consider the scherzo from his
Hammerklavier Sonata, which is based on the most innocent
little diatonic tune in the home key of B-flat [17]. But now
just listen to how the movement ends [18]. Whither have
we wandered? Far from home, into something like B minor
[19]. But with those last two notes Beethoven has arbitrarily,
dictatorially, proclaimed B-flat again. Are we home at last?

Disc
Side 3
band 8

[20]

[21]

a tempo (♪ = 76)

(A major)

cresc. — — — — accelerando — — — —

Prestissimo

ff

[cont'd]

Yes, we are [20]; but it was nip and tuck there for a minute.

And what about this mysterious passage, later on in the same Sonata, the bridge from the slow movement into the Final Fugue [21]? This is ambiguity rampant. We start thinking we're in A major, then go wandering, lost to the world, till we abruptly wind up in B-flat. But, mind you, all that blind wandering isn't so blind; it is all a modified series of tonic-dominant changes through the well-known circle of

[21 cont'd]

203

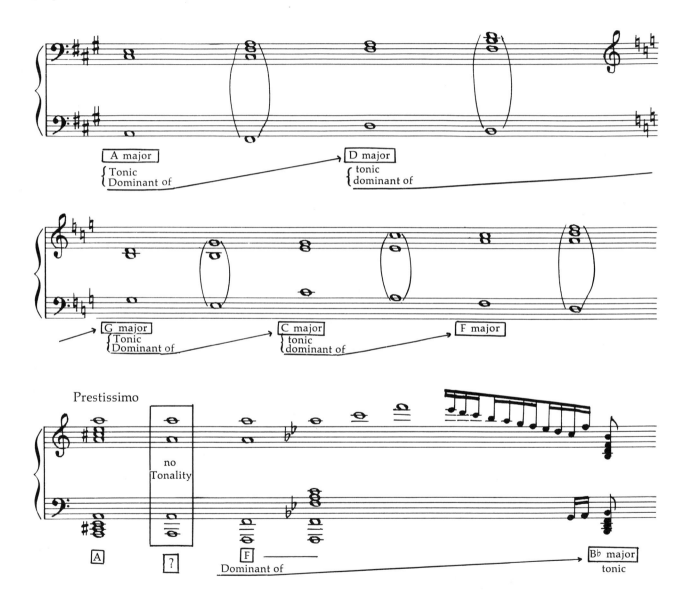

fifths [22], up to the *Prestissimo*, where we seem to get stuck on A major; but suddenly all tonality is suspended, and surprise, we're in F, which turns out to be the dominant of B-flat; and so home again, into the Final Fugue. Ambiguity by prestidigitation. And I'm sure I don't have to mention the obvious *structural* ambiguity of this incredible passage—the elusiveness of the rhythm, the almost savage intensity of the acceleration—and all written without a single bar line to point the way [see 21].

It's evident that with Beethoven the Romantic Revolution had already begun, bringing with it the new Artist, the artist as Priest and Prophet. This new creator had a new self-image: he felt himself possessed of divine rights, of almost Napoleonic powers and liberties—especially the liberty to break rules and make new ones, to invent new forms and concepts, all in the name of greater expressivity. His mission was to lead the way to a new aesthetic world, confident that history would follow his inspirational leadership. And so there exploded onto the scene Byron, Jean Paul, Delacroix, Victor Hugo, E. T. A. Hoffmann, Schumann, Chopin, Berlioz—all proclaiming new freedoms.

Where music was concerned, the new freedoms affected formal structures, harmonic procedures, instrumental color, melody, rhythm—all of these were part of a new expanding universe, at the center of which lay the artist's personal passions. From the purely phonological point of view, the most striking of these freedoms was the new chromaticism, now employing a vastly enriched palette, and bringing with it the concomitant enrichment of ambiguity. The air was now filled with volcanic, chromatic sparks. More and more the upper partials of the harmonic series were taking on an independence of their own, playing hide-and-seek with their sober diatonic elders, like defiant youngsters in the heyday of revolt.

205

The composers themselves now had something of the
defiant child in them, along with their Priest-and-Prophet
images. I wish we had time to explore their syntactic
adventures fully and comprehensively, ranging from the
highly personal tenderness of Schubert's enharmonic
modulations to the almost diabolical antics of Berlioz. We
can't do all that in one lecture; but we can touch on a few
salient peaks—Schumann, for example, gloriously mad
Schumann, a master of ambiguity. Only think of a Schumann song such as *Zwielicht*, with its twilit introduction,
or of the fascinating punning and anagramming that goes
on in a piano work like "Carnaval." But Schumann's most
exciting sallies into ambiguity are his *rhythmic* ones, such as
the festival of asymmetry at the end of "Carnaval" [23].
All that music is basically in 3/4 time, but you'd never know
it, because it's been beautifully distorted by an overlay of
two's and four's plus a superimposed meter of 3/2. The
mind reels with all these built-in ambiguities, these metrical
contradictions. Another typical Schumann device is treating
a string of syncopations as though it were a succession of
strong beats, as he does in this variation from his *Symphonic
Etudes* [24]. It's hard to believe that every one of those
accented melodic notes is *off* the beat, not *on*. Again, the
mind reels.

[24 cont'd]

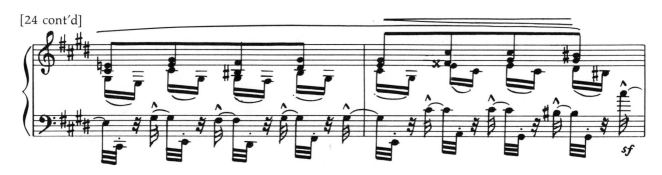

208

Another shining peak is Chopin, with his own delicious brand of chromatic ambiguity, which is rather like harmonic teasing, sensuous and seductive. Like this passage from his *Etude in Thirds*—mind you, an Etude: imagine being seductive in an Etude . . . [25]. Do you hear those implied harmonic gorgeousnesses? And all the implications arise from ambiguities. Are we in the major or minor? Or in the Phrygian mode? Is this music tonal or modal? Are we to infer ninth chords, or diminished sevenths?[26] You may not have understood a word I've just said, but no matter, as long as you feel how this music hovers between something and something else. It's enough that you feel the ambiguous quality.

Disc
Side 3
band 9

Perhaps *this* bit of Chopin will make the ambiguous point more clearly (if that sentence is linguistically possible). This is one of Chopin's fifty-odd Mazurkas—and very odd they are, quirky little masterpieces, every one. This is No. 4, and begins thus [27]. Now without recourse to the printed music, would you know whether that began on a downbeat, or an upbeat, or where? And besides, what key is it in? We don't know with certainty: it's sort of in F; it could be the subdominant of C; it could be the submediant

Disc
Side 4
band 1

[27]   Lento, ma non troppo (♩ = 152)

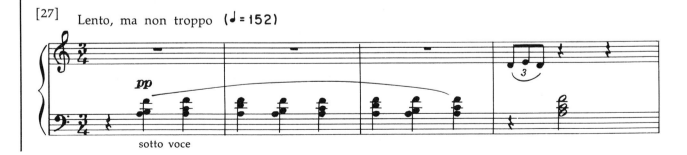

209

of A minor; it could be the Lydian mode; never mind, it's only the introduction. Now comes the tune [28]. Ah, E minor—there's a possibility. But no—chromatic side-slipping; little dying falls; again F, at least F-*ish*; again E minor, again chromatic straying . . . we're nowhere. Ah, at last a cadence in A minor. So it was in A minor all the time!

210

Talk of subtlety, elusiveness, seductiveness . . . And then, in the same little Mazurka, after contrasting sections, re-prises, after it's apparently all over, Chopin gives the final ambiguous twist: he has again arrived at A minor—this time we're absolutely sure it's A minor [29]. But then come the last four bars, which are exactly like the opening bars. The piece is over; but what key are we in? Sort of F? Lydian mode? Certainly not A minor. We are left hovering as we began, in a bliss of ambiguities.

I've been speaking of ambiguity as an aesthetic function; and this would seem to carry the implication that the more ambiguous music gets, the more expressive it becomes. But does that mean, for instance, that chromaticism is better than diatonic plain talk? Does it represent an advance in musical progress? Is Chopin better than Mozart because he's more chromatic than Mozart? If so, then shouldn't Bartok be better than Beethoven? And the Beatles better than Bessie Smith? Is Keats more chromatic than Shake-speare? And Swinburne more than Keats? And therefore *better* than Keats?

Foolish questions, needless to say. I don't have to point out that it's not a question of "better"; these questions relate not to qualitative changes in art but to quantitative changes. Of course Chopin is more chromatic than Mozart, but that doesn't make him a greater composer. And of course Swinburne is more chromatic than Keats. But in what sense is Keats chromatic at all? What do I mean by "chromatic" in terms of literature? What is chromaticism in poetry? I mean it to denote the terms in which one single phonological aspect of poetic language can be freely pursued—sound itself, indulged in for its own sake. A chromatic poet, as it were, seeks out new sonic relationships, just as a chromatic composer does—relationships that are subtler, more intricate, that exploit the alphabet to its sonic limits. Such a poet concentrates on assonance, alliteration, dark vowels or bright ones, smooth labial continuants or abrupt, plosive consonants—every kind of sonorific device; and by so doing he shifts his emphasis toward this phonetic area, away from syntax, away from semantics, even at the expense of structural clarity. All this, of course, makes for ever-increasing ambiguity, always in the name of greater and greater expressivity.

Two lines from Gerard Manley Hopkins' "The Leaden Echo" will show you what I mean:

> How to kéep—is there ány any,
>   is there none such, nowhere known
>   some, bow or brooch or braid or
>   brace, láce, latch or catch or key to keep
> Back beauty, keep it, beauty, beauty,
>   beauty, . . . from vanishing away?

Words, words, glorious words. Some say mud, mud,

glorious mud. I don't agree. If we didn't know that was Hopkins, we might almost think it was Joyce. But these words were written way back in 1880: "is there any any, is there none such, nowhere known some . . . " It's *almost* music, and chromatic music at that. Hopkins is wallowing in gorgeous sounds, and so are we, his readers. But what is gained thereby, and what lost? What is lost is easily told: structural clarity, immediacy of meaning. The basic meaning of those lines—from a purely semantic point of view — is simply this: *How to keep beauty from vanishing away?* But it's a long, long trail, a winding Joycean trail of thick sonorous beauty, that leads from "How to keep" to "vanishing away". What is gained, on the other hand, is an intense expressivity born of sheer sound, rich, complex, chromatic sound that doubles and redoubles on itself, creating new meanings of its own, sonorous meanings— nonsemantic meanings, so to speak. Listen to how the poem ends:

> When the thing we freely fórfeit is
>   kept with fonder a care,
> Fonder a care kept than we could
>   have kept it, kept
> Far with a fonder a care . . .

and this could well be *Finnegans Wake*:

> . . . finer, fonder
> A care kept.—Where kept? Do but
>   tell us where kept, where.—
> Yonder.—What high as that! We
>   follow, now we follow.—Yonder,
>   yes, yonder, yonder.
> Yonder.

213

This ecstatic poetry has a chromaticism that leads the ear
far away from the lucid, C-majorish meaning of "How to
keep beauty from vanishing away?" or "My heart leaps up
when I behold a rainbow in the sky". Instead, the ear is led
toward the new pleasures of sheer sonority, and on to bigger
and better ambiguities—to Ezra Pound, to Dylan Thomas,
to James Joyce, and to the ultimate *reductio*, Gertrude Stein:
"Let Lucy Lily Lily Lucy Lucy let Lucy Lucy Lily Lily Lily
Lily Lily . . ." Phonology has virtually taken over. Syntax
is all but vanished, leaving a semantic vacuum.

It would seem, with all this talk of chromatic poetry, that
I've strayed from the main line: music. But there's method
in the madness, because the Romantic Revolution we are
discussing brought with it a new interaction of poetry *and*
music, in fact, of all the arts. It's as though the arts became
more interested in one another, as did the artists themselves.
They began to intermingle, their diverse artistic media
drawing closer together in mutual influence. Artists were
now painters of words, composers of pictures, poets of
tones. Any aesthetic innovation, such as heightened
chromaticism in music, would immediately find its counterpart in painting, or exert an observable influence on poetry.
The chromatic outpourings of Berlioz are mirrored in the
slashing expressionism of Delacroix, or in the multicolored
visions of Shelley. We begin to see a movement taking
place, the Romantic Movement. We begin to see artists as
interrelated groups: Berlioz with Byron, Chopin with
Georges Sand and Delacroix, Schumann with E. T. A.
Hoffmann and Jean Paul. Stendhal was writing of Mozart
and Rossini; Schubert and Schumann were setting their
favorite poets, especially Heine. Composers like Liszt and
Wagner were omnivorous readers. And they not only read,

214

but they *wrote*—words!—criticism, memoirs, poetry, and in some cases, the entire texts of their own operas. This was a Romantic breakthrough: just try to imagine Bach or Haydn as literary buffs. *Ausgeschlossen.*

The pivotal point in this interdisciplinary action is, as we know, Beethoven. There he was, still the great master of the Classical Viennese School, already casting adumbrations of the musical and extramusical fusions that were to come. A detailed programmatic symphony such as the *Pastorale,* or the Ninth Symphony with actual sung words in it— these were truly romantic innovations. There had never been anything like them before. But it remained for Berlioz, who idolized Beethoven, to seize that extramusical concept, that new semantic ambiguity, and make it his banner. His first major work, the *Symphonie Fantastique,* written barely three years after Beethoven's death, mind you, was like the *1827* *Pastorale* Symphony raised to the nth power, in terms of programmatic content. And from there on it was literary attachment all the way, whether to Shakespeare or Byron, or to Virgil, from whose *Aeneid* he fashioned the libretto of his own opera, *Les Troyens.* Did you know that in all of Berlioz' output there exists only one little piece that does not have specific literary associations? One little violin piece, in a lifetime of composing—something called "Reverie and Caprice for Violin and Orchestra". Everything else he wrote was either opera, oratorio, cantata, songs, or very explicit program music.

So there is a dramatic change from Beethoven's program- maticism to that of Berlioz—a qualitative change. Literary ideas are now inextricably tied in with music. Berlioz wants us to be aware of definite extramusical meanings, not merely of suggested feelings, as in Beethoven's *Pastorale.* Those

jonquils and daisies, which in Beethoven were only suggested, are now blazing with color, and the mosquitoes really bite. This change forces the listener into a new auditory attitude: he must now listen on two levels at once —a purely musical level and an extramusical one. When we listen to Berlioz, we must perforce embrace this new semantic ambiguity; we are not permitted to ignore it, as we did last week—or tried to—with Beethoven's *Pastorale* Symphony.

Berlioz is the arch-Romantic; and it's always oddly surprising to recall how close he was to Beethoven, not only in terms of period, but in terms of stylistic and formal elements as well. We tend to think of Berlioz as the essential Romantic madman and of Beethoven as the Titan of Classicism: worlds apart. Actually their worlds are contiguous, even overlapping; and among the stylistic legacies inherited by Berlioz are, most strikingly, those very chromatic ambiguities we observed earlier in Beethoven's *Hammerklavier* Sonata. And, again, it was Berlioz' historic mission to seize on those ambiguities and magnify them to gigantic proportions.

So it is after all not so surprising that in the decade directly following Beethoven's death Berlioz was spinning this extraordinary series of notes [30]. This subtly tinted thread, as modern in its way as a contemporary tone-row, is the opening phrase of a movement from Berlioz' *Romeo and Juliet*, which he called a "dramatic symphony". By "dramatic" he meant that Shakespeare's drama is told musically, with added choral and solo voices. But all the great moments are purely orchestral—such crucial scenes as the street fight, Mercutio's Queen Mab speech, the ball scene, the balcony scene, the tomb scene—all these are told by

the orchestra alone, in highly pictorial terms. We are about to hear one of these symphonic movements performed on tape by the Boston Symphony Orchestra, and I would like to prepare you for some of the ambiguous beauties to come, not the least of which is the semantic ambiguity of having to listen to this music on two levels. This ten-minute excerpt depicts the scene, early in the play, where Romeo is about to meet Juliet at the Capulet ball. He is alone, love-sick, vague, restless, waiting for his imminent destiny. And Berlioz captures this ambiguous ambience by spinning those notes I just played—a solitary melodic line with no harmony at all to support it [31]. The harmonies are all implied—but which harmonies? What is implied by that E-flat, by that A-flat, or that D-flat? They are all nondia-tonic, chromatic tones on the fringes of F major. Or is it F minor? Both are implied: and that is already a basic ambiguity.

Notice that all three of those dubious notes I pointed out occur in little chromatic descents, "dying falls" that imitate lovesick sighs. Now that's tone painting—the very thing Beethoven insisted he was *not* doing. But Berlioz still reminds us that he is Beethoven's disciple by punctuating this vague opening phrase with a classical comma—a lightly plucked touch of the dominant triad [32]. His am-biguity, you see, is still being classically contained in a tonal framework. But, once having reminded us, he is immediately on to new ambiguities. Here's the second phrase: [33]—in a totally foreign key, E minor, and this time with *rising* chromatic sighs. Now we seem to land in E *major*—but no, more chromatic vagueness, and we're back in F. Again, this is adequate (just barely!) classical containment; but not for long: because here's F-sharp minor! Or is it? No, it's F major after all.

You see, the music is trying hard to establish this tonic key of F even as it wanders about, moody and unstable. And just when it finally succeeds in reaching a solid F-major cadence (which is already three or four minutes into the piece) [34] there is a sudden interruption [35], as very softly, the distant rhythms of the Capulet ball intrude on Romeo's consciousness—and here is a new ambiguity, surprising as an alarm clock. Observe: Romeo's reverie is just reaching that cadential close in F when it is interrupted by the dance music in D-flat major, which is not only interrupting, you see, but also *coinciding* with the end of the cadence. In other words, that final F of the cadence, which is the tonic note, is suddenly *not* the tonic, but the third degree of a whole other scale, D-flat. This sudden modulation is based on the well-tempered fact that the note F is common to both keys, F major [36] and D-flat major [37]. So that instant in musical time—of expecting one harmony and getting another, that mighty principle of the Violation of Expectation—is really a double instant, a millisecond of ambiguity, achieved through a device musicians call a "deceptive cadence". In that deceptive instant we sense both tonalities at once; we "hear" the F-major tonality [see 36] in our mind's ear because we expect it; but we really hear the D-flat major because it is actually sounded, violating our expectation [see 37]. This is the anatomy of one small ambiguity.

But only one. The dance tune over that D-flat rhythm [38] is created straight out of those sighing chromatic descents we heard in Romeo's reverie [see 31]. What a transformation: from lovesick sighs to highly rhythmic dance music! It's only a short flash—one phrase carried by the breeze from the Capulet palace; but it's just enough to stir up new ambiguities in Romeo, shifty chromatic tremors [39]—*shall I go to the ball? Or not? After all, I'm a Montague, an enemy. But I am strangely moved to go, drawn by that dance rhythm.* (You see how precise Berlioz is about his meanings, his extramusical semantics?) And so Romeo sings (or rather the oboe sings) a clear, diatonic love song [40]—diatonic, nonchromatic, because it is now a clear decision to attend the festivity, come what may. And this song is constantly punctuated by that distant, magnetic dance rhythm [41]—another ambiguity, but a

[39]

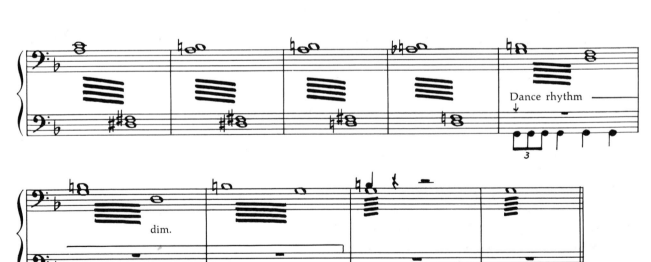

223

perfectly clear one, <u>belonging uniquely to the art of music.</u>
Romeo's song *and* the ball music together. Only in music
can two such disparate messages travel simultaneously, and
not only be distinctly perceived as counterpoint, but actually
reinforce each other. Certainly the most striking case of this
musical simultaneity—literally *double entendre*, hearing
double—occurs at the climax of this movement, when
Romeo has arrived at the ball. The dance music is now
brilliant and full-out; he sees Juliet, and dances with her, all
in clear, joyful F major. And at this moment we actually
hear two musics together: half the orchestra is batting out
the beat of the dance music [42], while the other half is
blaring out, in full cry, Romeo's love song [43]. This is, if
you recall, a clear case of contrapuntal syntax—a mechanism
of ambiguity that is possible only in musical terms. And
this double event is constantly reinforced by the simultaneous contradiction of bright diatonic sound against the
chromaticism of Romeo's yearning which persists throughout the dance music, right up to the end, in the bass [44].
The whole piece is a triumph of ambiguities, a brilliant
illustration of the deliberate exploitation of ambiguity for
increased expressive power.

*(At this point the Ball scene from Berlioz' Romeo and
Juliet is performed.)*

II

Ambiguous and beautiful as that *Romeo* music is, it's only a hint of what's to come two decades later. Take the lonely, sighing phrase that opened it, with its ascending fourth and its chromatic dying fall [45]; stretch that fourth to a minor sixth with the same dying fall [46], and what have you got? Tristan, of course. Now take Berlioz' second phrase, which does indeed begin with a rising sixth and continues in a chromatic climb [47], and you have Isolde. Now put them together [48]. And what have you got? Tristan *and* Isolde. The derivation of the Wagner from the Berlioz seems all too clear: for the history-making opening phrase of Wagner's *Tristan* is in fact the conjoining of two subphrases, dovetailed, and both straight out of Berlioz [49]. It seems a clear case of Wagnerian robbery, or to put it more politely, borrowing; but it's even subtler than that. It is rather a phenomenon of transformational grammar, in the most Chomskian sense, where one surface structure, namely Berlioz', has become the deep structure of another surface structure, namely Wagner's [50]. The transformations are extremely clear: the extension of the opening interval by enlarging the fourth to the sixth, and then the conjoining of the two strings. Quite unconsciously borrowed, of course, although we know of Wagner's almost envious admiration for Berlioz' *Romeo*. We might say—in the semantic terms of our last lecture—that *Tristan and Isolde* is a giant metaphor of *Romeo and Juliet*. It's a lot to say, but it's irresistible: there are just too many instances of this Romeo-into-Tristan metaphor throughout the opera.

1857-59

227

Only recall the dance music of Berlioz' ball scene [51], and
compare with it Isolde's panting anticipation in Act Two of
Tristan [52]. Just another remarkable coincidence? Well,

here's another, which we just heard: Romeo in love [53]; by the simple extension of a third to a fourth it has expanded into Tristan in love [54]. And these examples are only a few among many. We haven't even touched Berlioz' great Balcony Scene, with its throbbing, passionate climax [55]. I don't even have to play you Wagner's metaphor for that one. But here it is anyway [56].

My purpose in all this is not to expose Wagner as a plagiarist, but as a transformational magician. I want to show to what extent a tonal language can grow, from artist to artist—growing in expressivity and in magnitude, over a span of a mere twenty years, just as we could see it grow from Haydn to Beethoven, or from Scriabin to Stravinsky. The examples abound throughout musical history; this happens to be a particularly striking one. And with this growth comes the inevitable increase in ambiguity. *Tristan* is the very crux of ambiguity—the turning point after which music could never be the same; it points musical history directly toward the upcoming crisis of the twentieth century.

Tristan exploits ambiguity fully, in all three of the linguistic modes we have discussed. Phonologically, for example, the highly chromatic opening bars of the Prelude have fascinated analytical minds for over a century [57]. What key are we in? Or no key at all [58]? Did that cadence on the dominant seventh [59] indicate A minor? But the dominant never resolves to the A minor tonic. Instead there is a long pause, and the phrase is repeated, higher, more intense, with the rising minor sixth now stretched, transformed to a *major* sixth [60], again ending on a dominant, but in a different key. Again, pause. And then again, even higher [61], now stretched out in time, and ending on yet another dominant. Pause. And this cadence is now echoed [62], an octave higher, as if to say, "this could be the one." Is it? asks Wagner, fragmentarily reiterating the last two notes [63]. But the harmony has been dropped out, thus intensifying the ambiguity of the question. And yet again that fragmentation, an octave higher [64]. Is it the one? Then finally [65] this *is* it, says Wagner, the original dominant in A minor—but no [66], the resolution is a deceptive cadence, not A minor at all. In other words, the

231

[68]

[69]

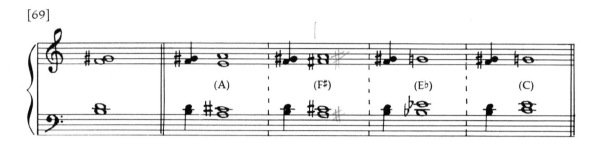

(A) (F#) (E♭) (C)

[70]

Allegro

pp

etc.

232

resolution of all this ambiguity is in itself ambiguous. Is this tonality, or toying with tonality, or simply nontonality? Wagner keeps you guessing. It's almost as if the extreme chromaticism of this music, with its fiercely unappeased sensual desire, can no longer be contained in a tonal frame-work. And this is why *Tristan* is the crisis-work of the nineteenth century.

While thinking about all this the other night, I made myself a diagram—just out of curiosity—to determine exactly the comparative frequency of the twelve chromatic tones as they occur in the first two phrases of this Prelude [67]. The results are curiously interesting: all twelve tones appear at least once—this in itself is significant, in the light of the twelve-tone music to come a century later—but there are four tones that predominate, in that they occur more than *twice*. And these four tones, G-sharp, F, D, and B, happen to form a diminished seventh chord [68]. Now don't fret; I'm not going to explain that. But it is worth your knowing that a diminished seventh chord is the most am-biguous of all tonal formations, and for that reason became the favorite harmonic ambiguity of all the Romantic com-posers. Maybe I should explain a bit, after all.

Every diminished seventh chord is capable of at least four different resolutions, which gives any such chord a minimum four-way ambiguity. Take this one we're looking at, for instance [69]. It can resolve to four different tonics: to A, to F-sharp, to E-flat, to C. What's more, each of those four tonics may be major or minor; and there are even more possible resolutions I won't go into. No wonder the Ro-mantics seized on this chord; it's so wondrously useful for all ambiguous situations, such as moody meandering [70] (where would Tchaikovsky be without that?) or noisy

[67]

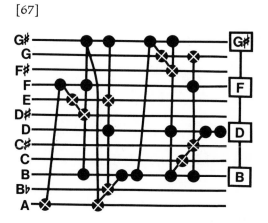

233

234

confusion [71] (where would Liszt be without that?) or abrupt dramatic suspense, as in *Carmen* [72]. Suspense. Tension. Ambiguity.

Now the remarkable thing is that no diminished seventh chord actually occurs in these first two phrases of the *Tristan* Prelude; the diminished seventh is only *suggested* by the prevalence of these four tones, G-sharp, F, B, and D, casting their ambiguous shadow. Thus their presence is felt hovering over the music as a diminished seventh chord, even though there is no such chord actually sounded. Now ask yourself, is that prevalence the result of calculation on Wagner's part? All my instincts tell me, No. It must have been an unconscious action. For me, this is a striking model of linguistic transformation at work, converting this hidden deep structure [73] into a metamorphosed surface structure in which the chord is no longer even perceptible.

All this chromatic ambiguity is reinforced to a great degree by the syntactic vagueness of the musical *structure*. Actually this Prelude is anything but a vague structure. It is very tightly knit together, but Wagner deliberately imposes syntactic ambiguities to make it seem languishing, mysterious, and timeless. Timeless—that's the clue. The utter *slowness* of it all [74]; "Langsam und schmachtend", he writes, slow and languishing . . . and then the interminable written-out silences between the phrases . . . and then the ambiguity of whether that first note is an upbeat or a downbeat. How can we tell it's an upbeat? There is no pulse to give us a clue. (And by the way, how did we know that the corresponding phrase in Berlioz' *Romeo* [75] began on a downbeat? Which it did.) All these ambiguities, and many more, conspire to plunge us into a new dimension of time, quite different from anything before in music. It is a time

236

which no longer ticks by, or even dances or saunters by: it proceeds imperceptibly, as the moon moves, or as leaves change their color.

And this is what gives *Tristan* its true semantic quality —quite apart from the obvious semantic facts of the text, of Wagner's own poetry; of chivalry and magic potions and betrayal; and apart from leitmotivs signifying desire or death. I am speaking of musical semantics as we have come to know it, as the sum of phonological and syntactical transformations, producing a highly poetic metaphorical language. And in this sense *Tristan* is supreme: it is one long series of infinitely slow transformations, metaphor upon metaphor, from the mysterious first phrase through to the climactic heights of passion or of transfiguration, right to the end. I could even devise a deep structure for that opening phrase that would show you the final *Liebestod* already present, in nucleus form. If we accept the customary assumption of A minor as the tonality of the opening phrase, we can discern two appoggiaturas, or "leaning tones", within that phrase [76], both resolving in conventional fashion. Now by simply deleting those two dissonant tones we get this series [77]. That is one possible deep structure nucleus, arrived at by deleting two appoggiaturas. Now we subject that embryo to transformations, including inversion and others I won't go into, and we arrive at this new series [78]. By further transformations, including metrical ones, we get this melodic phrase [79]. And once we support that line with pure diatonic triads, freed from all chromatic writhing and tortuous frustration, we reach the final transfiguration [80]. In my end is my beginning, said T. S. Eliot. Let's hear them both now, the beginning and the end of *Tristan and Isolde*. (*At this point, the Prelude and Liebestod from Wagner's* Tristan and Isolde *is performed.*)

III

And so music can never be the same again. The gates of chromaticism have been flung open—those golden gates of the Golden Age, which were the outer limits of ambiguity, standing firm in diatonic majesty. But now that they are open, now that Berlioz and Chopin and Schumann and Wagner have pushed them open, we are in new tonal fields that are apparently limitless. We are bounding and leaping from one ambiguity to the next, from Berlioz to Wagner, to Bruckner and Mahler, to Debussy and Scriabin, and Stravinsky. It is a dizzying adventure, this Romantic romp, shedding one inhibition after another, indulging in newer and ever more illicit ambiguities, piling them on, stringing them out, daring them to take over, for nearly a whole century. But how ambiguous can you get before the clarity of musical meaning is lost altogether? How far can music romp through these new chromatic fields without finding itself in uncharted terrain, in a wild forest of sharps and flats? Are there no further gates of containment—perhaps not golden ones, perhaps only dry stone walls or rude fences? Of course there are—or rather *were*, until they began to crumble under the attack of the new century. These tonal fences, walls of formality, somehow still managed to contain the rampage of chromaticism, even through the crises of *Tristan and Isolde,* of *Pelleas and Melisande,* and *The Rite of Spring.* But ultimately a supreme crisis did arrive, a crisis that remains unresolved to this day—and it's over half a century old. As I said way back in the first lecture, if we are ever to face up squarely to Ives' Unanswered Question, if we are ever to understand this crisis, we must first understand what brought it about. In the remainder of this lecture, I am going to try to give you a sense of this critical turn by examining, and then listening to, one short piece plucked out of musical history at a moment of particular stress—Debussy's *Prélude à l'Après-midi d'un Faune*—the *Afternoon of a Faun*, one of the last-ditch stands of tonal and syntactic containment, as was the Mallarmé poem on which it was based.

This enchanted faun came into being just before the turn of the century, at a moment when all the arts were standing on the brink of radical change—not just stylistic change; I mean radical change. The tugs and strains that were wrenching at figurative painting had already produced Impressionism; the representational object was fast disappearing into washes of color, suggestive formations, chromatic pointillistic fantasies. Cubism is around the corner, abstraction is in the wind. Poetry has begun to show a remarkable disintegration of syntax, a diffusion of meaning or of logical continuity that intoxicates the mind. The heart aches a bit too readily. A drowsy numbness pains the sense. A decadent aestheticism turns the horizon mauve. In this last mauve decade Salome, Des Esseintes, Dorian Grey are all standing in the wings. And everywhere hovers a delicious vagueness, a highly charged ambiguousness of dreams, images, and symbols. Baudelaire drifting in *volupté,* Rimbaud in his *bateau ivre.* And Mallarmé turning himself on with anti-semantic pills, turning himself into a sort of faun, sort of remembering, perhaps dreaming, perhaps dallying with sort-of-nymphs, perhaps a couple, or is he one of the couple, was it Sicily, where, when, who?—all are submerged into the how, the ever-present now. (Good Lord, I'm doing it myself.) Phonology is taking over; syntax is a

vague memory of something once learned. If all the arts, as Walter Pater said, aspire to the condition of music, then Mallarmé's poem is surely getting close.

And when Debussy turns the Faun into music, it is Mallarmé's dream come true. A drowsy numbness does indeed invade this opening bar [81]. Where are we? In what key are we hearing this flute of Pan? It's in no key at all— well [82], maybe E major. Oh, yes, definitely E major; but oh, no, here's vagueness again [83], resolving to the most unlikely chord possible [84], the dominant seventh of E-flat major. E-*flat?* But it was E major a second ago, wasn't it? Well, E-flat, E-natural—how easily they can be confused in this faunish dream. And now, where, what? Nowhere [85]. A bar of silence. Six slow silent beats of no music, just as in Wagner's Prelude to *Tristan.* But do we know they are six beats? How do we count silence? Do we care? No, we dream on. Again that delicious wash of vagueness [86] and again the dominant seventh [87] prolonged, prolonged . . .

It's lovely, this dreaming along with Debussy, but it's no way to analyze music. We want to understand the vagueness, not just bathe in it; and so we must wake up, and look clearly at what we have just heard. What about that opening phrase of Pan's flute? The first thing that strikes us is the highly chromatic nature of this phrase as it languorously dips and rises between the two poles of C-sharp and G-natural [88]. Now those two melodic poles tell us something crucially important to the whole piece: they define the interval of the augmented fourth [89], an interval known as the tritone, that is, a span of three whole-tone steps [90]. This tritone interval has always had a peculiar significance

Disc
Side 4
band 2

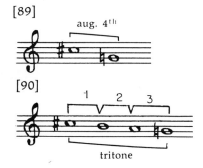

[89]

aug. 4ᵗʰ

[90]

1 2 3

tritone

[91]

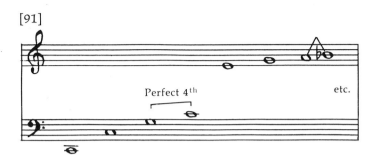

Perfect 4th   etc.

[92]

Augmented 4th

[93] Molto moderato

Fl.

[94]

p   dolce e espressivo

[95]   [96]

Hn.

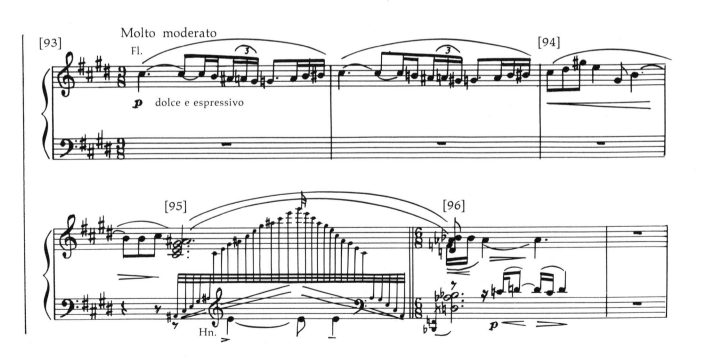

242

throughout musical history, since it bluntly contradicts the basic concepts of diatonic tonality, the tonic-dominant function that we found in the very first lecture to be at the heart of the harmonic series. Do you recall those early overtones [91] and the diatonic stability of those intervals? G to C, a perfect fourth; dominant-tonic, the root factor of all tonality, as we observed it last week in Beethoven's *Pastorale* Symphony—and even in the scene from Berlioz' *Romeo and Juliet* heard earlier this evening, although used much more ambiguously.

But now, in Debussy's *Faun*, that essential interval of the perfect fourth becomes an augmented fourth (G to C-sharp) [92] which is a tritone, the most unstable interval there is —the absolute negation of tonality. And it is this interval —so unsettled and unsettling that the early Church fathers declared it unacceptable and illegal, calling it *diabolus in musica* (the devil in music)—it is precisely this interval of the tritone that Debussy adopts as his basic structural principle. And this interval is our leading clue to penetrating the vagueness and ambiguity of the piece as a whole, which carries out, to the very end, all the harmonic implications of that initial tritone.

Disc
Side 4
band 3

For example, do you remember when we were dreaming along with Debussy [93], how after these two vague opening bars there came the first suggestion of a key [94]—E major? And how that briefly suggested tonality instantly slipped away in a wash of sound [95] that left us floating in distant waters [96], this dominant seventh chord? But now we can see *why* this of all chords was Debussy's choice; because the root of that chord is B-flat [97] and B-flat is exactly a tritone away from E [98], which is where we thought we were. The tritone [99]. The devil. And then in

[97]

[98]

[99]

tritone

243

[101]

E major   B major   A major   F♯ major   etc.

the ensuing bar of silence we are left to float in blissful indecision between the two possibilities [100], E major tonic and B-flat dominant. Then, silence.

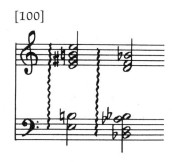

[100]

Do you begin to understand what I mean by Debussy's carrying out harmonic implications of the tritone? If you do, you will realize that this music is not just drowsily improvised, but carefully composed, intentionally designed to produce a specific ambiguous effect—a far cry from the conventional Hollywoodish idea of the moody composer improvising a vague dream in which anything can happen anywhere at all. On the contrary, the *Faun* is a masterpiece of structure.

In fact, the ending of this piece finally confirms that it *was* all conceived in the key of E major, right from the beginning, where that very key was first so tentatively suggested. In other words, it not only ends in E major, but throughout its course it is constantly referring to, reverting to, or flirting with E major or some diatonic relative thereof [101]. These clear tonal references occur every time there is a point of repose, the cadential close of an episode, or the arrival of a new one. Where the ambiguity arises is that between these points of tonal articulation Debussy is just as consistently misleading us (not unlike Gerard Manley Hopkins), deliberately leading our ears astray, away from those diatonic landmarks, by employing all kinds of phonological maneuvers and superchromatic freedoms, most of them evolving out of the basic tritone principle enunciated in the opening bars.

Let me show you briefly what I mean. Here we are in our
B-flat seventh chord [102] tritonically alienated from the
E-natural [103] that had been teasing us into tonality. And
now back we go to our opening tune—the exact same
notes [104], only now harmonized. But harmonized how? In
D major; foiled again. The promise of E major has been
broken; but wait, what's this [105]?—we *are* in E major,
after all! But only for a flirtatious instant; back we go to our
B-flat seventh chord [106], into it, and right out again.
More chromatic side-slipping [107] leading us into—not
again! Yes, that same B-flat seventh chord, only now differently spelled, in terms of sharps [108]. And yet again [109]!
Why this insistence? Why does Debussy want to stamp that
B-flatness (or A-sharpness) so firmly in our ears? Because
the promise of E major is now about to come true, and he
doesn't want us to see it coming: he wants to prepare us for
it as ambiguously as possible, as far away from it as possible, therefore—on the tritone, B-flat [110]. And when it
finally does come, the happy arrival [111], the opening tune
is heard for the third time, but now clearly and beyond all
doubt in our long-promised and hungrily-wished-for E major.
At last. This is what I meant by a point of repose, an arrival.

[110]

[111]

247

This new episode proceeds quite lucidly, in peaceful E-major tonality, up to its climax, which then subsides into the first real, definite cadence of the piece; and, wonder of wonders, this cadential point of repose is in B major [112], the dominant of E major, just as it's supposed to be in the books, following the most classical tradition. Where is ambiguity now? What has happened to vagueness, to the very point of this piece? Ah, but that *is* the point: that the larger, overall ambiguity derives from the interplay of all those chromatic wanderings with these carefully spaced landmarks of tonal articulation. It is the same phenomenon we observed in Mozart, and again in Berlioz and Wagner: chromaticism contained in diatonicism; only here the chromaticism is enormously magnified, and—if I may hop back to my earlier beat-up metaphor—there are still those tonal fences to contain it. They're a bit shaky, but they're standing.

Disc
Side 4
band 5

For instance, hardly have we had time to rest in our classical dominant cadence of B major [113], when a new contradiction breaks out [114], based on that original tritone of G-natural and C-sharp [115], only now elaborated into a new formation called the whole-tone scale [116]. Do you sense this new, special ambiguity? It's the sound of the whole-tone scale, a unique invention of Debussy's, directly derived from the original tritone. It's not difficult to see how this new scale came to exist, if you only recall that the interval of the tritone is actually a span embracing three whole tones. Let's say we start on C-sharp and proceed upward by whole-tone steps [117]; one, two, three, and we've landed on G-natural, the other pole of the tritone. Now watch: if we simply repeat the procedure, starting from this G-natural where we landed, and again go up three

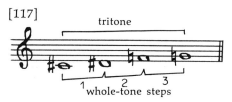

[117]

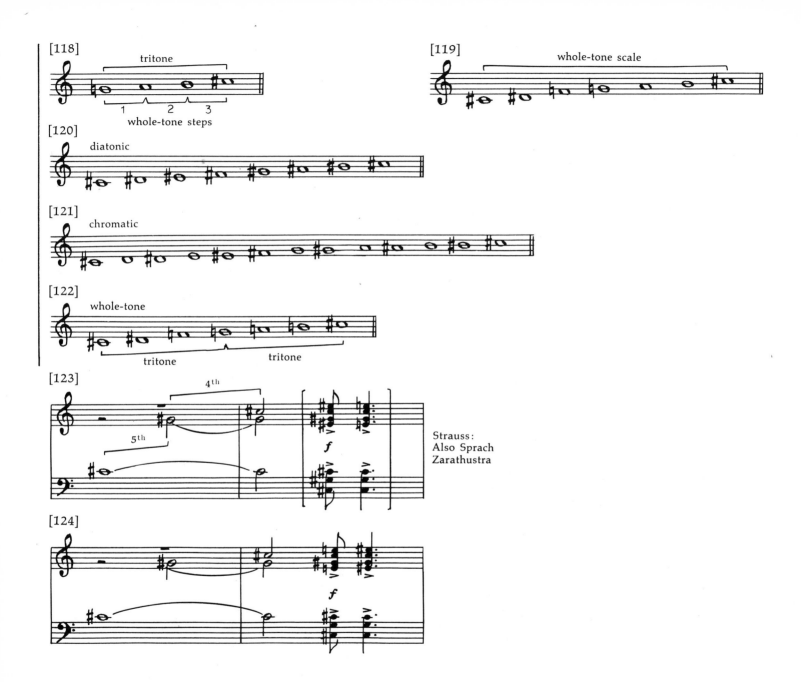

Strauss:
Also Sprach
Zarathustra

whole tones [118] lo and behold, we're back to C-sharp
again, only an octave higher. In short, we've got a scale, a
whole-tone scale [119]. What's actually happened is this:
the octave span, C-sharp to C-sharp, instead of being divided
diatonically [120], or chromatically [121] (which would be
twelve equal half-steps) is now divided into six equal whole-
steps [122], with that tritonic G-natural at the exact mid-
point of the octave, between the two C-sharps. What's most
important is that we've got a scale that cannot function
tonally, that cannot produce a tonic or a dominant relation.
Why is this? Because the scale by its very nature doesn't
contain intervals of the fifth and the fourth [123] which,
as you well know, are the first and strongest overtones of
the harmonic series, and therefore the bread and butter of
tonality. So, no fifths and fourths [124], no tonic and
dominant, no bread and butter, no Zarathustra. And, by
extension, there can obviously not be a circle of fifths, and
therefore no traditional modulations are possible. This
whole-tone scale is self-limiting, autistic, so to speak; in
short, it is *atonal*—the first organized atonal material ever
to appear in musical history. And because of its atonal
nature, this new scale suddenly produces the most ambiguous sounds ever heard in music. But they are controlled,
in the *Faun*, by those tonal landmarks; just when we're
beginning to feel utterly lost in Debussy's atonal woods
[125], the music again reaches one of its points of repose

[125]

251

Animato

E major

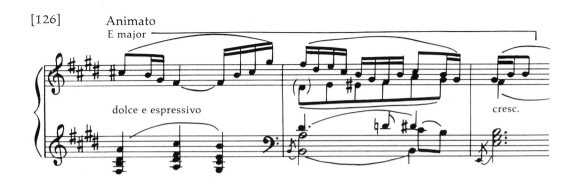

dolce e espressivo

cresc.

[126], and we're home again, in E major at that. Saved by the fence. But for a moment there we were on the brink; sheer phonology was becoming too important, too interested in its own chromaticism at the expense of semantic clarity.

It's almost exactly what happens in the Mallarmé poem, where the images and symbols pile up in such alliterative profusion, with such seeming irrelevance and incongruity, that, reading it, we often feel awash in sound, ravishing sound to be sure, but we feel equally at sea as far as comprehension is concerned. Again, in literary terms, it's a case of phonology threatening to take over at the expense of meaning—and in fact to produce a semantics of its own.

This is very subtle stuff, involving the mysteries of the creative process itself, and thus terribly hard to pinpoint; but let me have one stab at it. In Mallarmé's poem, the faun has just been recalling a dream image: on the banks of a calm Sicilian pool he has been "cutting the hollow reeds (to be) subdued by talent", "les creux roseaux domptés par le talent"—an image, in other words, of the birth of music; and at that moment, "et qu'au prélude lent", the moment he calls a "slow prelude", he has a vision of a flight of swans (no, naiads!) running away (or diving)—one ambiguity after another. And just at this point come the following two lines, as the faun recalls the dream:

> Sans marquer par quel art ensemble détala
> Trop d'Hymen souhaité de qui cherche le *la.*

Literally translated, and therefore even fuzzier in meaning, the lines say: "Without noticing by what art there ran off together too much Hymen desired by him who is seeking A-natural". I won't even try to interpret that further; I would like only to point out that the word "la", meaning the note

253

Offstage audience at a music taping session, WGBH studio

A, stands at the end of a line where it rhymes identically
with the last word of the preceding line, "détala", meaning
"ran off". And I am asking if it's not therefore possible that
the symbolic word "la" was born phonologically rather than
syntactically, that it was motivated by its inherence in the
earlier word "détala", which, coming so soon after the
musical idea of "Prelude", in turn suggested the musical
association of "la"? I'll try to ask it more clearly: might it
not be that the "la" image was created *not* because the poet
had intended to invoke it—because he had some meaningful idea in mind and was looking for a structural way of
saying it—but rather that the image was *phonologically*
suggested in the preceding line? And I am proposing that
this is only one of hundreds of such creative mechanisms in
this poem, all examples of a phonological impulse operating
at the expense of syntactic and semantic clarity.

But notice, also, that the example I've been discussing
involves rhyme, in fact a rhymed couplet; and so it becomes
instantly clear that Mallarmé too has his fences—his
structural and tonal fences, so to speak. Just as the vaguenesses of Debussy are protected by clear cadential resolutions, by classically stable, interrelated keys, so Mallarmé's
dream-within-a-dream is contained in equally classical
structural forms, in perfect Alexandrine rhymed couplets.
It's almost a shock to realize that this vaguest of poems,
with its elusive but strongly evocative images, is written
from beginning to end in strict hexameters. What's more,
Mallarmé clearly indicates distinct episodes within the poem
by putting them into italics and surrounding them with
quotation marks, and these episodes, curiously enough, are
analogous to similar episodes in Debussy's musical
counterpart.

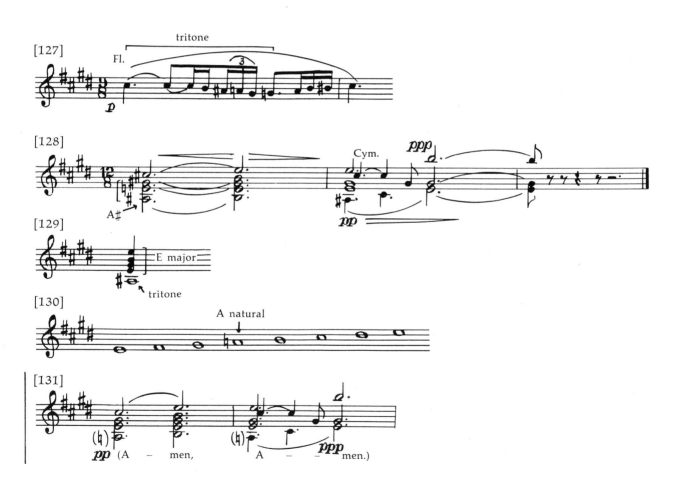

256

In other words, both the poem and the music preserve a clarity of structural articulation in spite of all vaguenesses. The poem and the music are both high on phonology-pills, but in both cases the high, or the heightened consciousness (or whatever psychedelic term you care to use) is rationally contained. Both works have definite beginnings and ends, for instance, which provide frameworks that greatly aid perceptibility. Mallarmé begins with a forthright statement: "I wish to perpetuate these nymphs"—though inevitably there is a little twist, an inversion of word order: "Ces nymphes, je veux les perpétuer". And in the same way, Debussy's opening is a clear flute melody [127], but with *his* little twist, our now-familiar tritone. And Mallarmé's ending is also clear enough in its intention: "il faut dormir", we must sleep; "couple, adieu", a clear farewell, though again with its dreamy twist: "je vais voir l'ombre que tu devins" (I go to see the shadow that you became). Similiarly, Debussy's ending is a clear farewell, yet sicklied o'er with the pale cast of the tritone.

It's amazing, this ending, because it's so definite and yet indefinite at the same time. It is, as I told you, in E major, and the closing bars are as clearly terminal as an Amen— in fact, they do say *Amen*, twice. Listen as I play those last bars; I am going to alter one note—this A-sharp [128] which is the tritone in our key of E [129]. This note is the twister, the "wrong" note, so to speak. But I'm going to remove the sharp from it, making it A-*natural,* which does belong to the key of E [130]; and through this simple alteration you will clearly hear two Amens—plagal cadences, as they are known—just as they are heard in church at the end of hymns [131]. Amen, Amen. But of course Debussy's version does have the twist, the tritonic

A-sharp, and so his Amens come out a bit mistier, more
ambiguous, but Amens nevertheless, and perfectly consistent with the tritone principle that has been operative since
the very first bar. And they sound like this [132].

So ends our *Faun*; now let's hear it, bearing in mind that
while it was first being introduced in this country by the
Boston Symphony, some seventy years ago, much of the
audience came streaming out of Symphony Hall, muttering
darkly of "crazy modern music". And now you know why.

(*At this point,* Debussy's Prélude à l'Après-midi d'un Faune
is performed.)

Crazy modern music? It's actually an essay on E major,
much as the *Pastorale* Symphony is an essay on the tonic
and dominant of F major. But still those people who seventy
years ago were muttering darkly of crazy modern music
were on to something. They sensed that this *Faun* was pointing in the direction of total ambiguity—one more step
and you're there, lost in fenceless chromaticism. It was to be
only one short decade before the crisis did in fact arrive;
and I hope that this analytic session has prepared you in
some ways to understand that crisis when we come to grips
with it in our next lecture.

*(The lecture begins with a performance of the fourth
movement of Ravel's* Rapsodie Espagnole.*)*

What a way to enter the twentieth century! Blazing with
self-confidence, back there in 1908, this Spanish Rhapsody
of Ravel's is totally unaware—or at least unconcerned—
that a crisis lurks just around the corner, a life-and-death
crisis in musical semantics. But this music has no worries
about the future; it's immensely pleased with itself; it has a
childlike faith that the tonality on which it feeds is infinite;
that tonality is immortal, as long as it is continuously
refreshed and enriched by bigger and better ambiguities,
both phonological and syntactic ones, chromatic and metrical
ones. They're all there in that music, all those elusive and
seductive Either/Or's that we found last time in Berlioz and
Wagner and Debussy; they're all there, and *then* some.

But so far the wandering chromaticism we've been
examining is still contained in a tonal framework; and Ravel
is telling us, through his music, that he sees no reason why
it can't go on forever similarly controlled and contained, to
the end of recorded time. The same is true of all the *rhythmic*
ambiguities that abound in this marvelous piece; no
matter how misleading they are, they can always ultimately
be heard and understood in the basic syntactic terms of
human symmetry. In other words, music seems to be safe:
it's only 1908, and there's still *Rosenkavalier* to be written,
and a few more Puccini operas, and the *Firebird,* and
other similar delights.

But 1908, if the truth be told, is not all that safe in its
tonal mansions. Far from it; there's something else in the
air; a disturbance, a prescient feeling that all this smug
optimism can't last—neither tonality, nor figurative painting, nor syntactical poetry, nor, indeed, the seemingly
endless growth of the bourgeoisie, or of colonial wealth, or

Studying Ives' score

of imperial power. Sensitive minds are hinting at a social collapse, a monstrous World War. A premature flicker of fascism is already perceptible: Marinetti's famous Manifesto of Futurism is about to appear, glorifying war, the machine, speed, danger, and calling for the destruction of the past with all its traditions, including music. At the same time, on the other side of the musical moon, Mahler is writing his Ninth Symphony, agonizing over his reluctant and protracted farewell to tonality. Scriabin in his *Prometheus* is waging a losing battle to contain his own mystic chromaticisms. Even Sibelius is writing a Fourth Symphony filled with unresolved doubts and terrors. This, too, is 1908.

These troubling presentiments are particularly intense in and around Vienna; the decadence and hypocrisy of the over-waltzed Austro-Hungarian empire are seen by the Viennese polemicist Karl Kraus as glaringly reflected in the degeneration of language, and are harshly exposed in the light of his critical writings. He knows what's coming. Mahler knows too, but he is about to die along with his beloved tonal music. And there is a new composer, still in his thirties, who also knows, but who will live to do something about it. He is Arnold Schoenberg, who has already written a masterly work, *Verklärte Nacht*, in which he has stretched those well-known Wagnerian tonal ambiguities to the snapping point. The problems presented by *Tristan and Isolde* have now grown to a point necessitating some radical solution. The works have become not only chromatically unmanageable, but unwieldy in sheer size as well. Like the dinosaur, they've simply grown too big. Composers like Reger and Pfitzner are vying with each other for some kind of Teutonic *grand prix*, to be awarded for the longest, thickest, and most complex piece in the world. Schoenberg too has made his bid, with an early super-Wagnerian monster work called *Gurrelieder*. They were all, including

265

Mahler, swept along by the mighty "wave of the future" that Wagner, in his hyper-romantic egomania, had predicted and initiated. But how big, how chromatically ambiguous, how syntactically overstuffed can you become without collapsing of your own sheer weight? There were just too many notes, too many inner voices, too many *meanings*. This was the crisis in Ambiguity.

So, now in 1908, Schoenberg is already giving up the struggle to preserve tonality, to contain post-Wagnerian chromaticism. In this very year he is writing a Second String Quartet that clearly announces the upheaval, the renunciation of tonality. In the last movement of this quartet he resorts to the human voice, a soprano who sings Stefan George's prophetic words: "Ich fühle Luft von anderem Planeten"—"I feel air from another planet". It sounds like

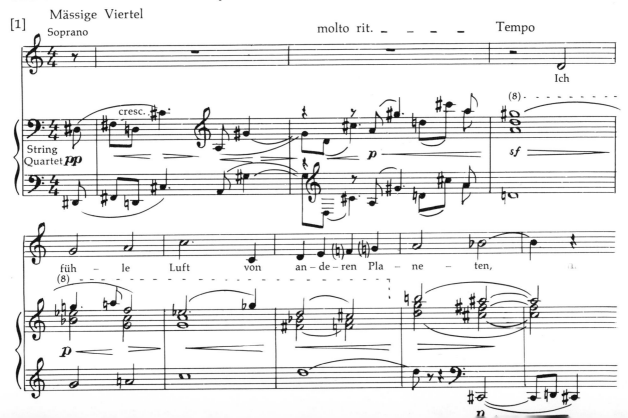

this [1]. Indeed, Schoenberg *does* feel that air, and we feel it too. This Opus 10 is to be his last tonal piece for many years to come; by Opus 11 (Three Piano Pieces) we are already breathing that new air [2]. This is atonality (to use that awful and frequently misunderstood word); not the atonality of Debussy's whole-tone scale, which, as we saw last week, was always tonally contained. This atonality is not contained, either diatonically or in any other way; for better or worse, nontonal music has been born. The history of music has suffered a sea-change.

[2]

But in that same crucial year of 1908, far away from all this—an ocean and a continent away, in Connecticut of all places—the sharpest comment, the most trenchant description of the tonal crisis, was made by an unheard, unhonored and unsung Sunday composer named Charles Ives. He also knew; though totally unaware of Schoenberg or any of that Viennese upheaval, he knew something was up, and he proclaimed it in his half-playful, mystical, quirky way through a marvelous little piece called "The Unanswered Question". This music says it all, and better than a thousand words. For this reason I'd like you to hear it now; it is an almost graphic representation of the conflict. Of course the question Ives proposes in his title is not a strictly musical one, by his own say-so, but rather a metaphysical one. Let me quote part of his descriptive foreword to the piece:

The strings play pianissimo throughout with no change in tempo. They are to represent "The Silences of the Druids—Who Know, See and Hear Nothing." The trumpet intones "The Perennial Question of Existence", and states it in the same tone of voice each time. But the hunt for the "Invisible Answer" undertaken by the flutes and other human beings [typical Ives cracker-barrel humor], becomes gradually more active, faster and louder . . . [These] "Fighting Answerers, as times goes on . . . seem to realize a futility and begin to mock "The Question"— the strife is over for the moment. After they disappear, "The Question" is asked for the last time, and "The Silences" are heard beyond in "Undisturbed Solitude".

A charming idea, naive and profound at once. But I've

always thought of Ives' *Unanswered Question* as **not a** metaphysical one so much as a strictly musical question: Whither music in our century? Let me try to reinterpret the piece in exclusively musical terms. There are three orchestral elements involved: the string ensemble, a solo trumpet, and a woodwind quartet.* The strings do indeed play "pianissimo throughout with no changes in tempo", as Ives says, but more important than anything about Druids, they are playing pure *tonal triads*. And against this slow, sustained, purely diatonic background, the trumpet intermittently poses his question—a vague, *non*tonal phrase; and each time it is answered by the wind-group in an equally vague, amorphous way. The repeated question remains more or less the same, but the answers grow more ambiguous and more hectic, until the final answer emerges as utter gibberish. But throughout it all, the strings have maintained their diatonic serenity, imperturbable; and when the trumpet asks his question for the last time, "Whither Music?", there is no further answer except for those strings, quietly prolonging their pure G-major triad into eternity.

Is that luminous final triad the answer? Is tonality eternal, immortal? Many have thought so, and some still do. And yet that trumpet's question hangs in the air, unresolved, troubling our calm. Do you see how clearly this piece spells out the dilemma of the new century—the dichotomy that was to define the shape of musical life from then to now? On the one hand, tonality and syntactic clarity; on the other, atonality and syntactic confusion. As simple as that, apparently; but not quite so simple, as we shall see. Tonal composers will be tempted into flirting with nontonality, and vice versa. And to cloud matters further, all twentieth century composers, however split they are, write what they

*During the remainder of this paragraph, Ives' *Unanswered Question* is performed in its entirety.

write out of the same need for newer and greater semantic richness; they are all, whether tonal or nontonal, motivated by the same drive, the power of expressivity, the drive to expand music's metaphorical speech, even if they do so in diametrically opposite ways, and split music apart.

We can therefore see this twentieth century split as having had a common impetus, much as a river divides into two forks. On the one hand, there were tonal composers, guided by Igor Stravinsky, who were seeking to extend musical ambiguities as far as possible by constant new kinds of transformations, but always somehow remaining within the confines of the tonal system; while on the other hand nontonal composers, led by Schoenberg, were seeking *their* new metaphorical speech through one huge, convulsive transformation—namely, transforming the entire tonal system into a new and different poetic language. But these two apparently hostile camps, with all their antagonisms and disputes about which side *really* represented "modern music", actually shared the same motivation: increased expressive power.

I have recently been reading a fascinating, nasty, turgid book called *The Philosophy of Modern Music* by the German sociologist and aesthetician Theodor Adorno. It's curious that a book with this title should turn out to be a double essay on precisely Schoenberg and Stravinsky, thus reducing "modern music" to that specific dichotomy. The double essay is, however, anything but even-handed: Schoenberg is all truth and beauty, while Stravinsky is everything evil. But Adorno confirms what I've been saying by pointing out, in his Hegelian way, that the Big Split is to be conceived dialectically, or, to use his language, as logical antinomies of the same cultural crisis.

To use simpler language, both Stravinsky and Schoenberg were after the same thing in different ways. Stravinsky tried to keep musical progress on the move by driving tonal and structural ambiguities on and on to a point of no return, as we will see next week. Schoenberg, foreseeing this point of no return, and taking his cue from the Expressionist movement in the other arts, initiated a clean, total break with tonality altogether, as well as with syntactic structures based on symmetry. It's interesting to note that Schoenberg was also a talented painter (this is one of his self-portraits) [3], and in those early years of the twentieth century, he was making the same kinds of experiments on canvas as he was making on music paper.

3

We've already referred to some of those early experiments, in Opus 10 and 11, where the break was made and free atonality came to be. But the clincher was Opus 21—that wild and spine-chilling masterpiece of expressionism called *Pierrot Lunaire*. This work is a cycle of twenty-one weird poems by Albert Giraud, set in German for voice and a small group of instruments. In the course of it Schoenberg not only goes over the cliff tonally, but introduces a new ambiguous wrinkle, which he called *Sprechstimme*, whereby the singer doesn't exactly sing. That is, each vocal note is clearly indicated, but the singer, having once attacked that note, must immediately let it fall or rise, as in speaking, producing something halfway between singing and speaking. In other words, if you can remember back four lectures ago to our discussion of heightened speech, the ictus of a syllable such as MA is not prolonged into a note but allowed to glide away, downward in a statement or upward in an interrogative (Ma↓ or Ma↗). *Sprechstimme* naturally strikes yet another blow at tonality, and lends a new spookiness to the music. For instance, here is one of the songs, entitled "Der Kranke Mond", The Sick Moon, and written for voice and flute only [4]. Notice how the *Sprechstimme* is indi-

cated, by crosses on each note-stem of the vocal line. And notice, too, how *Tristan*-like is the beginning of the flute line. But mainly, notice the general effect: haunted, meandering, rootless, psychotic.

In any case, it was soon to become clear that free atonality was in itself a point of no return. It *seemed* to fulfill the conditions for musical progress: it seemed to continue the line of romantic expressivity in a subjective way, from Wagner and Brahms through Bruckner and Mahler; the expressionism seemed logical, the atonality inevitable. But then: a dead end. Where did one go from here, having abandoned all the rules? For one thing, the lack of constraints and the resulting ungoverned freedom produced a music that was extremely difficult for the listener to follow, in either form or content. This remained true in spite of all the brilliant and profuse inner structures that abound in a piece like *Pierrot Lunaire*—canonic procedures, inverted phrases, retrogrades, and the like. Moreover, it was not easy for the composer to maintain his atonality, because of that innate tonal drive we all share universally. This was particularly true of Schoenberg, who was so gifted with his own innate musicality. Even the last song of *Pierrot Lunaire* finally has to yield to old triadic harmony, when Pierrot, or Schoenberg, if you will, sings 'O Alter Duft aus Märchenzeit": "Old fragrance from Once-Upon-a-Time" [5]. This is a deeply touching

[5]   Bewegt (♩ = ca. 60)   molto rit.

274

moment, this yearning for the past. It is as though Schoenberg were reaching back, in this final moment, for the universals of music itself.

But for all the reasons stated above, some new system had to be found for controlling the amorphousness of free-floating atonality. And so Schoenberg gradually evolved his famous twelve-tone method—gradually. Already before this, in his Opus 19 (a set of piano pieces) he was veering toward a concept of the twelve chromatic tones whereby they are all used constantly, but without the traditional tonal relationships to one another. For example, the Disc Side 5 band 3 first piece of the set begins with all twelve tones employed in the course of two bars [6], but there's still a ghost of tonality hanging over them. The chromaticism is still contained—just barely. Look at the melody alone [7]. Perfectly tonal; in fact, it outlines a B-major triad [8] with one not very startling appoggiatura [9], which resolves as conventionally as in Mozart or Mahler. (In fact it sounds rather like *Till Eulenspiegel*, doesn't it? [10]) Even as it continues [11] it still suggests B major; the chromatic wandering is not much more erratic than in the Berlioz *Romeo and Juliet* music we heard last week. Where the difference lies is in the left-hand accompaniment, which has very little to do with B major [12]. All the suggested B-majorness is now lost in a mix of atonality. But now listen to how it goes on [13].

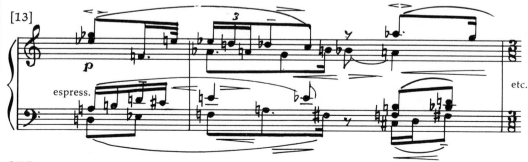

275

[14]

[15]

[16]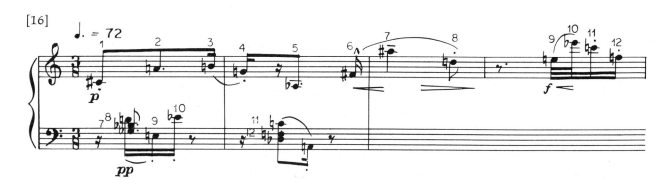

276

What is resonating in that phrase? Remember *Tristan?* [14]
And now listen again to Schoenberg [see 13]. "Son of
Tristan"; or is it perhaps "Tristan's Revenge"? Whichever
it is, there is still no escaping the past. The need for a con-
trol-system is pressingly clear. And so, by the early 1920's
Schoenberg had arrived at a twelve-tone *system* which
guaranteed, or your money back, that you would never slip
into old tonal habits (no more B major, no more *Tristan*),
and more important, that any piece you wrote could be
consistent, could make sense formally and stylistically, from
beginning to end. Aesthetic order had now been restored.

This crucial turn of events occurs in a piano piece from
1923 (and coincidentally numbered Opus 23; this happens
very frequently in the course of Schoenberg's writing, that
his opus numbers correspond to the year in which they
were written). In this highly significant work all twelve
tones are presented in a pre-established order, or series, with
no single tone repeated until all other eleven have been
sounded [15]. Read that last sentence again, for it is the
ground rule of the whole system (vastly oversimplified, of
course), and serves to give each of the twelve tones its equal
rights, rather like establishing a pure democracy among
them. Now of course the piece doesn't begin with a naked
presentation of this twelve-tone set, or "<u>row</u>", as it's called,
any more than the "Moonlight Sonata" begins with the presentation of the C-sharp minor scale. The first thing actually
heard is a transformation of the row with certain of its notes
combined into chords and others used as melody. In other
words, a surface structure has been evolved with all twelve
tones present in the first two bars [16]. (The twelve tones
are also presented in the right hand alone, if you notice,
extending over four bars.)

Disc
Side 5
band 4

277

278

Now once this row has been presented in its first transformational form, it's immediately heard again, but in a
new order; that is, the series has undergone a permutation.
Thereafter these permutations of the row continue in always
new ways, in new melodic, harmonic, and rhythmic combinations, which we might well call, in our now-familiar
linguistic terms, transformations of transformations.
Through this kind of perpetual variation or metamorphosis,
and through Schoenberg's inventive genius, the original

Disc
Side 5
band 5

row evolves into a piece in this case bearing the unexpect-
edly simple title of *Waltz*. Here are the first nineteen bars
[17].

Now this history-making little waltz may at first sound
not so very different in its nontonal style from earlier
examples I played you of *free* atonality. But there is all the
difference in the world; this piece is controlled by rules which
govern its consistent adherence to the original set of twelve
tones. In a sense, that tone row performs something like the
function of a scale in tonal music—that is, to provide a basic
source of "underlying strings", as the linguists say, which
evolve into a deep structure of musical "prose", out of which
ultimately arises this surface structure, Schoenberg's Opus 23.

These "rules", you understand, are not rigid: they were
advanced only as structural/philosophical guidelines. Indeed, Schoenberg himself was the first one to break them,
just as all great thinkers are rule-breakers. He used to tell
his composition students: Don't compose in my method;
learn my method and then just compose.

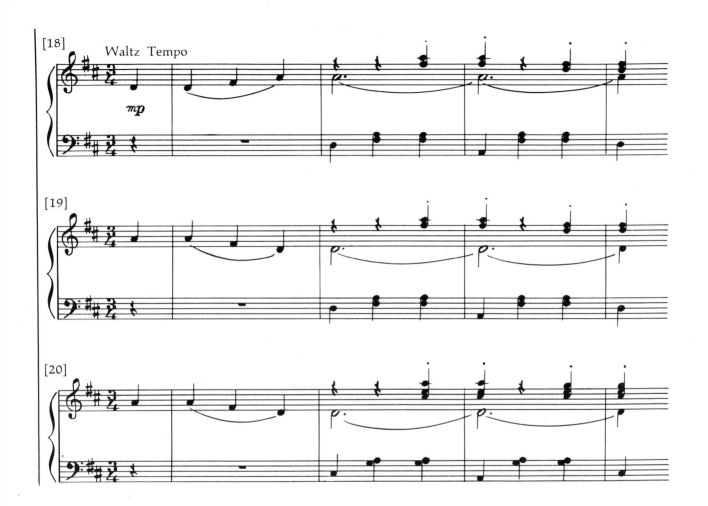

But to the extent that the row does provide certain functions analogous to those of a scale in the tonal system, this twelve tone, or *dodecaphonic*, method was indeed a viable replacement for tonal composition. It was such a welcome gift to the crisis-ridden twentieth-century composer that it took instant strong hold, capturing the imagination of such composers as Alban Berg and Anton Webern, both ardent Schoenberg disciples, and persisting to this very day (with evolutionary modifications,* of course) in the music of such composers as Stockhausen, Boulez, Wuorinen, Kirchner, Babbitt, Foss, Berio—and sometimes, though very rarely, even in mine.

It's as though a new covenant had been formed, replacing the old one of tonality. If we think of tonality as a kind of grammatical covenant, or agreement that there will be *sentences in speech*, then certain rules have to be obeyed. Only recall Alice's bemused sentence: "Do cats eat bats?" A puzzled but valid sentence. Then she wonders: "Do bats eat cats?" A *semantic* change, but still grammatically valid. But if we invert the sentence, by reversing its order, we get: Bats eat cats do? which is meaningless and chaotic. It's as though we took the opening phrase of the "Blue Danube Waltz" [18] and inverted it into this [19]. It's weak, though still acceptable. Maybe we could even call it a metaphor. But if we invert the *second* phrase [20], we're in chaos. It's cats

Disc
Side 5
band 6

* These include the extensions of serial techniques to parameters other than pitch: duration, dynamics, texture, rhythm, etc.

281

282

and bats again. Of course, that last phrase is conceivable as
what used to be called "crazy modern music", just as "Eat
do cats bats" is conceivable as a line of crazy modern poetry,
but in both cases there is an obvious crisis in syntax. A new
system of controls is clearly needed, a new covenant that
will guarantee order.

The trouble is that the new musical "rules" of Schoenberg are not apparently based on innate awareness, on the
intuition of tonal relationships. They are like rules of an
artificial language, and therefore must be learned. This would
seem to lead to what used to be called "form without content", or form at the expense of content—structuralism for
its own sake. That's exactly what Schoenberg is accused of,
for example, in the Soviet Union. *Formalism* they call it
there, strictly forbidden to the Soviet composer. We know
that Schoenberg never meant anything of the kind. He was
just too musical to hold such an attitude, too much of a
music-lover. Nor do I believe he really *meant* the extraordinary claim he is said to have made at a certain point
that it doesn't really matter how a piece of serial music
sounds; it is important only that the inherent structure of
the piece be logical. At least he couldn't have meant that for
more than a moment of excessive zeal. No matter how much
emphasis he placed on logical structure, that structure is
still derived from the same twelve tones of the harmonic
series, a universal we all share. This fact alone would account for Schoenberg's constant reversions to tonality,
whether overt or implied, as well as to traditional syntactic
structures. Even in this same Opus 23 *Waltz* we were just
hearing, where the serial system is being displayed for the
first time, we find a passage such as this, with a perfectly
symmetrical sequence: three bars [21] which are repeated in
a rhythmically exact sequence [22]. And not only is that

passage symmetrical, but there hangs over it a strong feeling of *tonality.* Do you sense that tonal quality, arising from the perfect fifths and fourths in the melodic line [23] and the "dominant" feeling in the accompaniment [24]?

This kind of tonal feeling haunted Schoenberg's music right up to the end of his life. Even his third quartet, Opus 30, which is a highly developed serial work, opens with repeated two-bar phrase groups that aren't very far from the procedures of Mozart [25]. And it's strikingly suggestive of a tonality, almost as if presenting the tonic and dominant of E minor [26]. (Of course that's vitiating the music, but I'm just trying to show you the tonal *implications* which are so strong.) Even in Opus 31, the *Variations for Orchestra,* a work rarely played because of its difficulty for performers and listeners alike—even here we find sequences that are symmetrical both tonally and structurally [27]. Left hand, right hand, clear as day. Such examples abound throughout the corpus of Schoenberg's work; in fact, as late as 1944, in the last decade of his life, he wrote an entire work in G minor, key signature and all.

[26]

tonic   dominant

[27]

Mässig ♩ = 88

Would you believe that this [28] is by the same composer whose dodecaphonic system we've been discussing? There is a famous quote from Schoenberg in which he says, "A longing to return to the older style was always vigorous in me; and from time to time I had to yield to that urge." He then went on to say that was why he had written so much tonal music even late in life, and then dismissed the whole problem by saying that these stylistic differences, as he called them, aren't really very important. This, imagine, after having spent most of his life tearing the musical world apart by denying tonality.

Of course, there are those who say that Schoenberg wrote this tonal piece out of desperation to have his music publicly performed; and indeed, this Theme and Variations in G Minor *was* given its premiere performance by the Boston Symphony under Koussevitzky, who rarely if ever played twelve-tone music, by Schoenberg or anyone else. Whether or not the story is true, its existence illustrates the heart-breaking situation of an unplayed master, seventy years old, most of whose major works were yet to be performed by most of our major orchestras, and that includes the great Violin Concerto, the Piano Concerto, and the Five Pieces for Orchestra, which may well be his orchestral masterpiece. But in whatever sense that story is true, it cannot detract from the evident truth of Schoenberg's continuing rocky romance with tonality, right up to his death in 1951. How else can we account for his orchestral transcriptions of Bach and Handel, and even Brahms' G-Minor Piano Quartet, which he also made late in his life? He loved music with such passion that the magnetic pull of tonality could never lose its hold on him. It conditioned his own music, to a smaller or greater extent, even through the whole revolutionary development of his twelve-tone method.

It seems somehow inevitable that the sense of tonality haunts his most beautiful works; even when it's not demonstrably present, it still haunts those works by its conspicuous absence. Does this sound paradoxical? It shouldn't, if you keep in mind that the twelve tones employed by Schoenberg are the same old twelve tones employed by everyone else, derived in the same way from the same natural harmonic series. They are the same twelve well-tempered tones of Bach, only their universal hierarchy has been destroyed— or, at least, an attempt has been made to destroy it. Schoenberg himself was the first to recognize this all-important truth, and, indeed the first to renounce the word "atonality", even to deny the possibility of atonality. Another paradox? Not at all. He knew—and we too must learn from him— that if ever a true atonality is to be achieved, some uniquely different basis for it must be found. The rules of the twelve-tone method may be nonuniversal and even arbitrary, but not arbitrary enough to destroy the inherent tonal relationships among those twelve tones. Perhaps a real atonality can be achieved only artificially, through electronic means, or through a truly arbitrary division of the octave space into something other than the twelve equidistant intervals of our chromatic scale—say, thirteen equidistant intervals, or thirty, or three hundred.

But not *twelve*, not the twelve tones of Bach and Beethoven and Wagner; with those twelve universals neither Schoenberg nor Berg nor Webern could ever escape the nostalgic yearning for the deep structures implied by, indeed inherent in, these notes. It's that "Alter Duft aus Märchenzeit," that nostalgic yearning quality that so often makes their music beautiful and moving.

[29]

[30]

[31] Andante
Commendatore

Tu m'in – vi – ta – sti a ce – na,

il tou do – ver or sa – i,

Is there possibly the beginning of a clue here to the Unanswered Question? How does the wild thought strike you that *all* music is ultimately and basically tonal, even when it's nontonal? Does this hypothetical notion touch off some innate response in you? I know it does in me; it gives me the same sort of electric charge I always feel when any two facts intersect and spark an idea; and the two facts here are the two givens of one series intersecting another—the harmonic series and any given tone row.

While we're on this subject of serial intersections, let's take a moment to remind ourselves that serial phenomena have been around for a long time, as far back, let's say, as the thirteenth century *cantus firmus,* and even including some significant stabs at actual tone rows, by (would you believe it?) Bach, Mozart, and Beethoven. Take for example the extraordinary chromatic subject of Bach's F-minor fugue from the *Well-Tempered Clavier* (Book I) [29]. That subject encompasses nine out of the twelve chromatic tones, or three quarters of all the notes we possess, and there's only one repetition in it—the first note. What's even more extraordinary is that in the course of the immediately ensuing fugal answer, Bach automatically picks up the three remaining tones [30], so that within these few bars all twelve tones are present and accounted for. It's not a Schoenberg row, but it comes remarkably close.

And what about this spooky passage from Mozart's *Don Giovanni* [31]? All twelve notes are in there, every one [32].

[32]

[33] Allegro energico, sempre ben marcato (♩ = 84)

p

Ihr   stürzt   nie — — der, Mil — li — o — — nen?

Ah — — nest du   den   Schö — — fer, Welt?

cresc.

Such'   ihn   ü — — ber'm Ster — — nen – zelt.

f

such'   ihn   ü — — ber'm Ster — — nen – zelt!

[34]

1 2 3 4 5 6 7 8 9 10 11

And what about the Finale of Beethoven's Ninth—that sudden awestruck moment of recognizing the Divine Presence [33]? Fantastic, that passage. Again, it's not Schoenberg, and admittedly it presents only eleven notes out of the possible twelve [34], but it *is* a row in the sense that for that brief duration Beethoven suspends all tonal harmony, leaving only harmonic implications; that's what makes it so suddenly awesome, unrooted in earth, extraterrestrial— so that when earthly harmony does return [35] that incandescent A-major triad does indeed cry "Brüder!"— Universal brothers, all emerging together from that non-earthly Divinity.

I have strayed from Schoenberg, but not without intention. For in going back to Bach and Beethoven we have had revealed to us a striking new ambiguity, which I was only suggesting earlier through the image of intersecting currents. Perhaps you can sense more strongly now what I meant by saying that all music is tonal even when it *isn't*. These early adumbrations of tone rows are clearly attempts to transcend tonality, to evoke mystery by momentarily denying, or ignoring, the universal roots of harmony, which are born in the harmonic series. And this sudden rootlessness, however brief, in every case suggests the mystic, the unearthly, whether it's Mozart's ghostly stone guest, or Beethoven's evocation of the Godhead. What then happens to music when Schoenberg, for example, constructs a whole system in terms of that rootlessness? Does that system therefore make all his music, and that of his followers, unqualifiedly mystic? Or only unqualifiedly intellectualized? What has happened to what Keats called the "Poetry of Earth," which ceases never? Is Schoenberg an end, or a beginning?

293

These are some of the problems we'll be confronting in the next and final lecture; right now what interests us is the fascinating ambiguity between the planned antitonal functions of the twelve-tone row and the inevitable tonal harmonic implications that innately reside in it, do what you will. Of course, a composer may construct any row at his own pleasure, either to emphasize harmonic relationships or to de-emphasize them, even to try to erase them. But either way, the relationships remain, whether overt (as in the Bach fugue) or implied (as in the Beethoven Ninth). And so there is always that resulting ambiguous tug-of-war between being rooted and partly rooted. But music can never be totally rootless as long as there are twelve equal tones in an octave. Not thirteen; twelve.

For example, one of the most famous pre-Schoenberg attempts at a twelve-tone row—dating from the 1850s, if you can believe it, is the opening theme of Franz Liszt's *Faust Symphony*. Here all twelve tones are immediately revealed, again with no harmonic support, and with no repetitions [36]. A pure tone row, as mystic as you could wish. But it's so constructed that each group of three notes in itself spells out a chord—a so-called augmented triad [37]—so that the whole row winds up outlining four such chords, and four times three is twelve. Now the harmonic implications in that row are so strong that obviously the whole piece is going to be filled with augmented triads, as long as that row has anything to say about it. And indeed it is filled with them, through all three movements. Now let's jump ahead seventy years to Schoenberg's crucial little Waltz, that same Opus 23 which officially announced the row as a linear string. What do we find? Harmonic implications galore, the most obvious of which is, curiously enough,

that same augmented triad. In fact, as we examine the piece, in terms of its groupings of the row, permutation by permutation, we find each new one clearly enunciating that augmented triad, in one way or another [38]. There it is, at the very beginning; clearly boxed in the left hand. Then the next permutation: the three notes in the next box form the same augmented triad. On to the next permutation, and here it is again—boxed. And yet again. And now do you see what I mean by "rooted and partly rooted"? Rejecting *and* embracing at the same time; denial *and* commitment: this conflict has engendered the most dramatic and the most critical semantic ambiguity we have found so far in all of music.

Is this perhaps why Schoenberg has still, to this day, not found his mass public—a large, concert-going public which loves his music? How many music lovers do you know who can say, today, in this fiftieth year of Opus 23, that they *love* to hear it, that they listen with love to it, as they might listen to Mahler or Stravinsky? Is it not perhaps that the ambiguity is simply too huge to be grasped, too self-negating to be perceived with our only human ears, ears which are after all tuned to our innate predispositions, in spite of all conditionings or reinforcements? Let's put it another way: have we not finally stumbled on an ambiguity that cannot produce aesthetically positive results? Is there conceivably such a thing as a "negative ambiguity"? And why, people ask me constantly, why *do* we listen with real response, with innate affective response, to the music of Alban Berg, the most fervent of Schoenberg disciples and an equally committed twelve-tone composer? Why does Berg succeed in producing a *positive* ambiguity out of the same tonal-atonal contradiction? Is it only that Berg is so

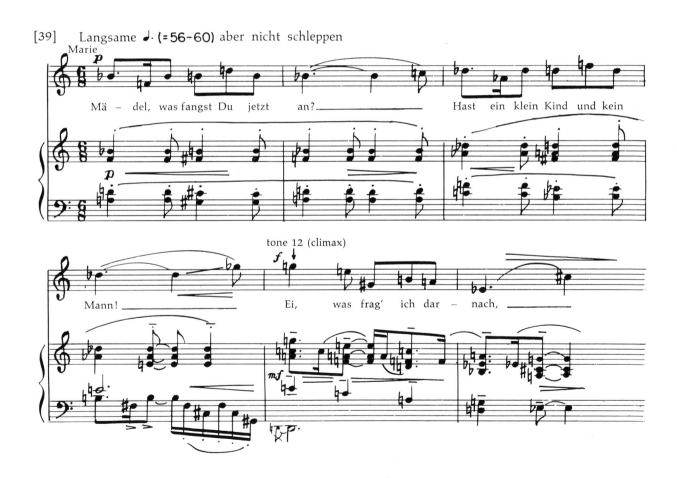

[39] Langsame ♩.(=56-60) aber nicht schleppen

Marie

Mä – del, was fangst Du jetzt an?_____ Hast ein klein Kind und kein

tone 12 (climax)

Mann!_____ Ei, was frag' ich dar – nach,_____

298

much more theatrical a composer than Schoenberg, that we are overwhelmed by the sheer drama of an opera like *Wozzeck?*

Many fine critical minds have claimed this to be true, and to some degree it is true. A good performance of *Wozzeck*, which is not easy to come by, can be a shattering experience in the theater. The fact is that Berg somehow found his own personal way to deal with that ultimate ambiguity of deep- and surface-rootedness; and what is more, he had an uncanny gift for dramatizing that ambiguity, for making drama out of dodecaphonic procedures embedded within universal tonal relationships. It would of course take a whole separate lecture to explain this clearly, in all its elusiveness and complexity; but let me try to give you a hint or two.

There is a moment in *Wozzeck* (Act I, Scene 3) where the poor, pretty Marie, Wozzeck's harlot-with-a-heart-of-gold, sits alone in her room, cradling their little illegitimate baby son with a lullaby. Granted, the lullaby is utterly simple and tonal, moving in conventional two-bar phrases—folk music, if you will. Amazingly enough, in the course of the first two phrases, all twelve tones are employed, and Berg's tone row is somehow embedded in that simple lullaby—all twelve tones but one, which he saves for the immediately ensuing climax [39]. This is twelve tone music—yet tender, moving, and totally accessible.

Then there is Marie, two acts later, abandoned and desperate, seeking comfort in random pages of the Bible. Do you remember *Sprechstimme* that ambiguous heightened speech device Schoenberg invented for his *Pierrot Lunaire?* Here it is again: as Marie reads dully from the New

Testament, she reads in *Sprechstimme* [40]; but then, as she
suddenly breaks off in despair, crying *"Herr Gott!* Lord
God, Don't look at me!"—then, she *sings* [40a]. The contrast is hair-raising music-drama. "Sieh' mich nicht an!"
Do you see how brilliantly the ambiguity is handled here?
Notice that while Marie was reading in *Sprechstimme*, the
orchestra was accompanying her in a purely tonal fugato.
But when she broke out in her anguish, it was the full dodecaphonic treatment, voice and orchestra both. Again, the
ambiguity is presented vividly, accessibly, tonally or non-
tonally according to the dramatic requirements.

But it's not only in his operatic works that Berg has
succeeded so remarkably where others have not. His sense
of drama, his deft and just balancing of these incompatible
elements, tonal and nontonal, carry over into all his com-
positions. For example, his very last work, the beautiful
Violin Concerto of 1935, solved that agonizing ambiguity,
to-be-or-not-to-be-tonal, in an equally satisfying way. First
of all, Berg chose for this concerto a tone row which is filled
with tonal implications [41]. Notice that the first nine notes
of that row all proceed in intervals of the third—mellifluous
thirds, major and minor ones. Moreover, these thirds are
symmetrically arranged, in "chiasmus" fashion, if you
recall, according to a pattern of AB:BA [42]—that is, minor-

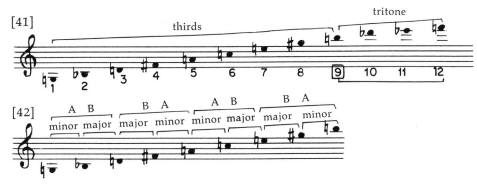

301

302

major: major-minor, etc. And what's more, the triads that are formed by these thirds [43] automatically alternate minor, major, minor, major, thus insuring all mellifluous possibilities. And what's even more tonality-making, every *other* note of these first nine combine into perfect fifths [44], of which the first four happen to correspond to the four open strings of the violin [45], a very handy tool to have around in a violin concerto. In fact, the first notes the violin plays in the concerto are these very open strings [46]. But all this issues from the first nine notes only. For then, starting with the ninth tone of the row [see 41] we find that the remaining four notes present us with our old Debussyan friend, the tritone [47], those three whole steps [48], which if you remember, generated Debussy's whole-tone scale.

So, all in all, Berg chose a row that has very strong roots in music's traditional past. And he adds to the strength of that traditional feeling with one device after another—a Bachian inversion, a Beethovenian fragmentation, a Schumannesque rhythmic ambiguity, to say nothing of that sine qua non of all Viennese composers, the waltz, in this case a rustic peasant waltz or "Ländler", as it is called in Austria. If you listen to the Scherzo movement (the end of Part I), and compare this waltz music with the little Opus 23 waltz of Schoenberg—no: strike that; don't compare it with anything; just enjoy it for its mellifluous, tender *Wienerisch*ness [49].

[49] see page 304

303

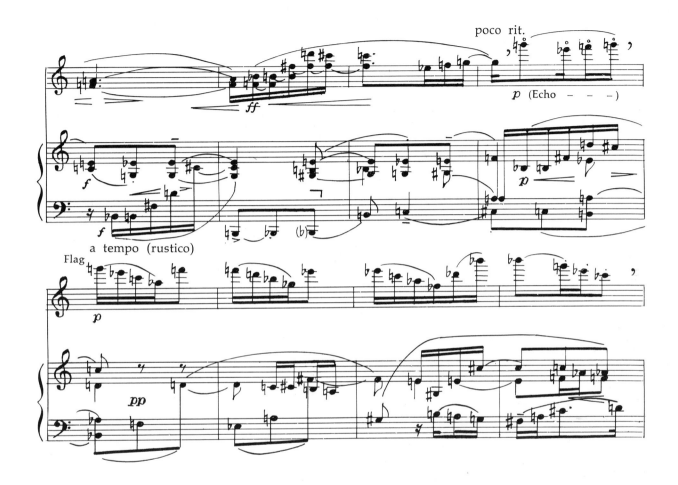

Isn't that delicious? Almost a *Sacher torte mit Schlag*. But it's far from mere Viennese whipped cream. It *is* twelve-tone writing; only it exists somehow in a tonal universe where it's accessible to us in all its warmth and charm. When you listen to the whole movement, observe how tonally it ends [50]. And that unmistakably tonic final chord is nothing but the first four notes of Berg's tone row [51], a lovely pile-up of sweet thirds, which results in an almost shockingly tonal G-minor seventh chord. And so, in these ways among others, the crucial ambiguity of tonality versus nontonality can manage to create a thoroughly positive aesthetic surface.

Needless to say, the Violin Concerto is not all sweetness and *Schlagobers*; anything but. It has stretches of almost unbearable intensity, dramatic brilliance, and Olympian calm. It is in a very real sense a tragic work. I didn't mean to get this deeply involved in it (after all, we were really talking about Schoenberg)—but I would dearly love to share with you just one other section of the piece, which presents the tonal-atonal ambiguity in a particularly positive way. This passage is the closing Adagio of the concerto, and is chiefly concerned with developing the tail end of the tone row, which, as you remember, consists of these four notes [52], spanning the tritone—the *diabolus in musica*, remember? But far from being the devil here, it is on the contrary angelicism itself; because, as it turns out, these four notes [53] happen to be identical with the first phrase of Bach's Chorale, "Est Ist Genug", which you all know and love. It's extraordinary, that initial phrase with its tritonic implications [54]; and that's the way Berg uses it—not only the first phrase, but the entire chorale. It comes at the point where there has just been a violent climax of shattering

hammer-blows [55]; and as it is subsiding we begin to hear,
emerging from the debris, murmurings of that four-note
phrase [56] intertwined with these gradually fading hammer
blows. The four-note phrase becomes more and more distinct
until suddenly the solo violin is playing the Chorale itself,
the first three phrases of it, note for note [57]. Of course,

[58]

Poco più mosso, ma religioso

[Mein Je – sus kommt: nun gu – te Nacht, O Welt! Ich

pp ma deciso   pp   doloroso   dolce

[59] a tempo

[Ich fah – re si – cher hin mit

poco *f* risoluto

fahr' in's Him – mels – haus]

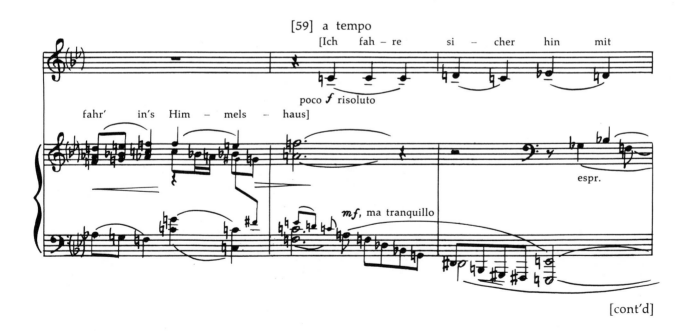

mf, ma tranquillo

espr.

[cont'd]

other things are going on at the same time, such as a
counterpoint of those thirds from the first part of the
tone row, a canon in the violas, and other things that I
won't bother you with; but then the most amazing thing
happens—a totally unexpected event in a twelve-tone
work. The first three phrases of the chorale are suddenly
repeated by four clarinets, imitating the sound of a Baroque
organ in Bach's pure B-flat major harmony. Of course there
are some little "wrong" notes hovering around in the background, but those four clarinets remain absolutely pure [58].
The solo violin then takes up the next phrase [59], again
with dissonant counterpoint; and again the clarinets
repeat the phrase in the Bach version [60]. And so on to
the end of the chorale. It's one of the most astonishing

[59 cont'd]   [60]

passages in all music, especially as it grows to its own dissonant climax, finally subsiding into an equally astonishing serene close in, of all things, B-flat major.

And so a great twelve-tone work has found its resting place in B-flat major; a compromise solution has been achieved. But does this hybrid represent *the* solution? Are you satisfied that the Ultimate Ambiguity was solved once and for all in 1935? In what way can I shed further light on this massive problem? Is it enough to have examined its origins, to have identified the great tonal split, to have traced one side of the split into the development of a Method that changed the history of music, to have attempted a dispassionate assessment of Arnold Schoenberg—only to have Alban Berg walk off with all the honors? No, there *is* further light to be shed, and that light is to be found in the mind and prophetic soul of Gustav Mahler. After a brief pause we are going to hear Mahler, specifically his last will and testament, the Adagio finale of his Ninth Symphony. And I think that after Mahler's Ninth, things may be suddenly clearer; we may have a new perspective.

II

During this interval certain sharp questions must have occurred to you. First of all, why Mahler? What has Mahler to do with Schoenberg? A great deal, and far more than the obvious fact that Mahler supported and encouraged his young colleague during those early years of the century. Then, why is Mahler's Ninth Symphony his last will and testament? What about the Tenth, that highly significant unfinished document? And in any case why invoke the Mahler Ninth to end a lecture on the twentieth century crisis? Isn't this back-tracking? Having moved with Berg and Schoenberg into the midcentury, why now retrogress to that fateful year of 1908? Because, like the Ives *Unanswered Question*, which was written in the same year, this Mahler Ninth is also a great question; but it's more: it contains a deeply revealing answer.

I had planned to prepare you for this music with my customary analysis at the piano, going in depth into the dualisms that tore Mahler apart: composer/conductor, Christian/Jew, sophisticate/naif, provincial/cosmopolitan —all of which contributed to the musical schizo-dynamics of his textures, and his ambivalent tonal attitudes. I had also hoped, by a detailed analysis of his treatment of appoggiaturas, for example, to reach the essence of the tonal crisis, through examining his nonresolution of tensions, his reluctant attempts to let go of tonality—which does shed further light on the inevitable split that was to occur between Schoenberg and Stravinsky. And so I picked up the score again, after some years away from it, filled with the sense of Mahler's torture at knowing that he was the end of the line, the last point in the great symphonic arc that began with Haydn and Mozart. I was again aware that it was his destiny to sum up the whole story of Austro-Germanic music, to recapitulate it and tie it up—not in a pretty bow, but in a fearful knot made out of his own nerves and sinews.

But while restudying this work, especially the final movement, I found more answers than I had expected (as we always do when we return to the study of a great work). And the most startling answer, the most important one—because it illuminates our whole century from then to now—is this: that ours is the century of death, and Mahler is its musical prophet. I want to talk to you about

313

that answer—without the piano, without visual aids, and on a somewhat different level of discourse from the one we've been following. Because this Ninth Symphony offers us a crucial, semantic explanation, an infinitely broader interpretation of what we've been calling the twentieth century crisis.

Why *is* our century so uniquely death-ridden? Couldn't we say this of other centuries as well? What of the nineteenth century, so poetically preoccupied with death, whether as late as Wagner's *Liebestod* or as early as Keats' *Nightingale:*

> I have been half in love with easeful Death,
> Call'd him soft names in many a mused rhyme . . .

Yes, true; poetically, symbolically, true. And haven't all centuries, all human histories been a long record of the struggle to survive, to deal with the problem of mortality? Again, yes; but never before has mankind been confronted by the problem of surviving global death, total death, the extinction of the whole race. And Mahler was not alone in his vision; there have been other great prophets of our struggle. Freud, Einstein, and Marx have also prophesied, as have Spengler and Wittgenstein, Malthus and Rachel Carson—all latter-day Isaiahs and Saint Johns, all preaching the same sermon in different terms: mend your ways, the Apocalypse is at hand. Rilke said it too: "Du musst dein Leben ändern."

The twentieth century has been a badly written drama, from the beginning. Act I: Greed and hypocrisy leading to a genocidal World War; postwar injustice and hysteria; a boom; a crash; totalitarianism. Act II: Greed and hypocrisy leading to a genocidal World War; postwar injustice and hysteria; boom, crash; totalitarianism.

Act III: Greed and hypocrisy—I don't dare continue. And
what have been the antidotes? Logical positivism, existen-
tialism, galloping technology, the flight into outer space,
the doubting of reality, and overall a well-bred paranoia,
most recently on display in the high places of Washington,
D.C. And our *personal* antidotes: Making it, dope, sub-
cultures and counter-cultures, turning on, turning off.
Marking time and making money. A rash of new religious
movements from Guruism to Billy Grahamism. And a
rash of new art movements, from concrete poetry to the
silences of John Cage. A thaw here, a purge there. And all
under the same aegis, the angel of planetary death.

What do you do if you know all this back in 1908, if
you're a hypersensitive like Mahler, and instinctively
know what's coming? You prophesy; and others pick up
your trail. And so both Schoenberg and Stravinsky,
Mahler's two continuing prophets, utterly different as
they were, spent their lives struggling in their opposite ways
to keep musical progress alive, to avert the Evil Day.
In fact, all the truly great works of our century have been
born of despair or of protest, or of a refuge from both. But
anguish informs them all. Think of Sartre's *Nausée*,
Camus' *Stranger*, Gide's *Counterfeiters*. *The Sun Also
Rises*, *The Magic Mountain*, and *Dr. Faustus*, *The Last of
the Just*, even *Lolita*. And Picasso's *Guernica*, Chirico, Dali.
And Eliot's *Cocktail Party*, *Murder in the Cathedral*, *The
Waste Land*, and the *Four Quartets*. Auden's *Age of
Anxiety*, and that supreme work of his, *For the Time Being*.
And Pasternak and Neruda, and Sylvia Plath. And on the
screen, *La Dolce Vita*; and on the stage, *Waiting for Godot*.
And *Wozzeck*, *Lulu*, *Moses and Aaron*, and Brecht's *Mother
Courage*. And, yes, also *Eleanor Rigby*, and *A Day In The
Life*, and *She's Leaving Home*. These too are great works in

315

miniature, born of despair, touched with death. And Mahler
foresaw it all. That's why he so desperately resisted entering
this twentieth century, the age of death, the end of faith.
And the bitter irony was that he did succeed in avoiding the
century only by himself dying prematurely in 1911.

It's very strange, how the pieces of the puzzle interlock.
Mahler and his message pervade everything he touches.
Think of *Kindertotenlieder*: the death of Rückert's children,
and then of Mahler's own. And Alban Berg, who adored
Mahler, dedicated his *Wozzeck* to Mahler's widow, Alma,
and his Violin Concerto to the memory of her beautiful
young daughter, Manon Gropius. It's all somehow tied in
with death. For instance, that Violin Concerto of 1935 was
Berg's last work; he died the same year, aged fifty, exactly
the same age at which Mahler had died. The coincidences
multiply; but let's not be tempted into mystical speculation.
The facts are potent enough: when Berg, as a young man,
happened to hear a performance of the Mahler Ninth, he
immediately wrote to his wife back in Vienna that he had
just heard the greatest music of his life, or some words to
that effect. I feel these connections very strongly and per-
sonally; a few years ago, when I was first reintroducing
Mahler's music to his own city of Vienna (where of course
it had been banned for years by the Nazis), there was Frau
Berg, the radiantly beautiful aged widow, sitting in rapture
at every rehearsal. We became acquainted; and she became
my living link back to the death-ridden intercrossing of
Berg, Schoenberg, and Mahler. As did Alma Mahler herself,
who attended my Mahler festival rehearsals in New York. I
began to feel myself in direct contact with Mahler's message.

Today we know what that message was; and it was the
Ninth Symphony that spread the news. But it was bad news,

and the world did not care to hear it. That's the real reason
for the fifty years of neglect that Mahler's music suffered
after his death—not the usual excuses we always hear: that
the music is too long, too difficult, too bombastic. It was
simply too true, telling something too dreadful to hear.

What exactly was this news? What was it that Mahler
saw? Three kinds of death. First, his own imminent death
of which he was acutely aware. (The opening bars of this
Ninth Symphony are an imitation of the arhythmia of his
failing heartbeat.) And second, the death of tonality, which
for him meant the death of music itself, music as he knew it
and loved it. All his last pieces are kinds of farewells to
music, as well as to life; think only of *Das Lied von der
Erde* with its final "Abschied." And that controversial
unfinished Tenth Symphony—even that one, which tried to
take a tentative step into the Schoenbergian future, and
which has undergone so many attempts at completion—
even that Tenth remains for me only the one completed
movement, which is yet another heartbreaking Adagio
saying Farewell. It was one farewell too many; I am
convinced that Mahler could never have finished the whole
symphony, even if he had lived. He had said it all in the
Ninth.

And finally, his third and most important vision: the
death of society, of our Faustian culture.

Now, if Mahler knew this, and his message is so clear,
how do we, knowing it too, manage to survive? Why are
we still here, struggling to go on? We are now face to face
with the truly Ultimate Ambiguity which is the human
spirit. This is the most fascinating ambiguity of all: that as
each of us grows up, the mark of our maturity is that we
accept our mortality; and yet we persist in our search for

immortality. We may believe it's all transient, even that it's all over; yet we believe a future. We *believe*. We emerge from a cinema after three hours of the most abject degeneracy in a film such as *La Dolce Vita*, and we emerge on wings, from the sheer creativity of it; we can fly on, to a future. And the same is true after witnessing the hopelessness of *Godot* in the theater, or after the aggressive violence of *The Rite of Spring* in the concert hall. Or even after listening to the bittersweet young cynicism of an album called "Revolver", we have wings to fly on. We have to believe in that kind of creativity. I know I do. If I didn't, why would I be bothering to give these lectures? Certainly not to make a gratuitous announcement of the Apocalypse. There must be something in us, and in me, that makes me want to continue; and to teach is to believe in continuing. To share with you critical feelings about the past, to try to describe and assess the present—these actions by their very nature imply a firm belief in a future.

I hope that answers the earlier question of why I am ending with Mahler a lecture that has been mainly on Schoenberg. Because Schoenberg is one of the great examples of the human spirit in our century, that spirit which is, after all, our only hope. He is a prototype of Ambiguous Man, compulsively engineering his own destruction, and simultaneously flying on into the future. We will find the same true of Stravinsky, in our next and final lecture. And this Ultimate Ambiguity is clearly to be heard in the finale of Mahler's Ninth symphony, which is a sonic presentation of death itself, and which paradoxically reanimates us every time we hear it.

As you listen to this finale, try to be aware of what has just preceded it: three other gigantic movements, each one a farewell of its own. The first movement in itself has been like a whole novel, a saga of tenderness and terror, of tortured counterpoint and harmonic resignation; it has been a farewell to love, to D major, a farewell to the tonic. In the second movement, a scherzo which is a sort of super-Ländler, we have experienced a farewell to the world of Nature, a bitter reimagining of simplicity, naiveté, the earth-pleasures we recall from adolescence. Then the third movement, again a kind of scherzo, but this time grotesque: a farewell to the world of action, the urban, cosmopolitan life—the cocktail party, the marketplace, the raucous careers and careenings of success, of loud and hollow laughter. And all three of these movements have been trembling on a tonal precipice, on the edge of death.

Only then comes the fourth and last movement, the Adagio, the final farewell. It takes the form of a prayer, Mahler's last chorale, his closing hymn, so to speak; and it prays for the restoration of life, of tonality, of faith. This is tonality unashamed, presented in all aspects ranging from the diatonic simplicity of the hymn tune that opens it through every possible chromatic ambiguity. It's also a passionate prayer, moving from one climax to another, each more searing than the last. But there are no solutions. And between these surges of prayer there is intermittently a sudden coolness, a wide-spaced transparency, like an icy burning—a Zen-like immobility of pure meditation. This is a whole other world of prayer, of egoless acceptance. But again, there are no solutions. "Heftig ausbrechend!" he writes, as again the despairing chorale breaks out with greatly magnified intensity. This is the dual Mahler, flinging himself back into his burning Christian prayer, then again freezing into his Eastern one. This vacillation is his final

319

duality. In the very last return of the hymn he is close to prostration; it is all he can give in prayer, a sobbing, sacrificial last try. But suddenly this climax fails, unachieved —the one that *might* have worked, that might have brought solutions. This last desperate reach falls short of its goal, subsides into a hint of resignation, then another hint, then into resignation itself.

And so we come to the final incredible page. And this page, I think, is the closest we have ever come, in any work of art, to experiencing the very act of dying, of giving it all up. The slowness of this page is terrifying: *Adagissimo*, he writes, the slowest possible musical direction; and then *langsam* (slow), *ersterbend* (dying away), *zögernd* (hesitating); and as if all those were not enough to indicate the near stoppage of time, he adds *äusserst langsam* (extremely slow) in the very last bars. It *is* terrifying, and paralyzing, as the strands of sound disintegrate. We hold on to them, hovering between hope and submission. And one by one, these spidery strands connecting us to life melt away, vanish from our fingers even as we hold them. We cling to them as they dematerialize; we are holding two—then one. One, and suddenly none. For a petrifying moment there is only silence. Then again, a strand, a broken strand, two strands, one . . . none. We are *half in love with easeful death . . . now more than ever seems it rich to die, to cease upon the midnight with no pain . . .* And in ceasing, we lose it all. But in letting go, we have gained everything.

(The lecture concludes with a performance of the Finale of Mahler's Ninth Symphony.)

The poetry of earth is never dead:
  When all the birds are faint with the hot sun,
  And hide in cooling trees, a voice will run
From hedge to hedge about the new-mown mead;
That is the Grasshopper's—he takes the lead
  In summer luxury,—he has never done
  With his delights; for when tired out with fun
He rests at ease beneath some pleasant weed.
The poetry of earth is ceasing never:
  On a lone winter evening, when the frost
    Has wrought a silence, from the stove there shrills
The Cricket's song, in warmth increasing ever,
  And seems to one in drowsiness half lost,
    The Grasshopper's among some grassy hills.

John Keats

(The lecture begins with a bit of the ballet music from Aida *played on the piano.)*

6. THE POETRY OF EARTH

I know what you're thinking: he's gone mad. Here we come to a lecture called "The Poetry of Earth" and he's playing he ballet music from *Aida*. [1].

You're right: I am a bit mad, *and* I'm playing the ballet music from *Aida*. It's my last lecture, and I hate the fact that it's my last lecture. Giving these lectures to you has become a way of life, and it's hard to give it up. So I warn you: this last lecture is going to be a long one; if you think the others were long, you've got another think coming, as my mother used to say.

etc.

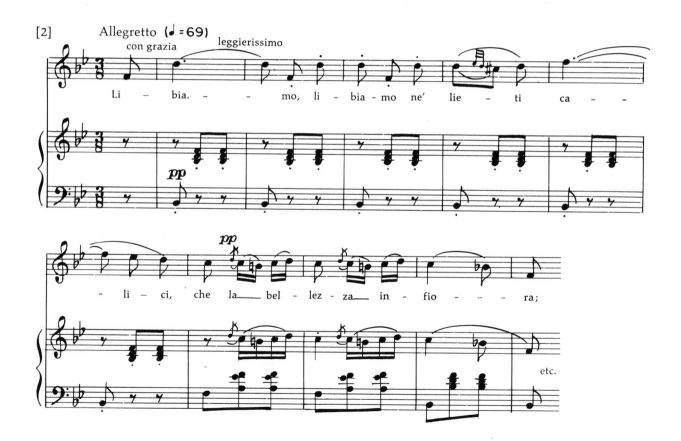

But my madness has method in it. I have a perfectly
serious question to ask you about this Verdi piece. Is this what
you'd call *sincere* music? Did Verdi write it out of a genuine
need for "self-expression"? Of course you'll argue: that's an
unfair question. You can't pretend to pass judgment on an
Italian writing fake Egyptian ballet music. But what about
this [2]? This *Traviata* tune is really Verdi's bag, isn't it? But is
it sincere? Or is it just to show off the tenor? And what about
this [3]? Are the "Kinks" sincere? And how about this

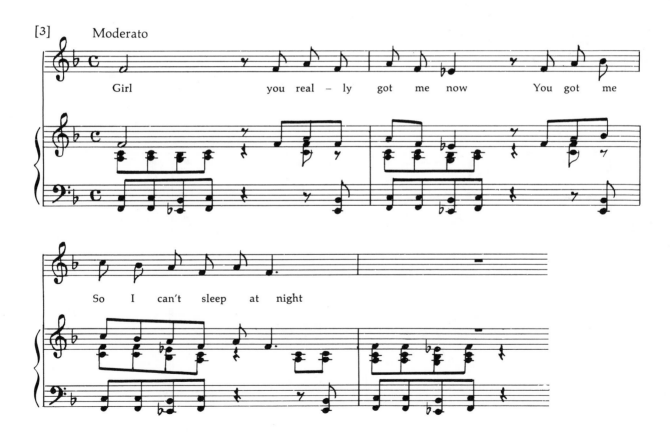

Mozart cadenza [4]? Is that sincere music, or is it written only to show off the pianist? And, as a matter of fact, how sincere is *Parsifal* [5]? There he sat, Richard Wagner in all his sybaritic splendor, in a dressing-gown of the finest silk brocade, in a room scented with rare perfumes and hung with the most sensuous fabrics, composing this penitential tale of the Saintly Fool. Is that a picture of sincerity? It certainly doesn't seem to be. But the fact is that every one of these pieces I've referred to is in its own way sincere. How can this be?

I'm plaguing you with this question because it's been plaguing me ever since the last lecture, while I've been thinking about Stravinsky and the other side of the great split. Do you remember my telling you about Theodor Adorno's book *The Philosophy of Modern Music*, in which he contrasts Schoenberg and Stravinsky? If you do, you may recall that he sees all modern music as a split between the two of them, each heading up a movement hostile to the other, with Schoenberg leading the righteous up the True Path, while Stravinsky was all deception and trickery, a veritable child of Satan. Why is Adorno so exercised over this twentieth century dichotomy, which, as we discovered through Ives' *Unanswered Question*, is basically a split between the tonal and the nontonal? Well, it's a lot more than that to Adorno; it evokes the whole question of sincerity. By "sincerity" he means direct expression of feeling, subjective, from the heart; and for him, the only way to continue the great sincere Wagnerian line, "Die heilige Deutsche Kunst", was via the Schoenbergian route, and not just through Schoenberg's early Romantic music, but through all his works, tonal, atonal, and serial. Against this he counterposes Stravinsky's cold intellectuality, his

rejection of expressiveness as mere heart-on-sleeve senti-
mentality, his over-elegant stylism, and so on, which for
Adorno meant everything vacuous and meretricious.

Of course what he's really talking about is the relationship
of art and artificiality. How artificial can art be, and still be
art? Well, it varies from one age to another, from one
stylistic period to another, from culture to culture. But
wherever or whenever, art always has, and still does, involve
the application of certain artifices. An artist is always to
some degree an artificer; to be artistic is to be artful. So it is
impossible to present a clear, black-and-white case, such as
Adorno's, where genuine art is that expression which is
subjective and sincere, and all else is artificial, hence false.
Art is more subtle than that, and much more interesting. If
we look at a Cimabue Madonna, for instance, fully understanding why he painted the head on the diagonal, that it's
an old Byzantine trick, or whatever—are we any the less
moved by the painting? Are we one whit less thrilled by
Dylan Thomas' "Fern Hill" because we know the traditional
Welsh syllabic count, line by line? Not one iota; couldn't
care less; "Fern Hill" flies. Blessings on the artifices that
give it wings, on all artifices that make emotions aesthetically
presentable and intelligible, whether they be simple
rhythm-and-rhyme or the most complex manipulations of
a twelve-tone row. In fact, it would be easy to make out a
case that the twelve-tone row is the most artificial device of
the whole twentieth century, it being a concept that fights
innateness: and that therefore the whole twelve-tone system
is one huge artificiality. I have no intention of making out
any such case because it would be pointless, and at least as
untrue as Adorno's case against Stravinsky, whom he
considers the apostate, the heretic, the devilish conjurer
with a bag of tricks.

But it was precisely this Stravinsky, this very child of
Satan, bag of tricks and all, who appeared like an angel of
deliverance, just in time to lead the great rescue operation,
the huge project of saving tonality in those critical years
before World War I. The death of Mahler, in 1911, and of
Debussy shortly thereafter seemed like the last-act curtain:
it was as though they had taken tonal music along with them
to the grave. But resuscitation was at hand; and even as
Schoenberg was renouncing tonality, Stravinsky was
glorifying it in a piece called *The Firebird*. While Schoenberg
was dedicating himself to saving music by continuing the
great subjective tradition, the chromatic, Romantic tradition,
Stravinsky was preparing to preside over a wholly new
movement, heralding a brilliant new group of composers,
all of whom stood ready to breathe life into what looked
like a moribund situation. Adorno would say: ah-ha,
artificial respiration. Merely a temporary expedient. So
what? What's so bad about a "temporary" rescue operation
that lasted a good half-century? What the great Igor did,
over that forty-some-year period, was to keep tonality
"fresh", by one means or another. Again, Adorno would
say that he kept it fresh by refrigeration, thus freezing the
life out of it. That would be a hostile way of describing
what was actually true; namely, a new objectivity, a cleaner,
cooler, slightly refrigerated kind of expression, which was
the result of placing the creative self at a respectful distance
from the created object, of taking a more removed perspective on music.

Now I've just used two words that may seem to be
mutually exclusive: "objectivity" and "expression". Can
something be both objective and expressive? Is there such
a thing as "objective expressivity"? Is this aesthetically
possible? It not only is, but always has been, and has

[6] Lent et douloureux

[7] ♩ = 76

332

produced some of the most beautiful music in history,
medieval, baroque, classical, and modern, not the least of
which is the music of Igor Stravinsky.

At the moment Stravinsky entered the musical scene,
this objective expressivity was already in the air; it seemed
not only right, but absolutely necessary. This new attitude
of personal disinvolvement was a predictable reaction
against the heavy, almost morbid subjectivism that had
informed Germanic music from Wagner to Schoenberg.
This reaction flourished centrally in Paris; Paris was the
new locus, and as early as the turn of the century—even
before, in 1898—the startlingly simple voice of Erik Satie
could already be heard [6], utterly *dégagé*, casually delivering
musical *objects*, purposefully avoiding what was then known
as "self-expression". There is a striking parallel here with
the advent of similarly antiromantic attitudes in Picasso's
art of painting, for example, an attitude that also shows up
at the same time in writing; think only of Cocteau.

In fact, it was Satie, Picasso, and Cocteau who all
collaborated in 1917, on a mad, scandalous ballet called
Parade, in which every possible anti-Wagnerian device was
exploited to the hilt. Perhaps I should say antisubjective, or
antiromantic device (because I don't want to cast aspersions
on the great Richard)—perhaps even antibourgeois. And
this is what made it seem anti-"sincere"—especially to the
bourgeoisie. To many people *Parade* seemed frankly anti-art,
and it was, in the sense of being opposed to that ponderous,
overblown, self-obsessed art of the late nineteenth century.
But in this sense, *Parade* must be said to be sincere art,
no less sincere, in its own loony way, than the ballet music
from *Aida.* Like this ragtime from *Parade* [7]. Perfectly
sincere triviality.

But this was mere whimsy compared to what anti-art *could* be. At its most extreme it was Dada-ism: it was kidding art, and kidding the public along with it. "Epater les bourgeois"—that was the slogan. The score of *Parade*, for instance, contains such musical innovations as the rattle of a typewriter, and an amplified puddle, whatever that sounds like. There is a lot of that sort of thing around these days, which makes me think that present-day dadaists and anti-artniks are probably the most conservative, even reactionary, element on the present cultural scene.

But our scene does not, alas, contain a Stravinsky in it. Stravinsky was then the genius-on-the-spot, the precisely right man at the right hour, the man who could make aesthetic objectivity work, who could produce beautiful music out of it. Even in such dynamic and "emotional" works as *Petrouchka* and *Le Sacre du Printemps* he keeps a certain distance. The composer is now not expressing himself any more, his inner conflicts or his psychic geography. He is, rather, contemplating a world to which he is affectively attached—as Stravinsky was, with deep love, to the specific world of a Russian carnival, as in *Petrouchka*, or to the dreamworld of a pagan Russia, as in *Le Sacre*— contemplating those worlds and recording musically what they expressed to him. The resulting music is then a kind of aesthetic document, unromanticized, an objective presenta-

Disc
Side 5
band 7

tion. You can feel it instantly with the first notes of *Petrouchka* [8]. This is not Stravinsky we are hearing, but an aspect of Russian life, recorded in Stravinsky's personal language. In other words, it is Stravinsky once removed— objective. And as the music goes on, with hurdy-gurdy [9], calliope, the ballerina's toy waltz, the trained dancing bear, the puppets' dance [10], and all the rest of them, object is

335

336

added to object, and the music becomes correspondingly more and more objectified. Even in the most emotional moments, such as Petrouchka's sadness [11], even here that sense of objectivity is maintained. It's so touchingly mechanical; and the more mechanically and pitilessly Stravinsky presents it, the more moving it is to us. Or take Petrouchka's despair [12]: objective as a bugle call. And the same is true of *Le Sacre du Printemps,* The Rite of Spring: that marvelous opening comes to us from a great distance [13]; Stravinsky brings it close to us, but he himself—the ego of Igor—remains at a respectful distance. That's why the Adornos of this world cannot see him as a Sincere Artist; a "sincere" composer should express his emotions directly, subjectively, like Schubert saying "Du bist die Ruh". That's how Wagner did it, and thus Schoenberg, as well. But Stravinsky? Can you imagine Stravinsky saying "Ich liebe Dich", just like that? Out of the question. He was too much the great artificer.

What were these artifices of his? What exactly was he carrying in that conjurer's bag of tricks? They were those bigger and better ambiguities I promised you last time, those constant fresheners which kept tonality alive and kept musical progress on the move.

[13] Lento ♩ = 50 tempo rubato
Bsn. solo (ad lib.)

For our purposes the clearest and most concise way to see these tonality-fresheners is via the three linguistic modes we have been following throughout these lecturers: phonology, syntax, and semantics. Obviously, the big phonological strides are to be found in the sharp increase of what used to be called dissonance. In other words, Stravinsky's kind of tonality has acquired some striking new additives— a new dissonantal freedom.

But what does this "free dissonance" mean? Is it simply an arbitrary use of wrong notes for shock value? Certainly not—although the shock element was undeniably a part of this rescue operation. Remember the old battle cry: *Epater les bourgeois!* But the origins of the new dissonance were more basic than that, and far more serious, premeditated, and organized. As briefly as I can put it, there are two ways of understanding the new dissonance. First, as an expansion of the triadic idea [14], so that a triad could now be thought of as a seventh chord, for instance, or a ninth chord, or a chord of the eleventh, or the thirteenth—all making for new *tonal* dissonances. That's why Petrouchka's puppet dance sounds the way it does [see 10]. It's just an extension of the triadic principle.

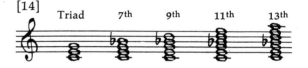

But there is a second key to this increase of dissonance, to be found in the new concept of *polytonality*—that is, employing more than one tonality at a time. It's as though tonalism could be saved, and freshened, by a sort of mitosis —by splitting any given tonality into two or more different and simultaneous ones. If there are two, we have bitonality; if more than two, then polytonality.

Musicologists are always pointing to a specific chord in *Petrouchka* as the primal statement of bitonality, because it's so clearly analyzable, and so dramatically effective.

It's this famous chord [15], which, again, is only two simple triads—pure triads, this time: C major and F-sharp major. Pure they may be, taken separately; but we know something about that C–F-sharp relationship, don't we?—something that instantly explains and clarifies the particular ambivalence of this chord—namely the tritone, that *diabolus* interval [16] on which you're all experts by now. That's the same tritone we found in Debussy's *Faun*, on which the whole piece was in fact constructed; and we also found it last time to be a crucial element in Alban Berg's Violin Concerto. And here is the tritone again, serving a wholly new purpose: to provide that unstable tritonic relationship between two absolutely pure triads, thus producing a marvelously distinct ambiguity [17]—a perfect musical evocation of the duality in the puppet Petrouchka himself, that bundle of sticks and rags concealing a passionate human heart.

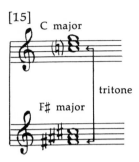

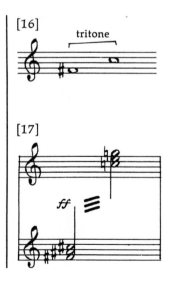

[18]

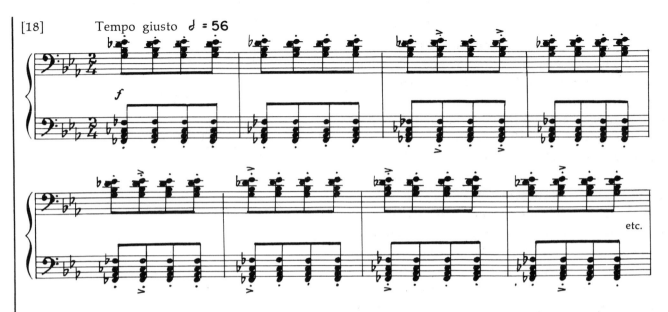

[19] E♭ dominant 7th

[19a] F♭ major (E major)

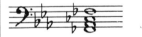

[20]

340

But bitonality does not only serve the function of producing dualisms; we must also recognize the obvious fact that the combination of two different chords automatically creates a third one, a new phonological entity. For instance, what are those famous primitive boom-booms in *The Rite of Spring* [18]? Is that just arbitrary banging, letting the fingers fall where they may? On the contrary, that repeated chord is carefully devised and structured through bitonality. Look at how clearly divisible it is into two separate but equal subsidiary chords, one [19] superimposed on the other [19a]. And each of them, mind you, is perfectly consonant in itself. The lower one spells out a pure E-major triad (or, in Stravinsky's orthography, F-flat, as you can see, which amounts to the same thing). And the upper chord is a plain old dominant seventh on E-flat. Each one by itself couldn't be more clearly tonal; but together [20]—wild dissonance. This is a wholly new way of looking at tonal harmony, a fresh Stravinskian way. He then plunges directly into a new bitonality, this time pitting notes of the same E-flat seventh chord against notes belonging to C major [21]. But there's something else going

Disc
Side 6
band 2

[21]

342

on at the same time: the cellos are plucking notes that outline the old E-major triad, so that there are now *three* simultaneous harmonic entities sounding together [22]. This is now the sound of polytonality, another fresh sound, acerbic, needling, like a cold shower—but still and always tonal.

   Of course, polytonality can (and does) become even more complicated than the mere family gathering of two or three tonal relatives. Do you know that masterpiece from World War I called "The Story of the Soldier"? *L'Histoire du Soldat*, a chamber ballet for seven instruments. If you don't know it, run, don't walk, to your nearest record shop, and grab it. It's the best cold shower of all. Here's the first phrase of the march that opens *L'Histoire du Soldat* [23]. Now that's a bit more subtle, polytonally speaking. There are two instruments playing: a cornet and a trombone. The cornet by itself is playing a tune [24] that seems to start in F major, suddenly switches to F minor, and cadences abruptly in a totally unexpected E major. So, F major, F minor, E major, all in the space of four seconds. Now let's see what the trombone is doing, down there below [25]—D-flat major, of all things, with its abrupt cadence in G major, without so much as a by-your-leave. So Stravinsky presents us, take it or leave it, with four seconds of music that encompass five different keys. Talk about bigger and better ambiguities!

[25]

[cont'd]

And look at how it goes from there [26].

Now what's going on? A new ambiguity, a new tonality-freshener; only now it's a syntactic one: rhythmic displacement. Did you notice how syntactically broken up that marching tune is, how asymmetrical it is? [26] We might say that this discontinuity of rhythm is a metrical or syntactic counterpart of the polytonality we've been talking about. We might even call it "rhythmic dissonance". My old friend Harold Shapero used to call it "Igor's Asymmetry Racket", meaning (affectionately, of course, in fact adoringly) that Stravinsky had developed asymmetrical procedure into an art of its own. Where would any Stravinsky piece be without asymmetry? Early works or late works, they all display this revivifying new art.

And now that we're in the syntactic department we can use strong Chomskian language again. What Stravinsky does is to take those transformational procedures we discovered weeks ago in Mozart's G-minor Symphony—those deep-structure deletions and the like, and make them into new surface structures of their own. His method is very much like the cubistic procedures of Braque or Picasso, who see an object through a prism, as it were, and exhibit the resulting optical fragmentation, bit by asymmetrical bit. Just so with Stravinsky: all those once-hidden deletions and permutations are now on brilliantly lit display, right up there on the surface.

[26 cont'd]

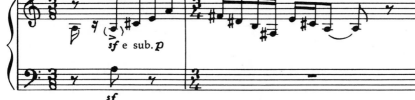

Oh, while you're in that record shop, you might as well stock up on *Les Noces,* which is maybe Stravinsky's greatest work, except for ten or twelve others. That's how it is with Stravinsky's music; it's like Schubert songs or Mozart piano concertos: whichever one you're hearing is the greatest one of all. You listen to the *Symphony of Psalms:* of course it's his greatest work—maybe the greatest of the century. But then listen to *Le Sacre*—same thing. Ah, but *Oedipus Rex;* what about *Threni?* You forgot *L'Histoire du Soldat!* They're all the greatest. And so it is with *Les Noces,* "The Wedding"—a combination choral cantata–ballet about a Russian peasant wedding which defies description. Just go listen to it.

But let me play a snatch of the opening scene, a strangely cruel and hurtful music that accompanies the ritual braiding of the young bride's hair [27]. What makes this music so barbarously cruel? The same bitonality as in the *Sacre* example [see 18, p. 340], only with the tonalities interchanged: instead of this dissonance [28], it's this one [29]. And this acid dissonance is mirrored in the *rhythmic* dissonance of the irregular meters [see 27]. Do you see how this sharply accentuated distortion of meter adds to the feeling of cruelty and pain, just as strongly as does the bitonal dissonance? It is exactly what happens in that barbaric passage of *Le Sacre,* where every accent comes at you like a body blow, always hitting when you least expect it. Left hook, right jab [see 18]. Of course, these asymmetries are not at all limited to Stravinsky's so-called "aggressive" works; they can be found just as strikingly in his gentlest, most lyrical pieces, such as *Perséphone,* or the much later *Scènes de Ballet.* Here is a simple but asymmetric passage from *Scènes de Ballet* [30]. It sounds almost like Mozart.

But there's a significant difference between the asymmetries of Mozart and Stravinsky: the difference—and what a difference!—between phrase structure and motivic structure. I know that's pretty dense language, but I mean by it a very simple thing: that Stravinsky's asymmetrical structures are mainly based on the juggling of motives, rather than what you ordinarily think of as melody. By "motives" I mean simply very brief melodic fragments, concise formations of two, three, or four notes which are then subjected to a kind of Cubistic treatment. Again in *Le Sacre du Printemps*, here's a motive we'll call "A" [31]. Here's another we'll call "B" [32]. Now look at how he juggles them [33]. Again, left to the jaw, right to the belly. But that's as nothing compared to the great Sacrificial Dance at the end of the ballet, the supreme brutality of all time. Brutal it may be, but it is fashioned with the precision of a master craftsman (artificer, remember?), fashioned out of tiny motivic cells, fragments like this [34] and this [35] and this [36]. All these cells are conjoined, embedded, permuted, expanded, and relentlessly repeated, always in different patterns, like jagged pieces of colored glass in some gigantic

[35]

[36]

kaleidoscope [37]. That's "Igor's Asymmetry Racket", in full glory.

Now, do you remember that we found these rhythmic asymmetries to be syntactic equivalents, so to speak, of phonological dissonance? In the same way, we can find a further syntactic equivalent with polytonality itself; and *this* syntactic equivalent is called polyrhythm. Another shot in the arm for tonality, another life-preserver. What are polyrhythms? Simply what they suggest: just as polytonality means more than one tonality at a time, so polyrhythms mean two or more rhythms going at the same time. For instance, if I start a tango rhythm in the left hand and superimpose a waltz on it we've got a simple polyrhythmic piece [38]. Now let's jump from that idiocy to great music: here's one fantastic page of *Sacre* which is all by itself a whole essay on polyrhythm [39]. The meter, as you can see, is 6/4, meaning six quarter-notes to a bar. But there is not a bar on this page that has anything to do with a sextuple rhythm. Every note of music on that page belongs to groupings of two, four, or eight beats; it is all conceived duply, in multiples of two. But the number six, you will say, rightly, is both duple *and* triple; six is after all two times three. So you can imagine the enormous complexity of the mathematical turmoil that results.

Let me try to explain it. There are two sets of rhythms embedded one within the other—not two rhythms, but two sets of rhythms. Let's call the first one Set A; it contains only groupings of fours and eights, superimposed on this basic meter of six. The main melody (which is not so much

[39] see pages 352-353

351

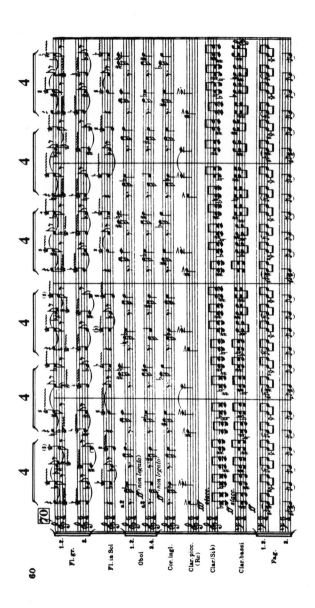

C-Fag.
*(Horns in F)
Cor. 1.2.
3.4.
5.6.
Tr. picc.(Re)
*(Trumpets)
1.2.
Tr. (Do) 3.
4.
(non legato)
sempre sf
Tr-boni
1.
2.3.
a 2
tenori
Tube (Si♭)
*(Tuba)
bassi
ff maestoso
Timp.
Gr. C.
*(Percussion)
Tamtam
Une rape Guero
etc. sim.
Viol.
1.
2.
fff sul pont. sino al segno
Viole
Celli
Bassi
70

a melody as a motive) is this scary fanfare in the tubas [40].
This is a primitive repeated motto in a regular pattern of
four beats, superimposed, remember, over a meter of *six*.
Then that tune, or whatever you want to call it, is em-
bellished by high shrieking trumpets, also following the
four-beat pattern [41]. In addition, the horns in their
highest register are screaming out a counter fanfare in eight
beats [42]. So far, so good; these elements are all rhythmical
blood-brothers, fours and eights, even though they ride over
sextuple bars.

But all that makes only one set; now let's have a go at
Set B, which contains groupings of twos and fours, not
superimposed over the meter of six, but operating *within* it,
within each separate bar of six beats. Are you still with me?
Just cast an eye on the percussion section, where all this
Set B is happening [43]. There's the timpani pounding
away in a steady cannonade of eighth notes, making,
needless to say, twelve of them per bar. And these twelve
notes are demarcated into four subgroups by a specially
violent accent on the first note of each [44]. Do you hear
how those four bangs per bar create four subgroups of three
notes each? And, mind you, those four subgroups are
contained within a six-beat bar. Thus, this counter-rhythm
of four against six constitutes a polyrhythm all by itself.
And to reinforce it, to electrify it even further, there are the
bass drum and tam-tam alternately whacking out the four
accents [45]. And just to top it off, so that you're all but

[44]

[45]

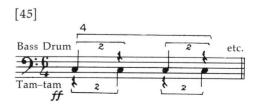

[46]

out of your skin with polyrhythmic ecstasy, there's a guiro, a kind of rasp such as you hear in Latin American dance bands, which further reinforces the four accents, but more than that, doubles them, so that there are now *eight* notes per bar [46]. So what have we got now? We have a single bar which simultaneously contains six beats, twelve beats, four beats, and eight beats. And that bar, repeated over and over, is only Set B; add to it all those superimposed fours and eights of Set A, and you've got yourself some polyrhythms.

That page is sixty years old [see 39], but it's never been topped for sophisticated handling of primitive rhythms, which is particularly striking in view of the fact that this *Rite of Spring* is a tonal piece, an old-fashioned tonal piece. People forget that too easily, in their zeal to acclaim it as revolutionary, the turning point, as crucial as Schoenberg's twelve-tone system. But it's not; it's only one of your everyday volcanic masterpieces, full of terrific tunes and marvelous harmonies and sensational rhythms and dazzling counterpoints and hair-raising orchestration and cathartic structure; it's also got the best dissonances anyone ever thought up, and the best asymmetries and polytonalities and polyrhythms and whatever else you care to name. It's also got a monumental objectivity, and a direct line to the vernacular, and a monopoly on primitivism; which of course leads us directly into the semantic department.

The primitivism which inhabits *Le Sacre* and *Les Noces* and so many other Stravinsky works is manifested not only phonologically, by the savage dissonances, and not only syntactically, by the convulsive rhythms, but also semantically, by the primitive "meanings" of the folk music which is the lifeblood of these works. This is one very obvious

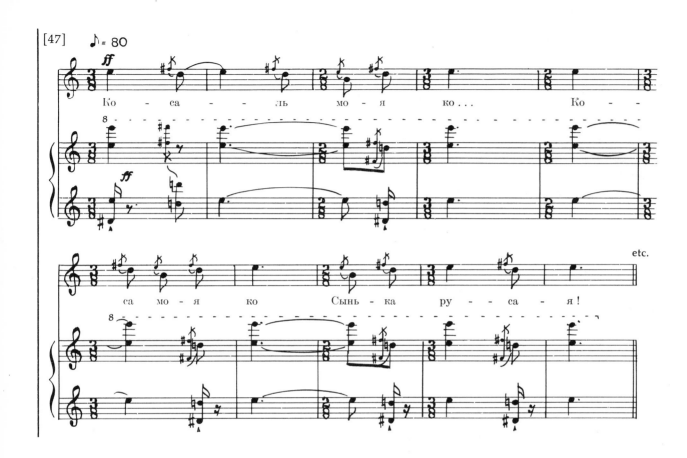

sense in which Stravinsky's music can be understood as Poetry of Earth; these pieces are deeply rooted in the earth of folklore, at times seeming to reach back even further than traditional folk music, reaching atavistically back to prehistory. There is a hypnotically primeval feeling to the opening notes of *Les Noces*, for example [47]. It sounds like ancient Chinese music, but it's even more primitive than that; it embraces not even a pentatonic scale, but only three-note and four-note constellations.

Pieces like *Les Noces* and *Le Sacre* are in themselves like attestations of monogenesis; they evoke responses in us that seem to demonstrate the identity of our human origins. Further, I suggest that this fiercely cherished bond that Stravinsky had with ancient folklore contributes largely to that special objectivity which we found to characterize all his musical expression; it is part of that "respectful distance" we were speaking of. The folk element naturally places great emphasis on the mythic—what Jung called the Collective Unconscious—which makes these early Stravinsky works seem like immense anthropological metaphors.

But the most striking semantic effects of Stravinsky's primitivism results from the utterly modern sophistication with which it is treated. There is an exciting friction here of conflicting forces: after all, here's a thoroughly twentieth century composer writing prehistoric music. It's a glorious misalliance, producing glorious offspring—a synthesis of earthy vernacular embedded in stylistic sophistication. This synthesis was to be a strong conditioning factor in all Stravinsky's music, throughout his composing life, even long after he stopped writing these so-called "Russian" works. Because it wasn't only the Russian vernacular that attracted him, but *all* vernaculars, old and new—an inter-

[cont'd]

national street language, so to speak, which ultimately included jazz, café music, and salon music, with all their attendant waltzes, polkas, foxtrots, tangos, and rags. Here was yet another department of fresheners for tonality, letting some fresh air into a stuffy post-Victorian room—a totally different air, chemically different from that other-planetary air, that "Luft von anderem Planeten" that Schoenberg was breathing at the same time.

But on Stravinsky's planet people now spoke in the vernacular; post–World War I aesthetic life could be relaxed, facile, and fun. This new aesthetic relaxation caught on like wildfire, so attractive was the sheer relief of it. It was to produce pieces like this delectable *Saudade do Brasil* by Darius Milhaud [48]; and the point to note is not only that it is bitonal, the left hand in G and the right hand in D, but that it is a Parisian speaking the Brazilian vernacular. Do you see how charming and relaxed bitonality can be?

[48 cont'd]

That's one vernacular: a Frenchman in Rio. But here's another Parisian, Francis Poulenc, talking his own lingo [49]. That's the famous little waltz from his opera *Les Mamelles de Tirésias*, and the vernacular this time is straight out of Montmartre.

Now here's an American, Aaron Copland, speaking *his* own lingo [50]. And again the point is not only that this bit of *Billy the Kid* is polyrhythmic [51], but that it is in the American language, and the cowboy vernacular to boot. Even some Germans are going to be affected by this

dose of fresh air. Here's one of them, Kurt Weill [52]. You all know where that comes from.

Disc
Side 6
band 5

But Stravinsky thought of it first, as usual. During the period of World War I he was already writing his phenomenal *L'Histoire du Soldat,* in which that unique objectivity of his showed itself in dry, witty take-offs: a cartoon of military pomp [53]; a wry tango [54]; a squeaky ragtime [55]. You can see how the transformation of these frivolous, lightweight materials, through Stravinsky's diamond-sharp intellect and sophisticated techniques, produced a music of unpredictable freshness, wit, and humor. Humor: there's another source of fresh air, another deep breath for tonality. Stravinsky had humor to spare; and he knew how to make the most of it musically. Only think of the enormous range of his humor, from *L'Histoire* through the needle-sharp wittiness of the 1923 Octet, to the Chaplinesque *boulevardier* elegance of the *Capriccio for Piano and Orchestra,* to the outright mockery of the *Circus Polka* he wrote for the balletic talents of Ringling Brothers' elephants.

But the fascinating thing for us to note about Stravinsky's wit is the way in which it results from mismatched semantic components. I suppose all humor does, in a way; jokes feed on incongruities. Those same dissonances that make *Le Sacre* barbaric can also be responsible for the "wrong note" sort of joke that tickles us so in *L'Histoire du Soldat.* It's the snark being a boojum; it's Groucho being the Prime Minister of Freedonia. Incongruous. Or, to use serious linguistic terms, it's the result of ill-matched semantic components. Chomsky gives a classic example of this: "Colorless green ideas sleep furiously". Now that sentence is phonologically perfect, syntactically impeccable, and semantically impossible. It's verbal salad, except—if you

[53] see page 366

[54] see page 366

[55] see page 367

recall—as poetry. Poetically it's perfectly acceptable, even witty or ironic, maybe even sort of beautiful—especially as twentieth century poetry. Just read the line aloud, slowly, with solemn intonation: "Colorless green ideas sleep furiously". Isn't that impressive? I could even make a prose deep structure for that line, as I did weeks ago for a line of Shakespeare; something like this: "Last night I slept badly; my usually *colorless* dreams were invaded by sort of dirty-*green ideas*, which caused me to *sleep* fitfully and to toss *furiously*."

The transformations are simple: delete all the prosy elements such as narrative sequences, and all connectives such as *and* and *which*. Condense *sleep* and *toss*, embed *fitfully* within *furiously*. The only remaining problem is that the ideas are now sleeping, instead of me. But delete the causal factor, as one does in dreams anyway, and you've got a dream image, a line of poetry born of metaphorical transformation.

What makes the whole thing possible is the basic implication of the dream; once that is implied, everything else works on that nonrealistic, hence aesthetic, level. And that is a valuable linguistic clue to our understanding not only of contemporary poetry, with all its colorless green ideas, but of contemporary music as well, Stravinsky's above all, which thrives on that very kind of incongruity and irony.

Very important, this ironic element; it becomes a concept essential to our understanding of Stravinsky, especially as his music developed stylistically from the so-called "Russian" works on. Just think of *Le Sacre*, that world-shaking, epic-making superpiece. Where could Stravinsky go from there? Don't forget, that was back in 1913, and he went on composing for another half-century. Where were the bigger and better ambiguities to come from now—those ever-refreshing gusts of bracing air that were to keep tonality alive? From his tonal colleagues, scrabbling around in an orgy of haphazard "modernism"? No, there had to be some great save, some definitive, durable preservative for tonal music, a topper to this Operation Rescue. And Stravinsky found it, in the concept we know as Neoclassicism. This was the concept that could finally impose some aesthetic order on the "modernistic" chaos. Neoclassicism: what is it, and why is it such a saving grace in our century? I wish I could assume that we all shared a single concept of what constitutes the neoclassic in art. Webster is no help; he defines neoclassic as the "revival or adaptation of the classical style, especially in literature, art or music". Well and good; but which classical style? And where revived? So many periods of cultural history have considered themselves neoclassic which we now regard as anything but. Even artists of the Renaissance thought themselves neoclassicists, both the Italian and the Elizabethan, on the grounds that they were inspired by the rediscovery of the glory that was Greece and the grandeur that was Rome. But we'd hardly call Da Vinci or Shakespeare "neoclassicists", would we? So let's accept the term in its broadest sense by identifying as "classical" any forms or styles regarded as classical by any given culture, and taking the "neo" prefix to signify the contemporaneous mechanisms by which the "classical" is adapted to that culture. In other words, "neo" equals whatever is "modern" in the language of its own time, including the current vernacular.

So it would seem that any neoclassical movement, being in the nature of a revival, implies something therapeutic, answering a need for revivification. But that's exactly the

369

need we've been finding all along—the sickness-unto-death
that has attended this century since its inception. In other
words, by the time the postwar twenties arrived, the ground
was all prepared for Stravinsky's neoclassicism, starting
with that new objectivistic reaction to the excesses of late
nineteenth century Romanticism. Even among those late
Romantics themselves there was already a flicker of interest
in the "neo": Strauss, for instance, was tuning into
Molière's world with his *Bourgeois Gentilhomme*; Reger
was writing mammoth variations on Mozart, Pfitzner an
opera on Palestrina. Even Busoni, Casella, and Respighi were
all convinced that they were somehow neoclassicists. And
the young Prokofiev had already written his elegant
"Classical Symphony." There was an all-round reawakened
interest in Bach, Handel, Haydn, and other so-called
classicists who had been all but swept away in the Romantic
undertow. And those bracing tonal fresheners were all
standing ready to help—all those exciting syntactic break-
ups and pile-ups we've been examining. Plus the chic,
sophisticated new focal point of Paris, with all its *enfants
terribles*, Apollinaire, Cocteau, Picasso, Nijinsky, and the
whole dizzy world of Diaghilev—all of this just waiting for
Igor Stravinsky to come along and tie it up into a neat
neoclassical package.

Disc
Side 6
band 6 And here it is, that exquisite, dry, neo-Bachian Octet
from 1923 [56]. It's chic, it's asymmetrical, it's just
dissonant enough—a witty linguistic transformation of
Bach into Stravinsky. But this neoclassic approach doesn't
have to be witty; it can be severely solemn, as in the Piano
Concerto, written in the same year as the Octet [57]. One
of the most curious aspects of both these pieces is that year
of 1923 in which they were written. Does 1923 ring a bell?

371

It was that year, if you recall, that Schoenberg, on his totally other side of the Great Divide, was presenting his twelve-tone concept for the first time, in that Opus 23 piano piece I played you last time. That was his version of the Big Save; and so we suddenly have a clear, eye-opening picture of these two great masters, in the same year, responding in their highly individual ways to the same crisis of the twentieth century.

I think this is again a moment to invoke literary analogy, which we've so often found useful and enlightening in the course of these lectures. In fact, it may well be that the best way to understand the neoclassic movement is through a sidelong glance at poetry. The poetic situation in the early twentieth century was remarkably similar to the musical one: there was the same feeling of surfeit with the Romantic excesses of such poets as Tennyson and Swinburne, to say nothing of the poets-laureate from Southey to Masefield. And so the ground was similarly prepared for the arrival of a poetic counterpart to Stravinsky—prepared not only by *les enfants terribles de Paris*, but by a solid international phalanx: in Russia, Mayakovsky; in Italy, Pirandello; in English, the crazy Sitwell family; and in America—*America*, think of it, the New World, which was musically so far behind the times as to be just discovering Brahms and Liszt—this same America was exploding with new poets, unfettered love-children of Whitman and Poe. Look at them: Ezra Pound, Amy Lowell, Hart Crane, Maxwell Bodenheim, e.e. cummings, dozens of them armed to the teeth with verbal "tonality-fresheners" —polyphonologies and supersyntactics.

But again, it's a "modernistic" orgy. Here's one tiny example. Do you know the little poem of William Carlos

372

Williams called "Nantucket"? It's not all that wildly modernistic, except for one thing: it doesn't have a single sentence in it, not a single independent clause.

> Flowers through the window
> lavender and yellow
>
> changed by white curtains—
> Smell of cleanliness—
>
> Sunshine of late afternoon—
> On the glass tray
>
> a glass pitcher, the tumbler
> turned down, by which
>
> a key is lying—And the
> immaculate white bed

It's the essence of Nantucket, bright and bare, like a clean, sparse painting. But the point is that this poetic transformation has been achieved by a process of deletion—the deleting of verbs. A whole poem of subjects without a predicate, a poem stock still, a framed image. Poetry for the eye, rather than for the ear. Which is why Williams was dubbed an imagist. He was also called a pointillist, an impressionist, accused also of postimpressionism, whatever that is. Do you realize how many isms we've had to contend with in our century, aesthetically alone? Not to speak of socialism or fascism, we are deluged with impressionism, expressionism, symbolism, futurism, vorticism, primitivism, fauvism, cubism, surrealism, motivicism, serialism—this proliferation of isms is clearly symptomatic of our sick century, of the many-faceted struggle to survive Mahler's apocalyptic prophecy by any or every means. Anything will

serve in this struggle, as long as it seems original, modern,
or, as they used to say, modernistic.

But a lot of it turned out to be first-class poetry. For
instance here is another great warrior against doom, the
irrepressible cummings.

my sweet old etcetera
aunt lucy during the recent

war could and what
is more did tell you just
what everybody was fighting

for,
my sister

isabel created hundreds
(and
hundreds) of socks not to
mention shirts fleaproof earwarmers

etcetera wristers etcetera, my
mother hoped that

i would die etcetera
bravely of course my father used
to become hoarse talking about how it was
a privilege and if only he
could meanwhile my

self etcetera lay quietly
in the deep mud et

cetera
(dreaming,
et
    cetera, of
Your smile
eyes knees and of your Etcetera)

This is a rather curious example of syntactic distortion, because in spite of its helter-skelter look it makes perfect grammatical sense, and it makes a deeply ironic antiwar statement based on the running gag of "etcetera". If this poem were rewritten as prose without changing a single word, it would turn out to be five excellent sentences, all syntactically valid, each perfectly set off according to the members of the poet's family: aunt, sister, mother, father, and himself. But cummings has transformed prose into poetry: by typographical metaphor; by the odd punctuation; by the apparently chaotic assortment of lines and stanza, such as ending one stanza with *et* and beginning the next with *cetera*. To say nothing of all those other "et ceteras" that make the beautiful dirty joke at the end work. All these antics are the metaphorical devices that make it a poem; and we can see that the very lack of syntactic clarity, through the mismatching of matter and manner, creates an irony which not only makes mincemeat of his entire family, but greatly strengthens the antiwar sentiment. Besides, when we read it aloud, we instantly recognize that it has become not only poetry, but modern poetry; and poetry for the ear, as well as the eye.

Why have I digressed into all this poetic analysis? I want to give you a feeling of the boiling poetic situation that was awaiting the messianic advent of neoclassicism, just as the musical situation awaited Stravinsky's neoclassicism. The ground is similarly prepared, just waiting for *its* neo-classic master, in this case, T. S. Eliot.

What was it that Eliot brought to poetry, that was so sorely needed? In short, why neoclassicism? Sorely needed, indeed; it was a security blanket for the whole literary world to clutch at in its sudden death-ridden distress. You see, we tend to view our century as so advanced, so prosperous

375

and swift in its developments, that we lose sight of its deeper, truer self-image, the image of a shy, frightened child adrift in a shaky universe, living under the constant threat of Mummy and Daddy about to divorce or die. And so we must cover up, we must hide our profound embarrassment at direct emotional expression; we can no longer say, like Schubert: Du bist die Ruh'', just like that, or like Matthew Arnold: "Ah, love, let us be true to one another!" We cannot afford that luxury; we're too scared. Now can you understand the vital necessity of <u>objective expression</u> in our time? Between the nineteenth and twentieth centuries "falls the shadow", as Eliot said. The new century must speak through a mask, a more elegant and disguising mask than any previous age has used. It is the obliquity of expression that is now semantically paramount; aesthetic perceptions are registered at a remove; they are, so to speak, heard around a corner.

see p 331

Eliot's first published poem was a love song, "The Love Song of J. Alfred Prufrock". What irony in the title alone. Where are the love lyrics? I remember Louis Untermeyer's old analysis of it, which went something like this: he sees the young Eliot writing "Let us go then, you and I, when the evening is spread out against the sky"—and suddenly stopping, embarrassed. Two rhyming tetrameters? Such old-fashioned, romantic words: "You and I", "evening", "sky"—it could be Wordsworth. But then came the inspired save: "Like a patient etherized upon a table". A real football save: it doesn't score directly, but it does prevent the opponent from scoring. And who is the opponent? Dreaded subjectivism, direct emotional expression, to be avoided at all cost. Untermeyer called this save "the triumph of the bizarre over the obvious". I thoroughly disagree; it is, if anything, the *rescuing* of the obvious by the bizarre; it is part of the great Operation Rescue, the filling in of "classical" forms and styles with unexpected modern ingredients. "Etherized". "One-night cheap hotels". "I have measured out my life with coffee spoons". "I shall wear the bottoms of my trousers rolled". A love song, indeed. It is a love song to youth, a threnody on growing old—again, the twentieth century disease. And the threnody is sung through the mask of a seamy-elegant life style. "Do I dare to eat a peach?" *Do I dare;* almost the mask is removed, but instantly replaced with another—the mask of allusion, of quoting from the past. "There will be time to ask 'Do I dare?' and 'Do I dare?' " Shades of Othello: "Put out the light, and then, put out the light." "Voices dying with a 'dying fall' ": exact quote from *Twelfth Night.* "I have heard the mermaids singing each to each": echoes of John Donne. We are now hiding behind the mask of once directly expressed emotion. That is the beginning of neoclassicism.

And with *The Waste Land* Eliot's allusiveness, with its mismatched semantics, becomes a *Ding an Sich.* "O O O O that Shakespeherian Rag." That says it all; that tells us everything. The tone is set for the neoclassic save; Ezra Pound the polyglot now interlards his Cantos with Chinese and Greek, and interlards *that* with jazzy jargon. James Joyce creates another polyglot masterpiece called *Ulysses,* which rests in the classic cradle of the *Odyssey,* but suckles on every style from Chaucer to Dickens to this morning's tabloid. And now Wystan Auden can spin his virtuosic rondeaus, villanelles, and even limericks, spicing them with drama or doggerel, as he chooses, resorting to the four-stress Anglo-Saxon line, or even to the Ciceronian oration in which he couches Herod's hip and heavy disclaimer in the *Massacre of the Innocents* (from that marvelous Christmas

Oratorio "For the Time Being"). Saved by the bell, the good old reliable classical past.

But the thing of it all is—and this is what's so extra-ordinary—the thing is that it can be so moving. Somehow that very indirectness, the very obliquity of expression, turns our hearts over inside us, when we're in the hands of such masters as Eliot, Joyce, and Auden. They speak for all of us frightened children, grasping for security in the past. Does it betoken an impoverishment of our resources, that we must have recourse to the past? On the contrary, it reaffirms our links with the past, our traditions and roots; only we disguise that relationship by coating it in our tough, cool vernacular. But it's a thin veneer; and when the underlying emotion shines through it hits us with doubled force, precisely because of our shy, frightened attempts to hide it. Again we are faced with the ultimate ambiguity. Living and partly living. Rooted and partly rooted, just as we found last time with Schoenberg; and so it is with Stravinsky, too, in his utterly different way. The one, Schoenberg, tried to control the tonal chaos of modernism through his twelve-tone method; the other, Stravinsky, through the decorum of neoclassicism, exactly like Eliot.

After this intermission we are going to hear and see—to witness really—the most awesome product of Stravinsky's neoclassicism, *Oedipus Rex*. I will of course try to prepare you for listening to it in my customary way at the piano. But for the moment, let me give you an epigraph for this work, something to ponder during the interval. Again, this is Eliot, the mature Eliot of the *Quartets*, speaking for himself, for Stravinsky, for all creative artists of our apocalyptic century:

So here I am, in the middle way . . .
Trying to learn to use words, and every attempt
Is a wholly new start, and a different kind of failure
Because one has only learnt to get the better of words
For the thing one no longer has to say, or the way in
    which
One is no longer disposed to say it. And so each venture
Is a new beginning, a raid on the inarticulate
. . . And what there is to conquer
By strength and submission, has already been
    discovered
Once or twice, or several times, by men whom one
    cannot hope
To emulate—but there is no competition . . .
For us, there is only the trying. The rest is not our
    business.

II

"One has only learnt to get the better of words/For the thing one no longer has to say, or the way in which/One is no longer disposed to say it." Thus spake T. S. Eliot. Now rewrite that as: "One has only learnt to get the better of *notes* for the thing one no longer has to say . . ." and you have Stravinsky speaking. He is no longer *disposed* to say "I love you", straight out from the heart, or, for that matter, "I hate you", "I miss you", or even "I defy you". Yet it's all in his music, including some of the strongest emotional statements ever made in music: pride, submission, tenderness, the fear of death and the love of God. How is this possible, especially in his neoclassic music, which is the extreme case, the very model of that objectivity, that obliquity, that mask we have come to know so well? This is the great aesthetic question of our time, the one question that must be answered before we can understand the real significance of *Oedipus Rex*, of Stravinsky in general, of his enormous influence on twentieth century music, and the very condition and future of music itself.

The question can be stated more briefly, though over-simplified: is great art still possible in our century of death? It's a staggering question, and in trying to answer it we can be led into endless discussions of the most abstruse kind. But we have no time for philosophical maundering; and so I propose to cut through the forests of heavy discourse by a direct visual approach. Do you recall those parallel ladder charts we used, long lectures ago [58] to help us discover how music and language ascend from their basic elements to deep structures, which then evolve into surface structures? You will recall that these ladders of ascent were not isomorphic, that at a certain point the one-to-one correspondence failed. That was at the point of surface structure in language, or the prose sentence, which is not equatable with the corresponding point in music, where, as you can see, we are still in deep structure. Language therefore has to take a further step, a metaphorical leap, into the super–surface structure of poetry. It is only then that the two aesthetic surfaces match, and we have finally achieved a level on which the words of Shakespeare and the notes of Mozart can be seen as analogous.

Now I propose to extend this hypothesis by taking yet another leap, on both sides of the chart at once. If we take the two top levels as our starting point [58a], the two aesthetic surfaces of language and music, and urge our minds still further upward (and we need imagination to do this), we find ourselves on an even higher metaphorical plane, perhaps the highest there is, on which we can almost

[58]

LANGUAGE	MUSIC
D. SUPER-SURFACE STRUCTURE (Poetry)	D. SURFACE-STRUCTURE (Music)
↑	↑
C. SURFACE STRUCTURE (Prose)	C. DEEP STRUCTURE ("Prose")
↑	↑
B. Underlying strings (DEEP STRUCTURE)	B. Underlying strings
↑	↑
A. Chosen elements	A. Chosen elements

[58a]

LANGUAGE	MUSIC
D. SUPER-SURFACE STRUCTURE (Poetry)	D. SURFACE-STRUCTURE (Music)

touch the essential being of both poetry and music [59]. We are now beyond surface analysis, or even super–surface analysis, beyond phonology, beyond syntax; we are into new areas of abstract semantics. It is on this plane of thought, a transcendental plane if you will, that the concepts of musical thought and verbal thought become comparable, where musical and nonmusical ideas can coincide. And it is because this level exists that I was able to talk to you last time of Mahler's Ninth Symphony in the way I did; that is what I meant by a "different level of discourse". But this level exists only in the case of such art as Mahler's, art which has the special power, the inner creative energy, to attain this philosophical level.

Now Mahler's music, and in fact all the music we've heard and discussed throughout these lectures, from Mozart and Beethoven to Ives and Ravel, whether intrinsically or extrinsically metaphorical, whether purely symphonic or programmatic—all of it has been only music. That is, we have not dealt with music which sets a verbal text, neither with a song nor an opera. Thus the semantic elements we have examined, however extramusical they may have been (as in Berlioz' *Romeo and Juliet* for example), were always confined to that right-hand side of the chart, on the level of musical surface structure. Now for the first time, as we approach *Oedipus Rex*, with music *and* words, we are facing semantic elements from the left-hand side, and they will not only be comparable with their companions of the right, but must now merge with them.

This union is possible only because we have reached this supra-level of abstract semantics, where concepts do coincide; and the expressive success of that union is obviously going to depend on the well-matched compatibility of the semantic components coming together from both the

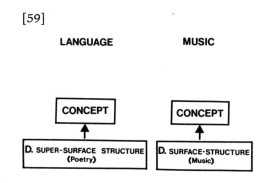

[59]

left and the right. In other words, a composer setting words to music seeks those notes which he considers most condign to the semantic values of the words he is setting. These well-matched components, verbal and musical, can be found happily married throughout the history of music, but particularly in the Romantic music of the nineteenth century, when as we found in an earlier lecture, the great wedding of words and music took place. A Schubert song like "Du bist die Ruh" is a perfect example [60]: the semantic components of Schubert's sublime melody-cum-harmony express all the tenderness and serenity of love-in-fulfillment, exactly as do the words of Rückert:

Du bist die Ruh
der Friede mild
die Sehnsucht du
und was sie
stillt.

And these identical ideas, musical and verbal (not the words and notes, mind you, but the ideas that underlie them) can be shown to combine in perfect consummation, and might be visualized thus [61].

It is here that the essences of Schubert's song exist as pure, abstract Being, to use a Platonic term: the pure idea of love, stillness, longing, and fulfillment. Notice that this meeting place of the two supra-levels is represented by a circle. By that perfect 0 (I don't mean to get into quasi-mystical diagramming, but I am constrained to if I want to be clear)—by that 0 I mean to suggest a unity, which is also an infinity, a realm within which all our responses to art can converge. It is the meeting place of our innate and our conditioned responses on the highest plane, both in terms of

[61]

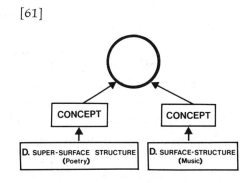

383

thought and of emotion; so that our circle is also the realm of pure *affect*, by which I mean love in conjunction with its opposite, death. All other affective responses are derived from this single antithesis; and I suppose that was the supreme metaphor that Wagner was seeking in Isolde's *Liebestod:* love-death, the ultimate synthesis of these two primal forces.

But what has all this to do with Stravinsky? Stick with it another minute and you'll see. Wagner tried to create his metaphor, and succeeded, by introducing into that supreme circle particular semantic components from his poetry and his music, components that matched perfectly. The love-death idea in Isolde's words correspond almost magically with the equivalent idea in the music. When she says "Ertrinken, versinken", she does literally seem to be drowning, her voice is submerged in the sea of orchestral texture that surges around her. When she sings the word "Wellen" you *hear* waves; when she is pouring out a progression of sexual verbs like "schwellen" and "schlürfen" and "wogenden", you experience them musically, in the orgasmic pulsings of the orchestra.

But enough. We now know what we mean by well-matched components, and what can result when they unite. But what happens when *ill*-matched components meet in that circle [62]? What happens is Igor Stravinsky. Stravinsky with all his musical incongruities: the modern with the primitive; tonality with wrong notes in it; one chord fighting another, rhythm against rhythm; the contradictions of asymmetry, of street vernacular dressed up in white tie and tails; classic forms filled with contemporary stylism, and classic styles in contemporary forms—name a mismating: Stravinsky's written it. His works are an encyclopedia of

[62]

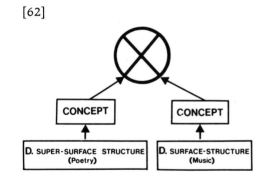

misalliances. And what do these mismatched components produce? Indirection, obliquity, the indispensable mask of our century—the objectified emotional statement delivered at a distance, from around the corner, and perceived, so to speak, second-hand. Second-hand? Stravinsky, that consummate original? Yes, second-hand; because the personal statement is made via quotes from the past, by alluding to the classics, by a limitless new eclecticism.

This is the essence of Stravinsky's neoclassicism: he is now the great eclectic, the Thieving Magpie, *La Gazza Ladra*, unashamedly borrowing and stealing from every musical museum. And this quasi-plagiaristic principle supported his compositional style over three long decades, in one way or another. It can be as overt as in *Pulcinella*, which is all based on actual pieces by Pergolesi, transformed by Stravinsky's personal modernisms. Or in *Le Baiser de la Fée*, where the same machinations are wrought upon Tchaikovsky's music. And in between come all those neo-classical works from the Octet of 1923 to *The Rake's Progress* in 1951, which may not boast direct quotes, but have equally strong stylistic references to Bach, Handel, Mozart, and Beethoven. Think of Stravinsky's two sym-phonies, the violin and piano concertos, all those Balanchine ballets: there's some composer from the past lurking in every page, leering at us through the dissonance of Stravinsky's own twentieth century language.

What's going on here, some kind of joke? Exactly: *some kind* of joke. Joke, imagine, right up there in our supreme magic circle, where those mismatched components are busily copulating. Remember: what's funny is what's incongruous; remember Groucho. And what's funny can bite deep: remember e. e. cummings. That was a *serious*

[63]

[64]   Tempo ♩=92

antiwar poem. There are all kinds of jokes: the humor continuum ranges all the way from slapstick burlesque through sardonic wit, through elegant satire, to black comedy and chilling dramatic irony. And it's all to be found in Stravinsky. In the most serious sense, humor, in one form or another, is the lifeblood of his neoclassicism. And I'm not talking about Elephant Polkas; I'm talking about his greatest works. Look: here is a joke and I assure you it's nothing to laugh at [63]. This is how Stravinsky begins his *Symphony of Psalms*, one of the most sublimely moving works ever written. In this opening movement he is setting Psalm No. 101, in Latin: *Exaudi orationem meam, Domine* —hear my prayer, O Lord, give ear to my supplication. Can you imagine how a Romantic composer might have set those words? Humble, supplicatory, introspective. Hushed, awestruck. Well-matched components. But not Stravinsky. He attacks: a brusque, startling pistol-shot of a chord, followed by some kind of Bachian finger exercise [64]. How mismatched can you get? It's the very antithesis of the Schubert-Wagner approach. It's loud, extrovert, command-ing. And that's incongruous, a sublime dramatic joke. It's a prayer with teeth in it, a prayer made of steel; it violates our expectations, shatters us with its irony. And that's precisely why we're so moved by it. It's exactly what we find happening in Eliot: in *The Waste Land,* for instance, there is a similar mighty irony when he invokes the image of Shakespeare's mad Ophelia, quoting her last words before she goes to drown. But he does it this way:

> Goonight Bill. Goonight Lou. Goonight May.
> Goonight. Ta ta. Goonight. Goonight.

and *only then:*

> Good night, ladies, good night, sweet ladies, good
> night, good night.

Chilling. Shattering. Neoclassic. And thus Stravinsky [65].
Yes, there is that imploring Phrygian incantation in the
vocal part; but underneath the orchestral accompaniment
is steel and chromium. It's a trick, a black joke.

In this sense, we've got to admit that our old friend
Adorno seems to have a point: Stravinsky is a trickster. It
was Schoenberg who was supposedly continuing the great
subjective tradition of the Romantics in the only way he
knew how—by his twelve-tone system; and it was therefore
Schoenberg who was the real radical, the true progressive. It
was Schoenberg who was *sincere,* fighting the fashionable
trends of the twentieth century; sincerity is not supposed to
be a twentieth century "thing". It's not chic. And for
Adorno, that's just what Stravinsky was—chic. He was a
facile virtuoso, a clever vaudevillian, a talented ballet-
composer parading as a symphonist, a thieving magpie,
and—the most unforgivable sin—he didn't restrict his
thieving; he was an eclectic. He wrote music about other
music, "music about music"; therefore, says Adorno bitterly,
music *against* music.

Stravinsky's own aesthetic pronouncements don't help
much to defend his case. With that intellect of his, one of
the sharpest and most agile of our time, Stravinsky kept
painting himself into a corner of aesthetic purism. In his
autobiography he insisted that music could express nothing
at all. I quote: "Music is essentially powerless to express
anything at all, whether a feeling, an attitude of mind, a

psychological mood, a phenomenon of nature . . . *Expression* has never been an inherent property of music." By this token, he would have to mean that all expressive verbal instructions—by Beethoven, for example—were useless and supererogatory, or at the very least redundant. If Beethoven marks the slow movement of his *Hammerklavier* Sonata "Adagio sostenuto; appassionato e con molto sentimento" (which of course he did), he is simply committing a four-way tautology. All that slowness and sustainedness and passionateness and sentiment should be contained in the notes themselves, and self-evident through them, needing only a mere metronome mark to indicate the tempo and a minimal number of dynamic indications for loudness and softness. But this clearly does not jibe with Beethoven's volition; nor, ironically enough, does it tally with Stravinsky's own expressive volition. Just open the score of that great neoclassic *Symphony of Psalms,* and what do you find? Right in the middle of a severe Bach-like fugue stand the words *dolce, tranquillo, espressivo. Espressivo!* Good Lord, it's enough to make you give up aesthetics for good— at least Stravinsky's aesthetics. Of course he was forced by the evidence of his own music to hedge over and over again on that famous statement I quoted, to modify it, rephrase it. But there is still this further contradiction: if his musical philosophy was so puristic, why was he so attracted by the theater, so devoted to ballet, to the setting of words? All extra-musical elements. If music can't express anything . . . but why go on? The crucial point of all this is that both Stravinsky and his Adornish detractors refused to acknowledge the power of that X-factor up there in the magic circle —the extraordinary power of dramatic irony that could be generated by those egregiously ill-matched components.

Stravinsky tried to deny it, but his music insistently confirms it. As for Adorno, he simply failed to perceive the X-factor at all, seeing it only as cleverness, showbiz, theatrical know-how (which was also true, in a way)—but not seeing the real meaning, which is the amazing proximity of comedy to tragedy in our time. He completely missed the joke, the big existentialist joke which is at the center of most major twentieth century works of art—namely, the sense of the absurd.

And now we are finally ready to understand *Oedipus Rex*. I had originally planned to present it to you in all its awesome grandeur, as a refutation of Adorno's attack. (Bear in mind that of all Stravinsky's music he most disliked the neoclassic pieces; and of all those he particularly loathed the *Symphony of Psalms* and *Oedipus Rex*—what taste!— on the grounds that they're so big (*Oedipus* being fifty-five minutes long), and that they're such pretentious bags of tricks, the *Psalms* posing as an ecstatic religious utterance, and *Oedipus* as monumental Greek tragedy.) My defense of *Oedipus* was to be based on frankly showing the tricks for what they are, exposing them as eclectic incongruities coexisting up there in the abstract sphere—misalliances that create ever more intense dramatic irony, ultimately producing a work of Aristotelian pity and terror by wholly original means.

For example, the initial misalliance of setting the Sophocles-Cocteau text in Latin, of all things (not even in Greek, another dead language: that would be too close to the subject) was deliberately done to create a distance, an objectivity which results from making the text all but unintelligible. You can't get more objectivistic than that—to write a whole musical drama, a combination opera-oratorio

lasting fifty-five minutes, in which the audience can't understand a single word.

Then, I was going to point out numerous quotes and allusions to specifically "classical" or "preclassical" composers—like these overwhelming opening bars, where the chorus is imploring Oedipus to deliver Thebes from the plague [66]. Those four notes [67] are like the head of a Bach fugue subject, but rendered stark and uncompromising (much more than they would be in Bach) by the "modern" dissonances used against it. And when Oedipus responds to

[67]

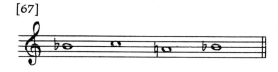

his people, "children, I will deliver you", is this not the
melismatic sound of seventeenth century opera, or even the
later *opera seria* [68]? It could be Rameau, or maybe Gluck.
And then Mozart appears. What could be more Mozartian
than the beginning of Creon's aria [69]? Pure classicism—
not even a "wrong note" in it—which then gets the "neo"
treatment, a slight case of wrong notes, when he sings: [70].

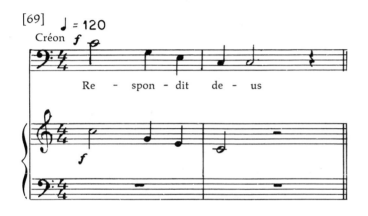

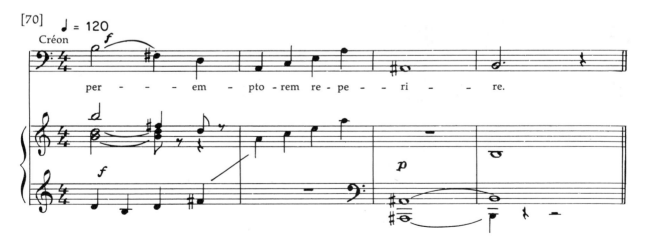

And what of Jocasta's great aria, beginning with this
Handelian Recitativo [71]? And later, when she is railing
against oracles, whose rhythms are those in the accompaniment [72]? Whose rhythms? Beethoven's, of course.

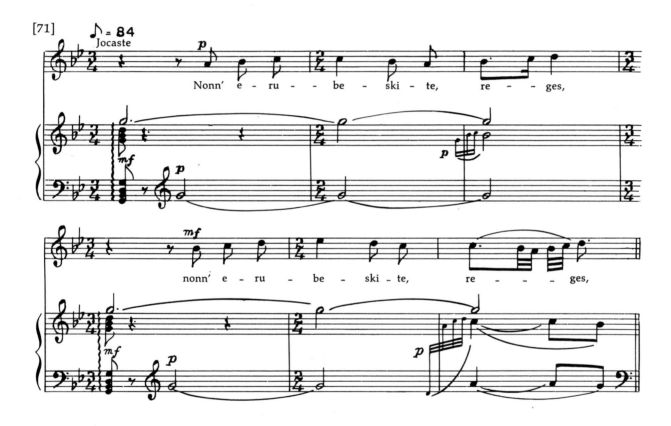

It's that Fifth Symphony pulse (∪∪∪ − /∪∪∪ −) over and over again, transformed by modern metaphor [73].

But the allusions are by no means limited to the classical composers. They can be more eclectic still. Remember that in this neoclassic world anything can pass for "classical" that the given culture chooses to regard as such. The main melody of Jocasta's aria, for instance, is rather like a hoochy-coochy dance, and might well have been one of Carmen's sexier moments [74]. And this is a queen, mind you, addressing the royal family. What a misalliance is

there. And what of the chorus hailing the queen's entrance
[75]? Shades of Boris Godunov.

But this eclecticism knows no bounds; the allusive
references can land anywhere, even outside the areas of
symphony and opera. Consider this later aria of Oedipus',
where he is singing of his determination to find out the
awful truth of his origins [76]. Is that a march? Or a

Russian Cossack dance? And what of the old shepherd who
brings Oedipus the awful truth [77]? Now that's a genuine
Greek dance—not the Greek of Sophocles' time, but the
Bouzouki variety that you can hear in any Greek restaurant
[78]. And what about that hair-raising chorus that tells
the grim news of Jocasta's suicide and of Oedipus' gouging
out his eyes? It's not exactly what you'd expect at this grisly
moment; it's more like a football song [79].

[79]

All this I had planned to tell you, and more. In fact, I even went ahead and made a deep structure for that chorus I just played, a deep structure that captures its hidden quality of a fight-song on the football field. I even went to the trouble of having the Harvard Glee Club record it; so I might as well let you hear it, even though it's part of everything I'm *not* telling you. You've just heard a bit of Stravinsky's version; in other words, the surface structure. Now here's my extrapolated deep structure, what we might call a "prose version". And I promise you: this is the last deep structure I'll ever extrapolate [80]. *Fight!* You think that's

[cont'd]

funny? I assure you, you won't think so when you hear
Stravinsky's finished product. It is a joke, true enough, but
a black, ironic one, bitterly and violently ironic.

So all this is what I was going to tell you, but won't.
Because last week I opened Stravinsky's score again, after a
year away from it; and when I reopened that monumental
score, hands trembling with reverence and awe, I experienced
that phenomenon of restudying a new vision—the same
phenomenon that occurred last time with the Mahler Ninth.
It was suddenly a new work to me; and as I played those
opening bars at the piano [See 66, p. 392], something
about those four notes [81] began to chafe at the back of
my mind—not a Bach fugue subject, but something from
another operatic work, another tragic situation, totally
different yet somehow similar. I began to rack my brain.
What was it—Gluck, Purcell, Weber, Wagner? What are
those four notes, suggesting a different but related dramatic
complex: pity and power, over and over again [82]? Power

[82] cont'd

and pity. And then, intensifying the pity of it all, those appoggiaturas in Oedipus' reply to his subjects: remember?
[83] Now what are all those appoggiaturas, those leaning notes, doing there in that neoclassic music, so romantic, so pathetic? And then I found those same appoggiaturas, strings of them, tension–resolution, tension–resolution, over and over again, in all the ensuing music sung by Oedipus. As in his next aria, where he sings: [84]. And again, later on in the same aria: [85]. Such pathos, such a broad, romantic line. And then, in his greatest aria, *Invidia fortunam odit* (Envy hates good fortune), Oedipus is pleading with the old prophet Tiresias for sympathy and support: You crowned me king, he says; I saved you all from the Sphinx. Who should have solved the riddle? You, the famous priest and prophet. But it was *I* who solved it, and *you* made me king. And he sings to the old man: [86]. Those pathetic

appoggiaturas again, so romantic as to be almost sentimental. Then finally, at the climax, he shouts: "It's a plot!"
"Creon wants my kingdom!" [87] . . .

. . . and suddenly I had the answer. That diminished seventh
chord [88]—remember? That favorite ambiguous tool of
suspense and despair in every romantic opera [89]? What
is it? Of course; *Aida*! It's Amneris pleading with the priests
who are judging Radames; same diminished seventh chords,
same notes, same key, the same appoggiaturas. So that's it!
And suddenly I knew why I had started this whole lecture
by playing the ballet music from *Aida*, thinking at the time
it was just an amusing way to introduce the question of
sincerity. Amazing, the power of the unconscious, so
accurate in its metaphors, so on-the-nose. But of course;
sincerity is the whole point of this Oedipus-Aida misalliance. Why Verdi of all people, who was so unfashionable at
the time Oedipus was written, someone for musical
intellectuals of the mid-twenties to sneer at; and *Aida,* of all
things, that cheap, low, sentimental melodrama, the
splashiest and flashiest of all the Verdi operas—*why?*
Then came the revelation: I remembered where those
four opening notes of Oedipus came from [90]. (I swear to
you, I had spent a week looking for them.) And the whole
metaphor of pity and power came clear: the pitiful Thebans
supplicating before their powerful king, imploring deliverance from the plague. Pity and power: an Ethiopian slave
girl at the feet of her mistress, Princess of Egypt; at the feet
of Amneris, at the shrine of power, imploring pity. Do you
remember the scene? Amneris has just wormed out of Aida
her dread secret: The slave girl loves Radames, as does

[90]

Amneris herself [91]. "Yes, you love him," says the Princess
(*Si, tu l'ami*). "But I love him too, do you understand? I am
your rival, I, daughter of the Pharaohs." And here comes
our indispensable diminished seventh chord, as Aida, who
has dared to reply "Then so be it; I am *your* rival", suddenly
realizes what she has dared to say, and screams [92]. *Pieta!*

Pity! And here come the great four notes [93]: have pity
on my grief; it's true I love him; but you are fortunate, you
are powerful; I have only this love to live for. *Tu sei felice.*

mor   Tu sei fe - li - ce tu sei pos -

sen - - te io —— vi - vo so - lo — per que - sto a - mor!

Pity and power of a wholly other kind, personal and inti-
mate, to be transformed by the metaphorical operations of
Stravinsky's genius into a huge, public, monumental plea
for pity [94].

But why this particular misalliance? Was Stravinsky
having a secret romance with Verdi's music in those
supersophisticated mid-twenties? It seems he was, or maybe
he just happened to catch a performance of *Aida* at the
Opéra in Paris. It doesn't matter. What does matter is that
somewhere deep in his inner musical consciousness the basic
metaphor contained in *Aida* registered, stuck, and connected
with the corresponding deep metaphor in *Oedipus Rex*.
Again, it's the amazing power of the unconscious at work,
not only connecting the two metaphors but combining them
into a single new metaphor at the abstract level of pity-and-
power, a single manifestation of that primal antithesis, love
and death.

How can we possibly describe what has happened?
Our words are helpless before such mysteries: they are
only a "raid on the inarticulate", as Eliot said. We can only
try to imagine this vastly complex interaction of metaphors,
and try to verbalize it, as taking place simultaneously
on the deepest level of the unconscious and on the highest
level of abstract idea. My words are poor, my diagrams
even poorer, but this one thing I know intuitively to be
true, and I will put my hand in the fire for it: that whatever
that creative mystery is, those mystical matchings and
mismatchings in that upper circle, it cannot exist, or come
to be, unless it is inextricably rooted in the rich earth
of our innate response, in those deep, unconscious regions
where the universals of tonality and language reside. The
Poetry of Earth is ceasing never.

417

It would now be a simple matter to trace this unlikely
marriage of Oedipus and Aida, page by page, diminished
seventh by appoggiatura. But I think we have gone beyond
that point. It is time to hear the Stravinsky work now; and
whatever few words of summary I have left I will save for
after the music. Only one last point: I don't mean for you
to listen to *Oedipus Rex* with *Aida* in mind; that would
utterly spoil the experience for you. What I do want is for
you to hear it in terms of its universality, that communality
of abstract idea, which permits the union of such unlikely
bedfellows as Stravinsky and Verdi, of classical tragedy and
Romantic melodrama, of direct, subjective expression and
neoclassic objectivity. And I leave it to you to decide
whether this work is a "bag of tricks" or one of the enduring
masterpieces of all time.

(*At this point Stravinsky's* Oedipus Rex *is played in its
entirety.*)

III

Va-le-di-co. What better cue could there be for a
valediction? Indeed, I have finally come to the valedictory
moment. And I don't like it; I am beset with problems and
conflicts. There is still so much to be said, and no time for
saying it. There are so many of those "underlying strings",
if the linguists will pardon me, waiting to be tied up; so
many cans of worms have been opened, and a lot of those
slippery little beasts are still wriggling around. There is
much further argumentation and clarification to be accomplished, enough for at least six more lectures. Maybe there'll
be six more, someday, or sixty more; perhaps you'll give
them. I hope so. But my main problem now is that there are

418

still summaries to be made, conclusions to be drawn, the present musical moment to be generalized upon, the future to be guessed at. All of this is clearly impossible to achieve in the five minutes I have allotted myself for this Farewell Address. So I must take a shortcut.

I am not ordinarily given to quoting myself, but I should like to make an exception now, for shortcut purposes. Back in 1966, not very long ago, really, I was writing an introduction to a book of mine, *The Infinite Variety of Music*, which was about to be published. That year was for me a low point in the musical course of our century—certainly the lowest I have ever experienced. Stravinsky had all but died creatively, around that summer, having converted a decade earlier to the serial faith. That conversion had begun, oddly enough, with Schoenberg's death in 1951, and had already precipitated a crisis, in the mid-fifties—a second twentieth century crisis; it was like the defection of a general to the enemy camp, taking all his faithful regiments with him. During that decade he produced some marvelous serial pieces, particularly *Threni* and the *Movements for Piano and Orchestra*; but the same cannot be said for his troops, who followed him blindly, like the children of Hamelin following their Pied Piper, right into the Schoenbergian sea. It took a genius of Stravinsky's multiplicity and authenticity to survive the conversion while maintaining his personal voice. For most of the others the conversion was a more negative one: the bald rejection of tonality and the embracing of the serial method. There were now more composers than ever, and more music was forthcoming, mainly because the new serial controls made it almost easy to write a good, presentable piece. All you had to do was go to school and learn how. But the frightened overcommit-

ment of the new converts caused this spate of new music
to emerge for the most part sterile and dry; there was so
much ordered precomposition involved, amounting almost
to a mathematical takeover. For some composers the serial
techniques succeeded in keeping their music alive (and
music in general, as a result) by enriching their vocabularies;
others were not so successful, and their vocabularies were
simply impoverished; still others stopped composing
altogether.

It was at this point that I wrote the above-mentioned
preface, from which I would like to read you one paragraph:

> I am a fanatic music lover. I can't live one day
> without hearing music, playing it, studying it, or
> thinking about it. And all this is quite apart from my
> professional role as musician; I am a fan, a committed
> member of the musical public. And in this role (which
> I presume is not too different from yours) in this role of
> simple music lover, I confess, freely though unhappily,
> that at this moment, as of this writing, God forgive
> me, I have far more pleasure in following the musical
> adventures of Simon and Garfunkel or of The
> Association singing "Along Comes Mary" than I have
> in most of what is being written now by the whole
> community of "avant-garde" composers. This may not
> be true a year from now, or even by the time these
> words appear in print; but right now, on the 21st of
> June, 1966, that is how I feel. Pop music seems to be
> the only area where there is to be found unabashed
> vitality, the fun of invention, the feeling of fresh air.
> Everything else suddenly seems old-fashioned: elec-
> tronic music, serialism, chance music—they have

already acquired the musty odor of academicism. Even jazz seems to have ground to a painful halt. And tonal music lies in abeyance, dormant.

What interests me about that paragraph is not what's true about it, but what isn't. In the few years that have elapsed since I wrote it, everything has changed. First of all, pop music is what I listen to least these days. What seemed fresh and vital then is now jejune and commercially grotesque. Second: it is jazz that is now alive and exciting, that same jazz that was then at a dead end. Third: those avant-garde techniques that seemed already dated have somehow outgrown their academicism; in some miraculous way, they are again living, viable techniques. How did this come to be? Because of the fourth and most important change: that tonal music is no longer dormant; it has been admitted into the avant-garde world, sneakily at first, and then with radical new approaches through which composers have found a way to share again in the fruits of earth.

But how did this come to be? First of all, the disappearance of Stravinsky from the creative scene, the loss of the Colossal Dad, as Auden said, made a whole new crisis, yet a third crisis of the twentieth century. Now both Schoenberg and Stravinsky were gone; where was a young composer to turn for guidance and inspiration? To himself, of course; composers were now suddenly thrown back on their own resources. And what they found there, naturally, was their innate and long-denied sense of tonality. And they could now be re-nourished by it. So the crisis turns out after all to be a solution, ironically enough, just as the earlier crisis of the mid-fifties can now be seen in retrospect to have been an occasion for synthesis, the merging of the two previously hostile camps. Thus, what was hitherto seen as the Great Split, as shown by Ives' *Unanswered Question,* can now be seen as a fusion of extraordinary force.

But this retrospective look at serialism changes Ives' question radically. Is it possible that far-off history may look back at the Schoenberg Method (which we must now also call the Stravinsky Method) as an evolutionary mutation, rather than a revolutionary one? Can it be that it simply occurred too rapidly for us to recognize it as a transformational phenomenon? If this is true, then music has undergone a qualitative change, a change in kind, a sea change. This is the first time in the entire history of music that such a drastic deviation has occurred, where the very nature of music has changed. But, as Ives reminded us so dramatically, tonality persists beyond the changes, imperturbable and immortal. And besides, as we have seen again and again, those magic twelve notes of dodecaphonic music are the same twelve notes nature gave us in the first place.

So all in all, things don't look so bad. We are in a position where one style can feed the other, where one technique enriches the other, thus enriching all of music. We have reached that supra-level of abstract musical semantics, of pure Idea, where those apparently mismatched components can unite—tonal, nontonal, electronic, serial, aleatory—all united in a magnificent new eclecticism. But this eclectic union can take place only if all the elements are combined with and embedded in the tonal universal—that is, conceived against a contextual background of tonality.

It's as though in the period since Schoenberg's death we have all had a vacation from tonality, and a somewhat shorter vacation from serialism since Stravinsky stopped composing. In any case, we are in a refreshed state: we have returned from these vacations fit, relaxed, and with a better perspective, which enables us to make the new synthesis, the new eclecticism. The bitterness is over; it is a time of reconciliation. All this is discernible in the music of these most recent years: the big avant-garde news of the moment is Steve Reich who can write for twenty minutes in D major. Stockhausen in his *Stimmung* spends seventy minutes in a B-flat world. There is tonality everywhere in the sonic environment of Berio; and I'm told that George Rochberg's most recent quartet is all tonal. Whereas Benjamin Britten and Shostakovich, who have always been tonal composers, have gone probing into serial techniques which they are absorbing into their own personal styles. And of course Gunther Schuller, who throughout his composing career has always been a pioneer of synthesis, is in fact the leader of what is known as the "third stream", which synthesizes the worlds of jazz and the concert hall. He is the incarnation of this new conciliatory spirit.

There is a general bubbling and rejoicing and brotherliness among composers that would have been unthinkable ten years ago. It's like the beginning of a new period of fresh air and fun, such as we discerned earlier in the century —a neo-neoclassicism, so to speak. In fact, why not, since these recent pieces are so often full of quotes and allusions? Only think of Berio's *Sinfonia*, the scherzo of which is literally the scherzo of a Mahler symphony overlaid with quotes from all of Berio's favorite symphonic pieces, including his own. And there is a new game-playing spirit, for example in recent pieces of Lukas Foss. All this "neo-neo" is still very much in the self-defensive spirit of the twentieth century, but it seems to be characterized by an ebullient renewed will to survive the apocalyptic, and to

make musical progress in friendly competition, or even—
as Stockhausen would have it—in communal effort. And I
believe all this has been made possible by the rediscovery
and the reacceptance of tonality, that universal earth out of
which such diversity can spring. And I believe that no
matter how serial, or stochastic, or otherwise intellectualized
music may be, it can always qualify as poetry as long as it is
rooted in earth.

I also believe, along with Keats, that the Poetry of Earth is
    never dead, as long as Spring succeeds Winter, and man
    is there to perceive it.

I believe that from that Earth emerges a musical poetry,
    which is by the nature of its sources tonal.

I believe that these sources cause to exist a phonology of
    music, which evolves from the universal known as the
    harmonic series.

And that there is an equally universal musical syntax, which
    can be codified and structured in terms of symmetry and
    repetition.

And that by metaphorical operation there can be devised
    particular musical languages that have surface structures
    noticeably remote from their basic origins, but which can
    be strikingly expressive as long as they retain their roots
    in earth.

I believe that our deepest affective responses to these
    particular languages are innate ones, but do not preclude
    additional responses which are conditioned or learned.

And that all particular languages bear on one another, and
    combine into always new idioms, perceptible to human
    beings.

And that ultimately these idioms can all merge into a speech
    universal enough to be accessible to all mankind.

And that the expressive distinctions among these idioms
depend ultimately on the dignity and passion of the
individual creative voice.
And finally, I believe that because all these things are true,
Ives' Unanswered Question has an answer. I'm
no longer quite sure what the question is, but I do know
that the answer is *Yes*.

The photographs on pages 1, 24, 38, 51, 94, 117, 132, 134, 142, 191, 261, and 323 are by Douglas M. Bruce; those on pages 66, 78, 146, 188, 264, and 320 are by Rick Stafford; those on pages 155 and 254 are by Milton Feinberg; the photograph on page 288 is by Grazyna Bergman; the photograph on page 32 is by Paul de Hueck.

ACKNOWLEDGMENTS

Acknowledgment is made for permission to reproduce portions of the following works.

Alban Berg: *Violin Concerto* (© 1936, Universal Edition A.G. Vienna); *Wozzeck* (© 1926, Universal Edition A.G. Vienna)—by permission of Universal Edition A.G. Vienna.

Leonard Bernstein: *Fuga a 3* (© 1974, Amberson Enterprises, Inc.); *Oedipus Rex* (Deep Structure) (© 1974, Amberson Enterprises, Inc.); Deep Structure—*Mozart G Minor Symphony* (© 1974, Amberson Enterprises, Inc.); *Music Playing* (© 1974, Amberson Enterprises, Inc.)—by permission of Amberson Enterprises, Inc.

Aaron Copland: *Billy the Kid* (© 1973, A. Copland and Boosey & Hawkes, Inc.); *Piano Variations* (© 1959, A. Copland and Boosey & Hawkes, Inc.)—by permission of Aaron Copland and Boosey & Hawkes, Inc.

Ray Davies: *You Really Got Me* (© 1964, Edward Kassner Music Co., Ltd.)—words and music by permission of Copyright Services Bureau, Ltd.

Claude Debussy: *Prélude à l'Après Midi d'un faune* (copyright 1916, Jobert et Cie.)—by permission of Elkan-Vogel, Inc., and Société des Editions Jobert.

Darius Milhaud: *Souvenir of Brazil*, No. 7 "Corvocado" (copyright 1950 by Editions Max Eschig)—by permission of Associated Music Publishers, Inc.

Maurice Ravel: *Rapsodie Espagnole* (© 1908, Durand et Cie.) —by permission of Elkan-Vogel, Inc., and Durand et Cie.

Francis Poulenc: *Les Mamelles de Tirésias* (© 1947, Heugel et Cie.)—by permission of Theodore Presser Company, and Heugel et Cie.

Erik Satie: *Gymnopedie #1* (© 1919, Rouart Lerrolle and Cie.); Ragtime from *Parade* (© 1919, Rouart Lerrolle and Cie.)— by permission of Editions Salabert.

Arnold Schoenberg: *Pierrot Lunaire*, Op. 12, No. 7, "Der Kranke Mond"; *Pierrot Lunaire*, Op. 12, No. 21, "O alter Duft"; *Streichquartett* II, Op. 10 IV, "Entrueckung"; *Drei Klavierstücke*, Op. 11, No. 1; *Sechs Kleine Klavierstücke*, Op. 19, No. 1;